Lecture Notes in Business Information Processing

469

More information about this series at https://link.springer.com/bookseries/7911

Massimo Marchiori ·
Francisco José Domínguez Mayo ·
Joaquim Filipe (Eds.)

Web Information Systems and Technologies

16th International Conference, WEBIST 2020, November 3–5, 2020
and 17th International Conference, WEBIST 2021
October 26–28, 2021, Virtual Events, Revised Selected Papers

Springer

Editors
Massimo Marchiori
University of Padua
Padua, Italy

Francisco José Domínguez Mayo
University of Seville
Seville, Spain

Joaquim Filipe
Polytechnic Institute of Setúbal/INSTICC
Setúbal, Portugal

ISSN 1865-1348 ISSN 1865-1356 (electronic)
Lecture Notes in Business Information Processing
ISBN 978-3-031-24196-3 ISBN 978-3-031-24197-0 (eBook)
https://doi.org/10.1007/978-3-031-24197-0

This Springer imprint is published by the registered company Springer Nature Switzerland AG
The registered company address is: Gewerbestrasse 11, 6330 Cham, Switzerland

Preface

The present book includes extended and revised versions of a set of selected papers from the International Conference on Web Information Systems and Technologies (WEBIST) events that took place in 2020 and 2021, which were exceptionally held as online events due to COVID-19.

WEBIST 2020 received 48 paper submissions from 22 countries, of which 2% were included in this book. WEBIST 2021 received 107 paper submissions from 35 countries, of which 9% were included in this book.

The papers were selected by the event chairs and their selection is based on a number of criteria that include the classifications and comments provided by the Program Committee members, the session chairs' assessment, and also the program chairs' global view of all papers included in the technical program. The authors of selected papers were then invited to submit a revised and extended version of their papers having at least 30% innovative material.

The purpose of the International Conference on Web Information Systems and Technologies (WEBIST) is to bring together researchers, engineers, and practitioners interested in the technological advances and business applications of web-based information systems. The conference has five main tracks, covering different aspects of web information systems, namely Internet Technology; Web Interfaces and Applications; Society, e-Communities, e-Business; Web Intelligence; and Mobile Information Systems. WEBIST focuses on real-world applications; therefore, authors should highlight the benefits of web information systems and technologies for industry and services, in addition to academic applications. Ideas on how to solve business problems using web-based information systems and technologies are discussed at the conference. Papers describing advanced prototypes, systems, tools, and techniques as well as general survey papers indicating future directions are also encouraged. Both technological and social-oriented papers are accepted. All papers must describe original work, not previously published or submitted to another conference. Accepted papers, presented at the conference by one of the authors, are published in the proceedings of WEBIST. Acceptance is based on quality, relevance, and originality. Both full research reports and work-in-progress reports are welcome. WEBIST typically features both oral and poster sessions. Special sessions dedicated to case-studies and commercial presentations, as well as tutorials dedicated to technical or scientific topics, are also envisaged: companies interested in presenting their products or methodologies, or researchers interested in holding a tutorial, workshop, or special session, are invited to contact the conference secretariat or visit the conference website.

The papers selected to be included in this book contribute to the understanding of relevant trends of current research on web information systems and technologies, including: natural language processing, document clustering, deep learning, decision making, knowledge representation and reasoning on the Web, applications, research projects and Web intelligence, recommendation systems, Web interfaces and applications, linked data, big data and applications in companies, and the Internet of Things.

We would like to thank all the authors for their contributions and also the reviewers who have helped in ensuring the quality of this publication.

October 2021

Massimo Marchiori
Francisco José Domínguez Mayo
Joaquim Filipe

Organization

Conference Chair

Joaquim Filipe   Polytechnic Institute of Setubal/INSTICC,
                                          Portugal

Program Co-chairs

Francisco José Domínguez Mayo   University of Seville, Spain
Massimo Marchiori   University of Padua, Italy

Program Committee

Served in 2020

Adelaide Bianchini   Universidad Simón Bolívar, Venezuela
Alvaro Figueira   INESC TEC and Universidade do Porto, Portugal
Andreas Kanavos   Ionian University, Greece
Andres Jimenez Ramirez   University of Seville, Spain
Angel Meseguer-Martinez   University of Castilla-La Mancha, Spain
Antonina Dattolo   University of Udine, Italy
Azza Harbaoui   RIADI Laboratory, Tunisia
Carlos Santos   University of Aveiro, Portugal
Chang-ai Sun   University of Science and Technology Beijing,
                                  China
Claudia Raibulet   University of Milano-Bicocca, Italy
Daniel O'Leary   University of Southern California, USA
Declan O'Sullivan   Trinity College Dublin, Ireland
Dominik Strzalka   Rzeszów University of Technology, Poland
Dongxi Liu   CSIRO, Australia
Dwight Makaroff   University of Saskatchewan, Canada
Esma Aïmeur   University of Montreal, Canada
Fan Zhao   Florida Gulf Coast University, USA
Hakima Mellah   CERIST -Research Center for Scientific and
                                  Technical Information, Algeria
Inaldo Capistrano Costa   ITA - Aeronautics Institute of Technology, Brazil
José Alfonso Aguilar   Universidad Autonoma de Sinaloa, Mexico

Served in 2021

Andreas Hinderks	Universidad de Sevilla, Spain
Andreas Klein	University of Seville, Spain
Angela Guercio	Kent State University, USA
Antonio Balderas	Universidad de Cádiz, Spain
Cesar Garita	Instituto Tecnológico de Costa Rica, Costa Rica
Christopher Turner	University of Surrey, UK
Costas Vassilakis	University of the Peloponnese, Greece
Davide Rossi	University of Bologna, Italy
Devis Bianchini	University of Brescia, Italy
Didik Dwi Prasetya	Universitas Negeri Malang, Indonesia
Ilan Kirsh	Object DB Software, UK
Jason Whalley	Northumbria University, UK
Luigi Di Caro	University of Turin, Italy
Michele Melchiori	University of Brescia, Italy
Paulo Alencar	University Waterloo, Canada
Petri Vuorimaa	Aalto University, Finland
Przemyslaw Falkowski-Gilski	Gdansk University of Technology, Poland
Santiago Meliá	Universidad de Alicante, Spain
Sokratis Katsikas	Norwegian University of Science and Technology, Gjøvik, Norway
Stavros Koubias	University of Patras, Greece
Vítor E. Silva Souza	Universidade Federal do Espírito Santo, Brazil
Victoria Vysotska	Lviv Polytechnic National University, Ukraine
Weiming Shen	NRC Canada, Canada

Served in 2020 and 2021

A. Henten	Aalborg University, Denmark
Abdelkrim Meziane	CERIST, Algeria
Alex Norta	Tallinn University of Technology, Estonia
Ana Margarida Almeida	Universidade de Aveiro, Portugal
Andrea Mauri	Delft University of Technology, Netherlands
Annamaria Goy	University of Torino, Italy
Bhanu Prasad	Florida A&M University, USA
Birgit Pröll	Johannes Kepler University Linz, Austria
Carlos Granell	Universitat Jaume I, Spain
Carolina Gallardo Pérez	Universidad Politécnica de Madrid, Spain
Christophe Cruz	University of Burgundy, France
Christos Troussas	University of West Attica, Greece
Claudio Schifanella	Università degli Studi di Torino, Italy
Clodoveu Davis Júnior	UFMG, Brazil

Comai Sara	Politecnico di Milano, Italy
Daniel Cunliffe	University of South Wales, UK
David Paul	The University of New England, Australia
Dickson Chiu	The University of Hong Kong, Hong Kong
Dirk Thissen	RWTH Aachen University, Germany
Ejub Kajan	State University of Novi Pazar, Serbia
Elarbi Badidi	United Arab Emirates University, UAE
Eliza Stefanova	Sofia University, Bulgaria
Enrico Denti	Università di Bologna, Italy
Faiza Belala	Constantine 2 University, Algeria
Fotios Kokkoras	University of Thessaly, Greece
Francesco Guerra	University of Modena and Reggio Emilia, Italy
Gabriela Bosetti	VeryConnect, UK
Georg Schneider	Trier University of Applied Sciences, Germany
Georgia Kapitsaki	University of Cyprus, Cyprus
Guglielmo De Angelis	IASI-CNR, Italy
Gustavo Rossi	Lifia, Argentina
Hanno Hildmann	TNO, Netherlands
Hiroshi Koide	Kyushu University, Japan
Ilche Georgievski	University of Stuttgart, Germany
Ingo Melzer	Daimler Truck North America, USA
Inmaculada Medina-Bulo	Universidad de Cádiz, Spain
Ioannis Hatzilygeroudis	University of Patras, Greece
Jari Veijalainen	University of Jyväskylä, Finland
Jesús Arias Fisteus	Universidad Carlos III de Madrid, Spain
Jim Prentzas	Democritus University of Thrace, Greece
John Garofalakis	University of Patras, Greece
Jose Gonzalez	University of Seville, Spain
Jose Herrero Agustin	University of Extremadura, Spain
Josep-Lluis Ferrer-Gomila	University of the Balearic Islands, Spain
Julián Grigera	Universidad Nacional de La Plata, Argentina
Kalpdrum Passi	Laurentian University, Canada
Karim El Guemhioui	Université du Québec en Outaouais, Canada
Karla Fook	Instituto Tecnológico de Aeronáutica, Brazil
Larbi Esmahi	Athabasca University, Canada
Laura Po	University of Modena and Reggio Emilia, Italy
Luís Ferreira Pires	University of Twente, Netherlands
Marco Aiello	University of Stuttgart, Germany
Marianna Sigala	University of South Australia, Australia
Martin Drlik	Constantine the Philosopher University in Nitra, Slovakia
Martine De Cock	University of Washington Tacoma, USA

Marzal Miguel Ángel	Universidad Carlos III De Madrid, Spain
Matthias Klusch	German Research Center for Artificial Intelligence (DFKI) GmbH, Germany
Miroslaw Mazurek	Rzeszów University of Technology, Poland
Monique Janneck	Luebeck University of Applied Sciences, Germany
Ombretta Gaggi	Università di Padova, Italy
Pankaj Pandey	Norwegian University of Science and Tchnology, Norway
Pasi Fränti	University of Eastern Finland, Finland
Philipp Brune	Neu-Ulm University of Applied Sciences, Germany
Roberto Saia	University of Cagliari, Italy
Sergio Ilarri	University of Zaragoza, Spain
Shanmugasundaram Hariharan	Vardhaman College of Engineering, India
Steven Demurjian	University of Connecticut, USA
Thomas Risse	University Library Johann Christian Senckenberg, Germany
Tony Wasserman	Carnegie Mellon University Silicon Valley, USA
Toon De Pessemier	Ghent University - iMinds, Belgium
Wieland Schwinger	Johannes Kepler University Linz, Austria
William Van Woensel	Dalhousie University, Canada
Xiang Fu	Hofstra University, USA

Additional Reviewers

Served in 2020

Francesco Del Buono	Università di Modena e Reggio Emilia, Italy

Served in 2021

Chiara Bachechi	University of Modena and Reggio Emilia, Italy
Jörg Thomaschewski	University of Applied Sciences Emden/Leer, Germany

Served in 2020 and 2021

Federica Rollo	University of Modena and Reggio Emilia, Italy

Invited Speakers

2020

Luc Moreau   King's College London, UK
Stefan Decker   RWTH Aachen University, Germany
Frank van Harmelen   The Hybrid Intelligence Center and Vrije
                              Universiteit Amsterdam, Netherlands

2021

Ian Horrocks   University of Oxford, UK
Dieter A. Fensel   University of Innsbruck, Austria
Oscar Corcho   Universidad Politécnica de Madrid, Spain

Contents

Virtual Testing Environment for Smart Automations in the Internet of Things

Anthony Savidis[1,2]([⊠]) and Yannis Valsamakis[1]

[1] Department of Computer Science, University of Crete, Rethymno, Greece
as@ics.forth.gr, jvalsam@csd.uoc.gr
[2] Institute of Computer Science, FORTH, Heraklion, Crete, Greece

Abstract. The Internet of Things (IoT) is a rapidly progressing domain, with solutions ranging from large-scale urban infrastructures shared by all citizens, to smaller scale home-based ecosystems targeted to individuals and families. While the choice of functionality in large ecosystems is the responsibility of respective authorities, in home setups smartness implies individualization of automations. In this context, the notion of end-user programming gains increasing attention as a promising way to allow users develop personalized automations by deploying visual programming tools. Since in an IoT ecosystem devices may be invisible, embedded or hardly locatable, sometimes physically inaccessible, testing becomes very challenging, as bringing physical devices to certain states may be either impractical (e.g. window and door sensors) or overall unsafe (e.g. fire or smoke sensors). For this purpose we implemented a virtual testing environment where trials are executed in a protected runtime, not confined to a particular location, disengaged from the physical ecosystem. All our tools run locally in a typical mobile machine and may operate in standalone mode without connecting to real smart devices. Finally, for automations involving time and scheduling, we introduce a virtual time tool, so that testing is done on demand, not following or waiting the actual pace of physical time.

Keywords: Internet of Things · Smart automations · Visual programming · Virtual testing environments · Digital twins

1 Introduction

The Internet of Things (IoT) is a rapidly-growing domain and relates to smart ecosystems at various scales, constantly evolving in terms of infrastructures, integrated solutions, development tools and best practices. Technically, the IoT domain rents its roots to ubiquitous computing, which in the late 90s envisioned that in the future there will be numerous ecosystems of distributed computation and interaction resources besides typical personal computers. In the context of user-interface software and technology, this idea was at that time abstracted by the concept of beyond the desktop interactions. Some interaction paradigms that appeared in this early period included the following features: treating environments as displays, projecting display output on various surfaces, using

M. Marchiori et al. (Eds.): WEBIST 2020/2021, LNBIP 469, pp. 1–25, 2023.
https://doi.org/10.1007/978-3-031-24197-0_1

physical objects for input, putting main emphasis on hand gestures and body postures, and deploying public shared screens and projectors. Such works tried to preserve computational ubiquity by treating interaction as an activity involving directly the environment. However, the entrance to the smartphone era caused a huge paradigm shift, with the vision of information and computation anywhere and anytime becoming fully instantiated. The user-interface technology for smartphones progressed rapidly, supported with novel interaction styles and advanced software libraries. The latter turned interaction in mobile user machines as the prevalent interaction paradigm in the new era, effectively disrupting past ideas and concepts related to beyond the desktop interactions.

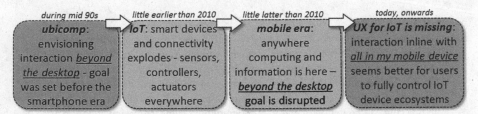

Fig. 1. Disruption of past concepts regarding the so-called beyond-the-desktop metaphor has been caused by the entrance in the age of smartphones and tablets (from [2]).

Simultaneously, IoT grew with a large variety of mission-specific devices, mostly in the category of sensors, actuators and controllers [19], while large-scale infrastructures started to proliferate [12]. The previous situation, which is depicted under Fig. 1 caused a technological gap: while device ecosystems constantly grow, the real benefits to daily life for individual consumers are lacking.

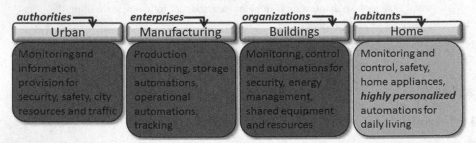

Fig. 2. Application of IoT technologies with smart device ecosystems at various contexts and scales, for different missions and owner users, showing how homes radically differ from all other infrastructures when it comes to end-user personalization demands.

As IoT technologies were incrementally adopted in various domains, it appeared that the eventual user experience is well differentiated according to the scale and range of the respective solutions and the need for sharing across many user populations. As outlined under Fig. 2, when it comes to the smaller-scale home-based infrastructures, that are assembled, controlled and administered by the habitants themselves, the need for highly personalized and configurable setups becomes crucial. The latter is explained by the fact that everyday automations are highly personalized in nature, being technically small-scale applications, something that also implies a niche-market with a small industrial interest. The latter is observed by a significant growth and proliferation of urban and building IoT solutions, however, with little penetration in the context of the home market. This also explains why the idea of end-user development quickly received attention and is now considered a very promising solution. Not only it may address this gap, but it is fully aligned to the need of everything in my mobile, enabling the management and execution of automations to be entirely handled via a typical smartphone device.

Our focus on personal automations requires distinguishing between smart environments shared by many people simultaneously, where either no access privileges are granted, or otherwise they are avoided to prevent conflicting configurations. For instance, in smart cities and smart working environments it is most likely that personalized automations are overall disabled, unless they affect the individual only. On the other hand, in homes, the support for personal automations is of key importance.

1.1 Contribution

The reported work follows our initial efforts reported in [17], where we introduced prototype testing tools for personal IoT automations. In this paper we discuss our transition towards an *integrated virtual testing environment* for personal smart automations, elaborating on updates regarding the architecture, scenarios and an early usability evaluation process with end-users. The layers of functionality are depicted under Fig. 3, with testing being the final stage that is underexplored in the context of end-user IoT development. Due to the distributed nature of IoT ecosystems, it is crucial that testing may be carried out in a protected, virtual environment, not the physical one, since bringing physical devices to certain states may be either impractical (e.g. window and door sensors) or overall unsafe (e.g. fire or smoke sensors). In this context, out contribution is the full-scale implementation of a virtual testing environment for IoT, enabling end-users carry out isolated testing and debugging of smart-automations, with virtual devices and virtual-time control, independently and physically away of the actual IoT device ecosystem.

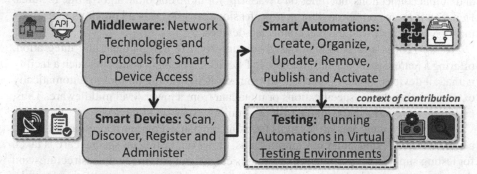

Fig. 3. End-user tool layers required to enable crafting of personalized smart automations (from [17]) with testing being the focus in the paper.

2 Related Work

In general, virtual testing environments relates to the ability of testing a software system outside its deployment (physical) environment by virtualizing all resources on which it depends. For domains like IoT, with numerous dynamic distributed resources, the importance of virtual testing is crucial, something that has been recently acknowledged in [3]. While virtual testing is not limited to personal automations, due to the involvement of end-users as the primary developers [14], in our context it is even more important. Based on this, we judge IoT development systems regarding their testing support facilities.

HomeKit [5] from Apple allows control connected home accessories (if compatible with the system), and supports to some degree user-defined automations as combinations of accessory control actions. Not an end-user solution as such, focuses mostly on premade smart home solutions with emphasis on advanced configurations.

Puzzle [11] is a visual development system for automations with smart IoT objects adopting the jigsaw metaphor. The system is primitive, without the full-scale capacity of common VPLs, entirely lacking testing or simulation tools.

Wia [6] is a cloud-based IoT development platform for linking devices, services and sensors using Wia Flow Studio. This system is better for service composition, while for testing only the real service elements can be deployed.

Embrio [7] offers a drag-and-drop visual programming interface for Arduino, requiring connection to the actual circuit and peripherals upon testing, lacking any debugging facilities.

XOD [8] is a microcontroller programming platform with a visual interface. It is based on the node model, which can represent sensors, motors, or a piece of functional code like comparison operations, text operations, and so on. As with all previous systems, testing requires connectivity of the real devices.

Zenodys [9] allows developers create IoT apps by organizing dataflow connections. It is an advanced platform for predictive maintenance, real-time control systems and product line automation, rather than typical non-professional end-users and personal automation development. All testing is done in the field by professionals.

Node-Red [13] is a visual flow-based system for wiring hardware devices with input and output connections, but relies on JavaScript for more elaborate algorithmic features. Hence, it is more complicated for non-professionals while, as in all previous tools, tests must be performed with the real connected devices.

IoTify [20] is a recent cloud-based solution for IoT development and integration, offering a feature to model and simulate IoT devices. The main issue with such a facility is that all devices should be introduced from scratch, offering no tool to automatically extract existing device specifications or metadata from a lower-level middleware. Thus, end-users are overloaded with the task of detailing every smart device.

In summary, there are various tools focusing on visual programming, some of which could be used to build smart IoT automations. However, testing no special care is taken for testing support, treated as a process that is carried out within real infrastructures and device ecosystems. The latter is impractical, unsafe and for certain cases even infeasible.

3 Case Scenarios

To validate our testing environment, we designed case scenarios requiring visual programming and testing on behalf of the end-users. The main scenario involves of automations to be performed early in the morning, so that people earn more sleep while their water for their bath and their coffee is getting automatically prepared. Additionally, for elderly people, they may like to be reminded to get a pill, while they would like to have peace of their mind when they leave their home to go for work by ensuring home safety, security and economy. Moreover, people would like to clean their home, however, their free time is limited and they would like to automate this task by using smart devices. All the aforementioned automation tasks are able to be served based on their daily life and needs.

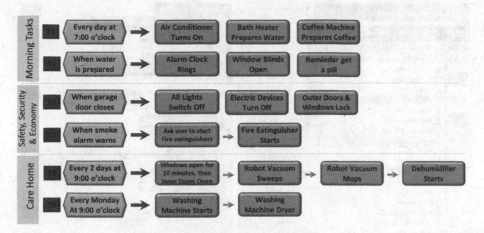

Fig. 4. Morning home automations for our case scenario.

An outline of these tasks is provided under Fig. 4, all separately visually programmed through our IDE (see Fig. 4). Now, to make all such automations of Fig. 4 ready for virtual testing, it suffices to provide just once a simulated implementation with visual programming of the following operations involved in the code blocks:

- Window Blinds: *Open, Close*
- Air Condition: *TurnOn, TurnOff*
- Bedroom/Main Light: *TurnOn, TurnOff*
- Bathroom Light: *TurnOn, TurnOff*
- Coffee Machine: *TurnOn, TurnOff*
- Window: *Open, Close*

Once this step is performed, end-users are able to test all types of automations with virtual devices, in isolation, locally in their smartphone, by defining test suites, opening the calendar and dashboard, interacting directly with virtual device GUIs, viewing history logs, playing with virtual time, and opening the debugger on-demand as needed. All these activities are possible without ever connecting to real devices. Moreover, the exact same tools are usable and available when the real device ecosystem is involved, when testing is carried out in the field. Having completed the definition of the smart devices for the morning automations, the next step is to define for each of the tasks (*T1-T6*, one project element Morning Automations, either scheduled or conditional, as it is shown in Fig. 5). Defining the smart devices in the project, respective Blockly blocks have been defined in order to handle their behavior.

These blocks are available in each of the tasks (i.e., *'Automations for Basic Tasks'*, *'Automations for Conditional Tasks'* and *'Automutions for Scheduled Tasks'*) as it is shown in Fig. 5. Using these blocks, visual code has been developed for each of the defined project elements as it is indicated through the *T1-T6* tags in Fig. 5.

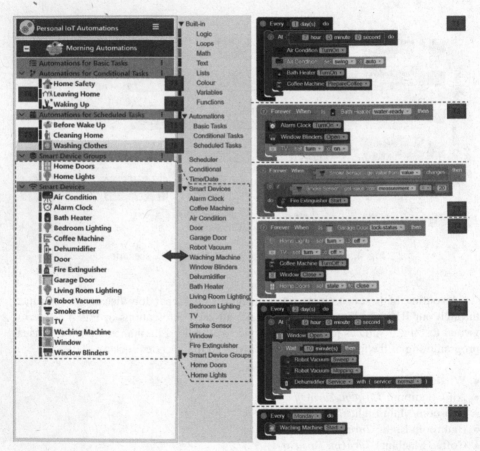

Fig. 5. Home automation case scenarios for helping in everyday life and healthy living.

4 Software Architecture

Our integrated testing tools, comprising the virtual testing environment, are all part of a large-scale Integrated Development Environment (IDE) for visual-programming, which relies on the [4] visual programming editor and the [10] middleware for smart objects. The software architecture of our integrated test runtime is illustrated under Fig. 6 (the rest of the IDE components are skipped for clarity). The components shown in blue background are the key elements supporting isolated out-of-environment testing of smart automations.

In the IoT era, heterogeneity is a fundamental and likely unavoidable characteristic, concerning networking, protocols and device APIs. In this context, diversity is expected to further proliferate, but it can be technically confined to the lower levels, with extra decomposition, better middleware and more service layers. In our architecture, for this purpose there is a specific layer named abstract object access (AOA). This layer sits on top of the IoTivity middleware, which is already a level of abstraction over device protocols. The entire backbone of our testing tools sits on top of the AOA layer, something that makes testing instruments resilient to scaling and tolerant to change. In particular, to accommodate device virtualization we had to allow switching between physical and virtual device access, at the backend, something that we introduced as a built-in feature of the AOA API.

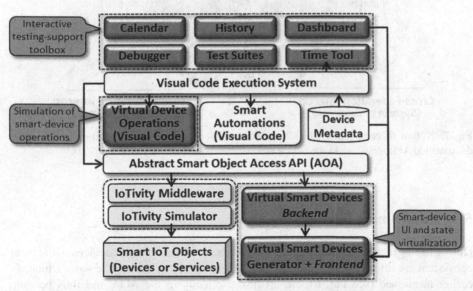

Fig. 6. Software architecture of the entire testing infrastructure – components shown in blue in red dashed rectangles comprise the virtual testing environment.

To support virtual testing, we needed to simulate device front-ends (GUIs), something which, as we discuss latter, is handled automatically by a User-Interface generator. However, as we explain latter in the paper, a similar automatic simulation of the device operations (backend) is not possible, since, besides function signatures from service

APIs, no other semantic information is given. For this purpose, we allow the visual programming of simulated operations, something we elaborate with detailed scenarios. Overall, in IoT solutions, device ecosystems are expected to constantly grow and proliferate, with decentralization becoming a necessity so as to break or avoid system monoliths. However, certain infrastructures, as those mentioned in urban and large building contexts, are naturally huge and cannot be reasonably constrained to a smaller scale. In this framework, the notion of ecosystem federations appeared (see Fig. 7), with cross-federation interoperability becoming a viable solution, enabling the disciplined orchestration and control of the various emergent constituent ecosystems. In our work, the Abstract Object Access (AOA) layer of a local ecosystem is the gateway to other ecosystems, playing the role of a cross-federation API. The AOA is already visible to, and deployable by, the entire IoT testing runtime, something that effectively results in the notion of cross-federation testing.

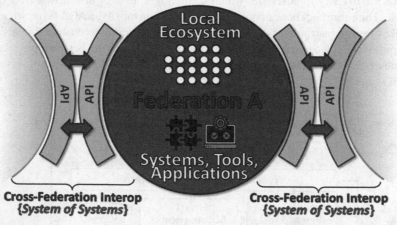

Fig. 7. Notion of ecosystem federations and cross-federation interoperability through well-documented APIs, resulting in the notion of system-of-systems (adapted from [17]).

5 Virtual Smart Devices

During testing mode, complete virtual GUI counterparts for all smart devices of the local ecosystem are offered by the testing environment, on top of the middleware, which, as earlier mentioned (see Fig. 6), are all linked directly to the AOA and thus become inseparable to the physical devices for rest of the runtime.

5.1 Automatic GUI Generation for Smart Devices

Smart device information (JSON descriptions or metadata) is retrieved via the middleware, during every device scanning process that is regularly initiated on-demand by the end-user inside a particular local device ecosystem. Such information is gathered by the

AOA and populates an up-to-date local database of smart-device meta-data, containing information regarding device properties and operations in the form of typed records and typed function signatures. Based on such device meta-data, we apply an automatic widget generation technique similar to [15], where the device GUI is composed by mapping device field data-types to corresponding widget classes (see Fig. 8, left part).

Besides GUI creation, it is crucial to keep the GUI state always synced to the backend, when the system is running in real-operation mode, holding a database of the virtual device state records. This ensures that when visual code fragments update any device, the change is also instantly mapped to the respective device GUI. For this purpose, upon creation of the widgets corresponding to device properties, the GUI generator will also install an internal event handler that keeps the two device images (GUI and backend) always synced to each other (see Fig. 8, right part).

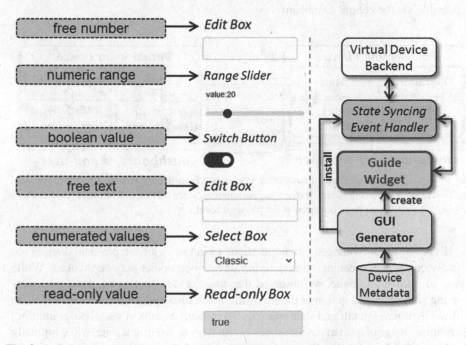

Fig. 8. Left: automatic GUI generation for devices relies on the mapping of device property types to specific widget classes; Right: auto-syncing between the device GUIs and the respective backend device state via a common event handler propagating state updates.

The reason for such syncing between physical and real devices is that, even when no system testing is carried out, virtual device instances exist as part of the dashboard, effectively as *digital twins* [21] for their corresponding physical smart devices of the real devices. The latter enables end-users not only to collectively supervise all currently connected devices locally, in their mobile device, but to also control them directly with GUI, besides using the typical physical device panel wherever possible (i.e. provided, accessible and reachable).

5.2   Simulating Smart Device Operations with Visual Programming

When trying to virtualize smart devices there is one issue that cannot be automatically addressed via algorithmic GUI generation. More specifically, besides device properties, the actual operations are also enlisted within device meta-data with typed function signatures. Now, with such information, we may directly generate a GUI so that end-users can supply all required argument values (if any) including a push-button to directly invoke the underlying device operation with the supplied arguments. As we elaborate latter, this feature is fully supported when physical devices are deployed, as part of the live device dashboard, and enables end-users to directly affect the physical devices using the graphical dashboard. Effectively, when such a GUI button is pressed, an invocation to the respective operation is posted via the middleware. As mentioned earlier, even for smart devices offering a hardware user-interface, such as a touch display, remote control is possible via the central dashboard.

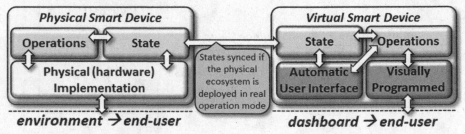

Fig. 9. For testing, to simulate smart device operations it suffices to visually program them as functions directly altering smart-device <u>state</u> parameters, since all respective event handlers will be invoked as if the changes occurred at the physical level.

However, when running smart automations in in test mode, no physical devices are actually connected, meaning no underlying device operations may be invoked. While trying to resolve this issue, we observed that most device operations, apart from performing some physical action at the hardware level, also update device state values to indicate their new operational state (see Fig. 9). In fact, in terms of visual programming, the runtime image of a smart device relates exclusively to its current state, while typically event handlers for state changes are defined as part of the smart automations logic. As also shown in the middle of Fig. 9, even during real operational mode the virtual images of physical devices become available, remaining interactive and fully synced to them.

In a virtualized testing setup, it suffices to cause changes to such device state properties to make, in terms of the software implementation of smart automations, virtual devices look conformant to their respective physical operational mode. Based on these remarks we enabled end-users simulate the behavior of such operations by implementing them through visual code. Essentially, the visual code for such simulated operations will only have to accordingly modify the state of the respective state device properties. Examples of such visually-programmed simulated operations are provided under Fig. 10.

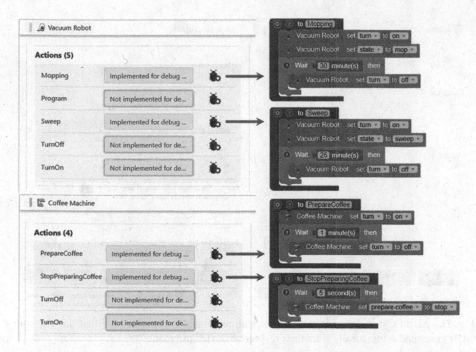

Fig. 10. Simulating the logic of operations for the *Vacuum Robot* and *Coffee Machine* smart devices to schedule respective state changes.

5.3 Virtual Smart-Device Access and Control

As mentioned earlier, device meta-data provides enough information to generate a fully-functional GUI through which device property updates and device operation invocations are directly possible. Effectively, such a GUI offers live device access and control, with state synced to the virtual device state, and invocation of operations resulting in the execution of the code for simulated device operations supplied by end-users (as explained in the previous section). An example of such a GUIs for the Alarm Clock and A/C devices is shown under Fig. 11. It should be noted that the same GUI *cannot* be used exactly as it is in case of physical device usage. In particular, for most smart devices, all property changes will occur either in response to normal device functioning or as a result of operations requested by the end-user, but never directly as internal system-level requests for explicit property updates. In this sense, when the GUI is embedded inside the global device dashboard (as will be discussed latter) for real physical device deployment, all device properties become read-only, and all respective *Update* buttons are removed.

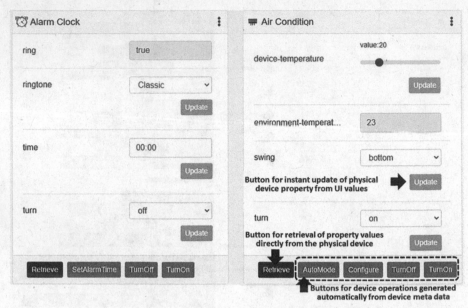

Fig. 11. Alarm Clock (left) and A/C (right, with annotated explanations) virtual devices with GUIs generated automatically from their respective device metadata.

6   Testing Toolbox

6.1   Action Calendar and Virtual-Time Tool

The action calendar offers a live view of all scheduled automation actions (see Fig. 12, bottom part). Every scheduled action, specified through the custom visual blocks in our IDE, is internally reported at start-up to the action calendar serving a twofold role for the end-user: (a) it provides an overview of all scheduled activities; and (b) shows which of such activities have been already invoked, with entries shown in green and a tick icon at right. The brief messages that appear on the calendar (right column, next to time or date) are the actual brief textual descriptions inserted by the developer in the corresponding scheduling visual blocks at development time.

As an add-on component of the activity calendar, our test environment also includes a virtual-time component, which enables very easily the testing of any scheduled automations, which, otherwise, would have to wait for action triggering following the normal time flow (see Fig. 12, top part). The reason this does not interfere with system time is due to the way we have developed scheduling logic in our toolbox: there is a time-access API, used throughout our runtime for querying the current time. In normal execution this is implemented to directly return the system clock time. However, during simulation, this API is implemented by the time simulator in a special way, enabling control the pace of time interactively and thus apply the current speed factor the user has chosen over the returned value of the current time. This allows far easier and quicker testing of scheduled tasks, especially when sequentially scheduled automation are defined, thus avoiding to wait for the real time to pass for respective actions to be triggered.

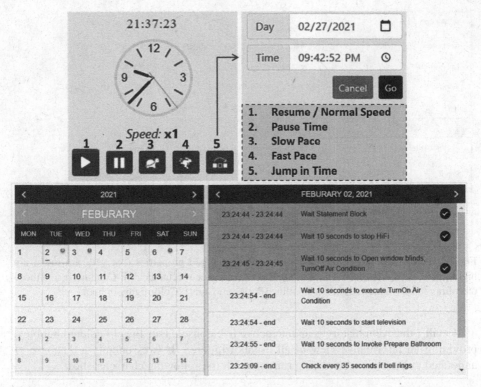

Fig. 12. Top: Virtual time tool, enabling to control pace of time and jump to a specific time and date; Bottom: Action calendar with all scheduled automations, showing in green and with a tick icon those already triggered.

6.2   Live Dashboard and Activity History

The dashboard is a useful tool (see Fig. 13) displaying live in real-time an up-to-date view of all smart-devices involved in the currently running set of smart automations, and behaves as follows:

- As new devices are discovered, they appeared in front, temporarily shown with a green border (e.g. *Air Condition* device)
- Devices out of range are shown with a red border and after a while they disappear (e.g. *Bedroom Light* device)
- When device properties change, they are highlighted (e.g. *Air Condition*, *swing* state or *Alarm Clock*, *ring* state)

The smart-device dashboard is always synced to actual device sate during runtime, while it is fully interactive, enabling directly select any device and change property values (only in test mode) or invoke operations (test mode or real operation mode). It is also important to note that all such changes are committed instantly on the smart device itself via the abstract object layer, so that the end-user visual code will indistinguishably treat them as genuine device-level state updates.

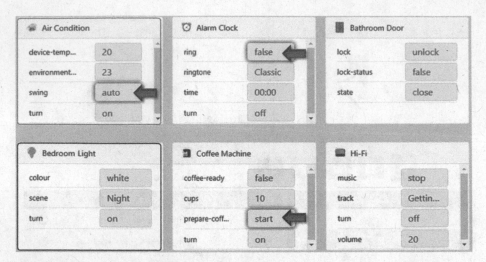

Fig. 13. Part of the device dashboard – recently changed properties (see yellow arrows) are highlighted, newly discovered devices are shown with green rectangle (Air Condition), and those out of range (disconnected) in a red outline (Bedroom Light) (Color figure online).

Finally, the event history is an interactive live console (see Fig. 14 colored bubbles) providing an informative view of all events triggered. It is essentially a database of annotated events that occur during runtime with the following characteristics:

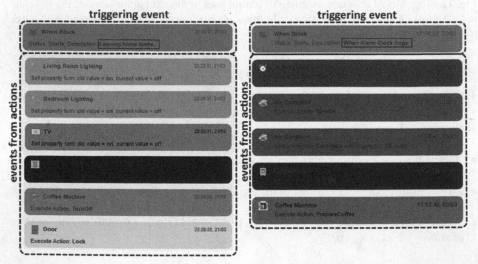

Fig. 14. Live history with event bubbles, including informative descriptions, for both device-level events (usually the triggering events) and events from all automation actions (Color figure online).

- All events are sequentially sorted in time, while they can be logically grouped following the smart automation they concern
- Color encoding (with chosen colors being interactively configurable) is deployed to differentiate between scheduled actions, device state changes and shifting of operational modes

Finally, the respective visual code block that actually handled an event appearing in the history can be directly tracked in the IDE by just clicking on the respective device icon appearing at the top left of every event bubble.

6.3 Input/Output Console

End-users are well familiar with instant messaging software tools (e.g. Skype, Messenger etc.). Based on this, we simulated the output console for the applications as a chat user-interface. In particular, when an output block is executed, the users receive the corresponding messages via the console. The input text area is disabled by default and when the end-user developer has to input text in the application, it alters to the enabled state, as depicted in Fig. 15. Moreover, the output console interacts with the project manager. In particular, when a Blockly input block is executed the project manager opens the respective project elements of this block. In addition, the bubbles (i.e. text messages) are interactive too. When the end-user developer clicks on each bubble, the project manager opens the respective project element which triggered the message in the run-time output console.

Additionally, based on the configuration of visual programming language elements, the developer can define alternative user interfaces of the messages by replacing the bubbles. For example, input could be a form of element(s) completion. This functionality is possible thanks to the API provided by the Console Output component which enables functionality to adapt input and output messages. Moreover, the developer is able to custom input/output visual programming language elements by adding extra I/O devices (e.g., gamepad, Joypad, microphone, camera etc.) with their respective third-party libraries as required.

6.4 Block-Based Debugger

Our additional testing tools include the debugger, the interactive definition of automatic test suites and the support for custom checking blocks. The combined testing process using these tools is outlined under Fig. 16 and commonly entails the following designated steps:

1. Setting breakpoints on blocks
2. Defining a test suite
3. Running tests and stopping in breakpoints
4. Observing changes due to the test suite
5. Tracing with the debugger like step-in
6. Observing execution events in the history

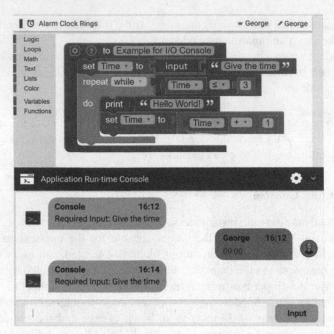

Fig. 15. Console input is enabled and immediately the corresponding triggering/invoker visual block is displayed and may be browsed.

In our IDE we have incorporated and appropriately adapted the user-interface of an open source block-level debugger for Blockly from the public repository of [16]. In particular, as part of the traditional variable watches tab of the original block-based debugger, we have inserted all smart devices, while we have grouped all variables under their respective smart automations code block. Finally, we also grouped breakpoints under smart automations, so that end-users can more easily and intuitively browse and manage breakpoints.

6.5 Embedded Explanations

In order to give an extra helpful facility in the end-user debugging of smart automations, we have introduced a new special visual programming elements whose purpose is only to support the debugging process. In particular, we have defined a new category of *Blockly* blocks called *Explanations*. These blocks can be inserted at various points of the automation program in order to explain what will happen or will occur in the associated visual code fragments (see example of Fig. 17). Using such blocks, context-specific or event-related messages can be posted in the input-output console of the IDE during the test execution of the smart automations. Additionally, there is the option to choose if the explanation block will alternatively popup a modal dialogue (message box), pause the execution of the current automation and display the message, instead of posting it to the input-output console.

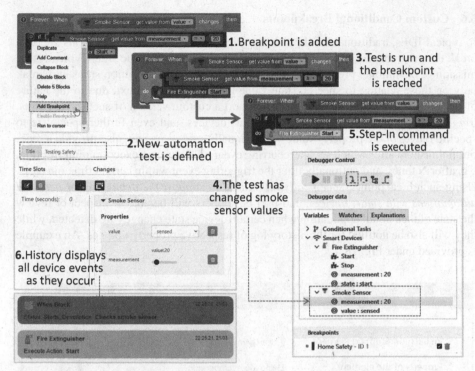

Fig. 16. Defining, running and debugging automations through previously edited scheduled automation tests (from [17]).

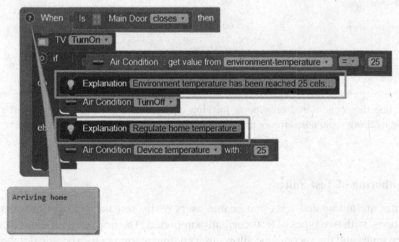

Fig. 17. Two explanations blocks (red rectangles) inserted before specific actions for the A/C device (in this case they will issue modal popups).

6.6 Custom Conditional Breakpoints

In typical IDEs, traditional breakpoints encompass programming expressions and will break the program execution only when upon entry they evaluate to true. Typically, the mission of conditional breakpoints is to constraint the cases execution stops and break only on those relating to specific state value ranges. In our context, due to the nature of personal automations, we decided to support a custom version of such breakpoints, triggered according to state changes of smart devices, and even further specialize to specific ranges of the property values. Additionally, end-users may also provide a repetition threshold after which such a recurring event will cause an execution interruption, e.g. after N times, and optionally filter the triggering event within certain time intervals. Using such breakpoints, *specifically introduced to support the debugging of personal automations with smart devices*, end-user developers will be able to inspect or review the state of their small application when certain device state changes are detected, while they will also be notified for the history log of respective property updates. An example is provided under Fig. 18.

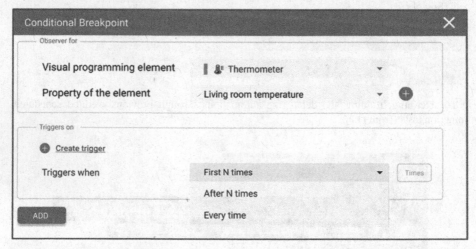

Fig. 18. Inserting conditional breakpoint tracking changes of the *thermometer* smart object regarding its *living room temperature* property, occurring only the first number of times.

6.7 Authoring of Test Suites

Test suites are automated tests that enable users easily test the visually programmed automations, with two types of tests currently supported. The first one schedules changes in device states and the second one allows users define warnings for specific device state modifications, by optionally suspending running automations. Every test can be either set as active directly after its creation, or at the beginning of the next execution session. For the first test type (scheduled) we provide a user-interface through which the user may define the elapsed time after which a device state will be triggered (see Fig. 16, label 2), or alternatively define repeated device changes at regular time intervals.

Multiple device properties may be also modified as part of a single test. It should be noted that in all such cases the virtual devices are only involved, something that gives end-users the opportunity to update even read-only device fields so as to test the respective associated automations.

More specifically, having replaced the smart devices with simulated devices, the system has to enable simulation and handling their properties and actions at specific time periods. In this context, we enabled the end-user to set smart device functionality tests (see top of Fig. 19). When users decide to insert a new test, or edit an existing one, they may choose specific time ranges and to schedule changes on smart device properties accordingly, as outlined under Fig. 19 (in *Times Slots* and *Changes* forms). Moreover, they should also provide a title for the test which will be automatically displayed on the tests management page and a color which is rendered in the execution, in the test control panel. Based on the supplied time ranges and the virtual time and date of the debugging process, the behavior of involved smart devices will change in order to enable the end-user developers to test their automations.

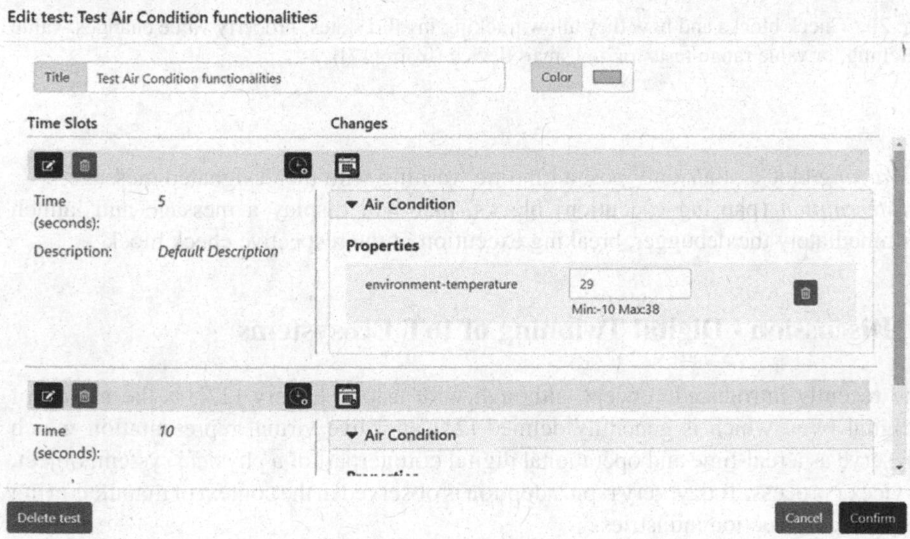

Fig. 19. Defining the test behavior of an A/C smart device within different time ranges.

6.8   Introducing Check Blocks

Check blocks are a new category of visual programming blocks that we introduced in Blockly to allow more elaborate and easy testing of smart automations. They generally look similar to conditional breakpoints in debuggers or to assertions in programming languages. In our case, they are more close to data breakpoints which capture unwanted or suspicious data changes in a program and issue automatically a breakpoint, so that developers can either capture the root of a cause or trace improper handling logic. More specifically, they allow users define conditions involving *device state fields*, which are evaluated with every respective device state change. Once such conditions are satisfied (i.e. become true), the runtime will issue a warning or pause execution and immediately open the debugger (see Fig. 20). As part of the condition placeholder for check blocks, any logical expression can be visually programmed or dropped in, as shown at the bottom part of Fig. 20. For our purposes, we have introduced two types of check blocks illustrated in the top part of Fig. 20:

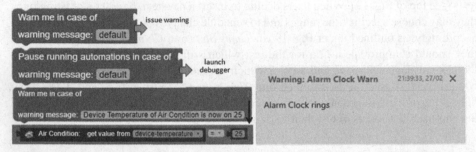

Fig. 20. Check blocks and how they allow tracking invalid states, property value changes, value matching, or value range-tests for any smart device (from [17]).

- *Warning* blocks, thus only post a runtime warning with the designated message
- *Interruption* (pausing execution) blocks, that will display a message and launch immediately the debugger, breaking execution at the respective check block

7   Discussion - Digital Twinning of IoT Ecosystems

One recently introduced concept, although with a long history [22], is the notion of a digital twin, which is generally defined [21] as a live virtual representation which can serve as a real-time and operational digital counterpart of a physical system, object, service or process. Today, very rapid adoption is observed in the context of manufacturing [18] and construction industries.

Amongst the various technologies involved in enabling digital twinning of physical systems is the Internet of Things, combining various devices that can be embedded or attached to physical assets, for data sensing, information collection, monitoring, actuation, control and even intervention. This crucial role of mission-specific IoT ecosystems is outlined under Fig. 21, middle and right part (*Digital Twin-1*), indicating a few of the key features offered, being simulations, visualizations and analytics. In fact, even in subject areas where the need for digital twins was not originally conceived as prominent or critical, such as smart cities and smart buildings, digital twins can facilitate added-value virtualizations, enabling to treat entire large-scale physical ecosystems, at an urban or even rural scale, as a unified living observed organism.

The previous trend reflects perfectly the idea that digital twins are essentially dynamic software models of physical things or systems that can offer insights and perspectives

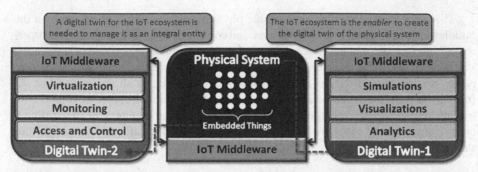

Fig. 21. How IoT ecosystems, which serve as enablers in creating digital twins for physical systems (e.g. buildings, cities, factories, etc.), also require their own digital twins in order to be managed and supervised as an integral and unified entity.

that may be only derived with the help of software computations. Now, while IoT infrastructures can be utilized for the development of such digital twins, they also constitute themselves entire systems, that can be also independently tracked and observed digitally as a complex physical entity, irrespective of their particular purpose and mission when being part of the larger container physical system. In other words, IoT ecosystems as enablers of digital twinning tend to be highly complex infrastructures that deserve their own custom digital twin as well. This concept is also outlined under Fig. 21, middle and left part (*Digital Twin-2*), outlining a few primary functions that might be provided, including virtualization, monitoring, access and control, not only over individual smart objects, but also over device groups or the smart ecosystem as a whole.

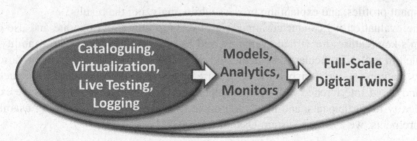

Fig. 22. Progressing from the basic components of our virtual testing environment (left) towards full-scale digital twins for IoT ecosystems.

Such operations offered by a IoT digital twin entail a basic backbone that is very close to the functionality of our virtual testing environment, in particular device cataloguing, virtualization (GUIs), live testing and debugging, and tagged histories or logs (see Fig. 22, left part). We consider this is a very interesting remark, since in building our virtual testing environment we had to simulate many aspects of the actual smart devices, effectively building a local mirror of the device ecosystem so as to enable end-users carry out testing in a protected environment.

Then, we allowed syncing between the physical and the virtual ecosystem via the middleware to allow end-users also observe and control their ecosystem during real operation from a single mobile device. Effectively, since simulation and mirroring are two key ingredients of digital twins, it is clear that the virtual testing environment encompasses a large part of the IoT digital twin core. The latter, as shown within Fig. 22 (middle ad right part), can be appropriately extended towards a full-scale digital twin by developing custom models, data analytics and operational monitors. Such IoT digital twins can model the *collective behavior* of an ecosystem and offer add-value facilities such as:

- provide information on its overall *digital health*
- offer notifications on aspects relating to firmware expirations or potential conflicts
- display live networking reachability aspects
- present physical placement information
- show warnings regarding almost end-of-life equipment
- query and outline grouping by device vendors, categories or location
- mark devices for which updates with improved capabilities are available
- indicate devices whose relocation or substitution is constrained by practical reasons, such as relating to location, embedding or installation complexity

8 Usability Evaluation

Having designed the case study with a set of home automations, we needed to evaluate the virtual testing environment in the context of an actual development and testing process. In this section, we discuss the aims and setup of our study, based on the scenarios, brief participant profiles, and explain the process while analyzing the results.

The evaluation we conducted aimed on observing how users operate and use our system's key features for virtual testing as well as on assessing the system usability as a whole (all tools). Particularly, we dedicated our focus on evaluating the use of various testing features, so we designed the basic case scenario to reflect natural home activities and avoid interference with new concepts and devices that would introduce extra complexity to participants, and likely add noise to our results. For obtaining usability measurements, we used the System Usability Scale [1].

8.1 Participants

We asked 15 participants (M = 10, F = 5) aged between 13 and 32 to be involved in the usability trial. Most of the participants were from our university departments (i.e. Computer Science, Mathematics and Physics). Additionally, 6 of the participants were high school students that have previous experience with *Scratch* or *Lego Mindstorms*. Moreover, we found 3 individuals that had no previous experience with programming, including visual programming.

8.2 Process

Each participant acted individually. We firstly discussed and presented the basic IDE and the main development tools. Then, we presented our virtual testing environment, discussing the dashboard, operation simulation, block-level debugger, event history log, activity calendar and the time tool. Next, each of the automations involved in the case scenario were described in detail, providing initial incomplete implementations with the *Blockly* editor, and they users were asked to deploy the tools in order to complete the virtual setup, testing and finalize each of them. For each task and participant, we measured the time required for completion and we recorded the user behavior. Finally, the users were asked to fill-in the SUS questionnaire.

8.3 Results

We summarized and further analyzed all the answers given from our participants (see Fig. 23). The SUS questionnaire was designed in order to export results in two main dimensions. The first was focused on the usability of the testing tools involving virtual devices and simulation, and the second on the testing process itself, including debugging and time simulation. Results showed that the vast majority of participants were overall satisfied with the testing tools. In general, they are satisfied with the use of the smart object dashboard to interactively control devices. However, some users found difficult the direct use of a debugger for testing. In this context, we realize that extra helpful

	SD	D	N	A	SA
Q1. The smart device dashboard framework is well integrated into the workspace.	0	1	2	6	6
Q2. I find the simulation of smart device operations unnecessarily complex.	6	8	1	0	0
Q3. I find the event history log user interface intuitive and easy to use.	0	0	2	8	5
Q4. I don't feel confident using the block-level debugger without guidance.	5	9	0	1	0
Q5. I feel confident using device dashboard to control devices.	0	1	3	5	6
Q6. The action calendar offers limited options for testing.	7	6	2	0	0
Q7. I find visual programming for simulating device operations complex to use.	5	7	2	1	0
Q8. I would like to use these tools for my personal projects with my family/friends.	0	1	2	7	5
Q9. I found easy to use and control the virtual time tool.	0	2	6	5	2
Q10. I found difficult to inject and use check blocks for testing.	8	6	1	0	0

Fig. 23. SUS responses with values *Strongly Disagree* (SA), *Disagree* (D), *Neutral* (N), *Agree* (A), *Strongly Agree* (SA) - numbers indicate how many participants gave the response.

functionality and user interface improvement was necessary. Moreover, the users were satisfied very much with the event logs and the virtual time tool.

Furthermore, based on the aforementioned measurements we focused on the average, the best and the worst time recorded for each testing step. All the users completed the tasks and most of the worst time measurements are not far from the average, while the best are not far from the average too. Moreover, during the evaluation, we realized that after half of the basic morning automations were tested task, most of the users were more familiar with the testing tools.

9   Conclusions

The Internet of Things (IoT) is a rapidly progressing domain, with solutions ranging from large-scale urban infrastructures shared by all citizens, to smaller scale home-based ecosystems targeted to individuals and families. Currently, IoT hardware becomes rapidly available for home setups, but the chances for open adoption with personalized configurations of cross-vendor resources are yet limited. Since smart devices may be invisible, embedded or hardly locatable, even physically inaccessible, testing is challenging, as bringing physical devices to certain states may be either impractical (e.g. window/door sensors) or overall unsafe (e.g. fire/smoke sensors).

For this purpose we implemented a virtual testing environment where trials are executed in a protected runtime, not confined to a particular location, being disengaged from the physical ecosystem. Our work reflects the recent adoption of end-user programming for smart IoT automations and the emphasis on local control from a mobile device of the entire IoT functionality and resources on small-scale personalized automations. We also carried out an evaluation trial from which we observed that end-users are very pleased by the ability to early test their automations in a protected virtual environment with worrying on physical operational aspects.

Finally, we investigated the linkage of our work with the emerging field of digital twins and we noticed two important aspects: (a) that IoT ecosystems progress as independent physical systems likely deserving a digital twin for improved management and monitoring purposes; and (b) that the virtual testing environment encompasses functionality that appears to be at the core of implementing such digital twins. Overall, we consider that more work is required for more user-friendly and comprehensive virtual testing environments to enable home automations crafted by end-users, and also for exploring how such tools can be shared by digital twins of IoT ecosystems.

References

1. Brooke, J.: SUS: a quick and dirty usability scale. In: Jordan, P.W., Thomas, B., Weerdmeester, B.A., McClelland, A.L. (eds.). Usability Evaluation in Industry. Taylor and Francis, London (1996)
2. Savidis, A.: Back to the Internet of Things future: when everybody crafts personal smart automations. In: Keynote Speech. IISA 2021 Conference (2021). https://doi.org/10.13140/RG.2.2.20423.83365

3. Farahmandpour, Z., Versteeg, S., Han, J., Kameswaran, A.: Service virtualisation of Internet-of-Things devices: techniques and challenges. In: IEEE/ACM 3rd International Workshop on Rapid Continuous Software Engineering (RCoSE), Buenos Aires (May 22), pp. 32–35. IEEE (2017)
4. Blockly: Google Inc. A JavaScript library for building visual programming editors (2021). https://developers.google.com/blockly. Accessed May 2022
5. HomeKit: a software framework to configure, communicate with, and control smart-home appliances using Apple devices. Apple Inc (2022). https://www.apple.com/shop/accessories/all/homekit. Accessed May 2022
6. Wia: a cloud platform that makes creating IoT apps easier by linking IoT devices and external services (2022). https://www.wia.io/. Accessed May 2022
7. Embrio :visual, real-time, agent-based programming for Arduino (2022). https://www.embrio.io/. Accessed May 2022
8. XOD: an open-source visual programming language for microcontrollers (2022). https://xod.io/. Accessed May 2022
9. Zenodys: a fully visual IoT platform for industry (2022). https://www.zenodys.com/. Accessed May 2022
10. IoTivity: An open-source software framework enabling seamless device-to-device connectivity to address the emerging needs of the Internet of Things (2022). https://iotivity.org/. Accessed May 2022
11. Danado, J., Paternò, F.: A mobile end-user development environment for IoT applications exploiting the puzzle metaphor. ERCIM News **101** (2015). http://ercim-news.ercim.eu/en101
12. Open Interconnect Consortium – OIC. Standards for the development of the Internet of Things (2022). https://openconnectivity.org. Accessed May 2022
13. Node-Red: Low-level programming for even-driven applications (2022). https://nodered.org/. Accessed 05 2022
14. Myers, B.A., et al.: Making end user development more natural. In: Paternò, F., Wulf, V. (eds.) New Perspectives in End-User Development, pp. 1–22. Springer, Cham (2017). https://doi.org/10.1007/978-3-319-60291-2_1
15. Dewan, P.: A demonstration of the flexibility of widget generation. In: Proceedings EICS 2010, pp. 315–320. ACM (2010). https://doi.org/10.1145/1822018.1822069
16. Savidis, A., Savaki, C.: Complete block-level visual debugger for blockly. In: Ahram, T., Karwowski, W., Pickl, S., Taiar, R. (eds.) IHSED 2019. AISC, vol. 1026, pp. 286–292. Springer, Cham (2020). https://doi.org/10.1007/978-3-030-27928-8_43
17. Savidis, A., Valsamakis, Y., Linaritis, D.: Simulated IoT runtime with virtual smart devices: debugging and testing end-user automations. In Proceedings of the 17th International Conference on Web Information Systems and Technologies (October 26–28), WEBIST 2021, pp. 145–155. Scitepress (2021). ISBN: 978-989-758-536-4
18. Yang, C., Shen, W., Wang, X.: The Internet of Things in manufacturing: key issues and potential applications. IEEE Syst. Man Cybern. Mag. **4**(1), 6–15 (2018). https://doi.org/10.1109/MSMC.2017.2702391
19. Dachyar, M., Zagloel, T., Saragih, L.: Knowledge growth and development: Internet of Things (IoT) research, 2006–2018. Heliyon **5**(8) (2019). https://doi.org/10.1016/j.heliyon.2019.e02264
20. IoTify: Intelligent Test Automation for Enterprise IoT Apps (2022). https://iotify.io/. Accessed May 2022
21. Fuller, A., Fan, Z., Day, C., Barlow, C.: Digital twin: enabling technologies, challenges and open research. IEEE Access **8**, 108952–108971 (2020)
22. Gelenter, D.H.: Mirror Worlds: or the Day Software Puts the Universe in a Shoebox—How It Will Happen and What It Will Mean. Oxford University Press, Oxford (1991). ISBN 978-0195079067

Machine Learning Based Finding of Similar Sentences from French Clinical Notes

Khadim Dramé[1,2(✉)], Gayo Diallo[3], and Gorgoumack Sambe[1,2]

[1] Université Assane Scck de Ziguinchor, Ziguinchor, Senegal
{kdrame,gsambe}@univ-zig.sn
[2] Laboratoire d'Informatique et d'Ingénierie pour l'Innovation, Ziguinchor, Senegal
[3] SISTM - INRIA, BPH INSERM 1219, Univ. Bordeaux, 33000 Bordeaux, France
Gayo.Diallo@u-bordeaux.fr

Abstract. Finding similar sentences or paragraphs is a key issue when dealing with text redundancy. This is particularly the case in the clinical domain where redundancy in clinical notes makes their secondary use limited. Due to lack of resources, this task is a key challenge for French clinical documents. In this paper, we introduce a semantic similarity computing approach between French clinical sentences based on supervised machine learning algorithms. The proposed approach is implemented in a system called CONCORDIA, for COmputing semaNtic sentenCes for fRench Clinical Documents sImilArity. After briefly reviewing various semantic textual similarity measures reported in the literature, we describe the approach, which relies on Random Forest (RF), Multilayer Perceptron (MLP) and Linear Regression (LR) algorithms to build different supervised models. These models are thereafter used to determine the degrees of semantic similarity between clinical sentences. CONCORDIA is evaluated using traditional evaluation metrics, EDRM (Accuracy in relative distance to the average solution) and Spearman correlation, on standard benchmarks provided in the context of the DEFT 2020 challenge. According to the official results of this challenge, our MLP based model ranked first out of the 15 submitted systems with an EDRM of 0.8217 and a Spearman correlation coefficient of 0.7691. The post-challenge development of CONCORDIA and the experiments performed after the DEFT 2020 edition showed a significant improvement of the performance of the different implemented models. In particular, the new MLP based model achieves a Spearman correlation coefficient of 0.80. On the other hand, the LR one, which combines the output of the MLP model with word embedding similarity scores, obtains the higher Spearman correlation coefficient with a score of 0.8030. Therefore, the experiments show the effectiveness and the relevance of the proposed approach for finding similar sentences on French clinical notes.

Keywords: Sentence similarity · Machine learning · Random forest · Multilayer perceptron · French clinical notes

1 Introduction

Computing semantic similarity between sentences is a crucial issue for many Natural Language Processing (NLP) applications. Semantic sentence similarity is used in vari-

M. Marchiori et al. (Eds.): WEBIST 2020/2021, LNBIP 469, pp. 26–42, 2023.
https://doi.org/10.1007/978-3-031-24197-0_2

ous tasks including information retrieval and texts classification [11], question answering, plagiarism detection, machine translation and automatic text summarization [6,34]. Therefore, there has been a significant interest in measuring similarity between sentences. To address this issue, various sentence similarity approaches have been proposed in the literature [1,6,7]. The commonly used approaches exploit lexical, syntactic, and semantic features of sentences. In the lexical approaches, sentences are considered as sequences of characters. Therefore, common shared characters [40], tokens/words or terms [18] between the source and the target sentences are usually exploited for measuring sentence similarity. Some other approaches attempt to take into account synonymy issues and/or to capture semantics of sentences using external semantic resources or statistical methods [8]. In statistical approaches, different techniques are used to capture the semantics of sentences, among them latent semantic analysis [22] or words embedding [23,29]. On the other hand, knowledge-based approaches rely on semantic resources such as WordNet [31] for general domain or UMLS (Unified Medical Language System) [4] for the biomedical specific domain.

In recent evaluation campaigns such as SemEval, supervised learning approaches have been shown to be effective for computing semantic similarity between sentences in both general English [2,6] and clinical domains [37,39]. We noted also the emergence of deep learning-based approaches in more recent challenges such as n2c2/OHNLP challenge [42]. Moreover, deep learning-based models have achieved very good performances on clinical texts [42]. However, in the context of French clinical notes, because of the use of domain specific language and the lack of resources, computing effectively semantic similarity between sentences is still a challenging and open research problem. Similarly to international evaluation campaigns such as SemEval [6], BioCreative/OHNLP [37] and n2c2/OHNLP [42], the DEFT 2020 (DÉfi Fouille de Textes - text mining) challenge, aims to promote the development of methods and applications in NLP [5] and provides standard benchmarks for this issue [16,17].

This paper aims to address this challenging issue in the French clinical domain. We propose a supervised approach based on three traditional machine learning (ML) algorithms (Random Forest (RF), Multilayer Perceptron (MLP) and Linear Regression (LR)) to estimate semantic similarity between French clinical sentences. We assume that combining optimally various kinds of similarity measures (lexical, syntactic and semantic) in supervised models may improve their performance in this task. In addition, for semantic representation of sentences, we investigated word embedding in the context of French clinical domain in which resources are less abundant and often not accessible. This proposed approach is implemented in the CONCORDIA system, which stands for COmputing semaNtic sentenCes for fRench Clinical Documents sImilArity. The implemented models are evaluated using standard datasets provided by the organizers of DEFT 2020. The official evaluation metrics were EDRM (Accuracy in relative distance to the average solution) and Spearman correlation coefficient. According to the performance and comparison from the official DEFT 2020 results, our MLP based model outperformed all the other participating systems in the task 1 (15 submitted systems from 5 teams), achieving an EDRM of 0.8217. In addition, the LR and MLP based models obtained the higher Spearman correlation coefficient, achieving respectively 0.7769 and 0.7691. An extension of the models as proposed in the context of the DEFT 2020 challenge has significantly improved the achieved performance. In particular, the MLP-based model achieved a Spearman correlation coefficient of 0.80. On the other hand, the LR based model combining the predicted similarity scores of the MLP model with the word embedding similarity scores obtained the higher Spearman correlation coefficient with 0.8030.

The rest of the paper is structured as follows. Section 2 gives a summary of related work. Then, Sect. 3 presents our supervised approach for measuring semantic similarity between clinical sentences. Next, the official results of our proposal and some other experimental results on standard benchmarks are reported in Sect. 4 and discussed in Sect. 5. Conclusion and future work are finally presented in Sect. 6.

2   Related Work

Measuring similarity between texts is an open research issue widely addressed in the literature. Many approaches have been proposed particularly for computing semantic similarity between sentences. In [14], the author reviews approaches proposed in the literature for measuring sentence similarity and classifies them into three categories according to the used methodology: word-to-word based, structure-based, and vector-based methods. He also distinguishes between string-based (lexical) similarity and semantic similarity. String-based similarity considers sentences as sequences of characters while semantic similarity take into account the sentence meanings.

In lexical approaches, two sentences are considered similar if they contain the same words/characters. Many techniques based on string matching have been proposed for computing text similarity: Jaccard similarity [18,32], Ochiai similarity [33], Dice similarity [10], Levenstein distance [24], Q-gram similarity [40]. These techniques are simple to implement and to interpret but fail to capture semantics and syntactic structures of the sentences. Indeed, two sentences containing the same words can have different meanings. Similarly, two sentences which do not contain the same words can be semantically similar.

To overcome the limitations of these lexical measures, various semantic similarity approaches have been proposed. These approaches use different techniques to capture the meanings of the texts. In [7], authors describe the methods of the state of the art proposed for computing semantic similarity between texts. Based on the adopted principles, methods are classified into four categories: corpus-based, knowledge-based, deep learning-based, and hybrid methods.

The corpus-based methods are widely used in the literature. In general, they rely on statistical analysis of large corpus of texts using techniques like Latent semantic analysis (LSA) [22]. The emerging word embedding technique is also widely used for determining semantic text similarity [13,21]. This technique is based on very large corpus to generate semantic representation of words [29] and sentences [23].

The knowledge-based methods rely on external semantic resources. WordNet [31] is usually used in general domain [15] and sometimes even in specific domains like medicine [39]. UMLS (Unified Medical Language System) [4], a system that includes and unifies more than 160 biomedical terminologies, is also widely used in the biomedical domain [37,39]. Various measures have been developed to determine semantic similarity between words/concepts using semantic resources [19,25,38]. In [27], an open source tool (called UMLS-Similarity) has been developed to compute semantic similarity between biomedical terms/concepts using UMLS. Many approaches are based on these word similarity measures to compute semantic similarity between sentences [26,35]. The knowledge-based methods is sometimes combined with corpus-based methods [28,35] and especially with word embedding [13]. One limitation of the knowledge-based methods is their dependence on semantic resources that are not available for all domains.

However, in recent evaluation campaigns such as SemEval, supervised approaches have been the most effective for measuring semantic similarity between sentences in general [2,6] and clinical domains [37,39].

Recently, we noted the emergence of deep learning-based approaches in semantic representation of texts, particularly the word embedding techniques [23,29,30,36]. These approaches are widely adopted in measuring semantic sentence similarity [8,13] and are increasingly used. More advanced deep learning-based models have been investigated in the most recent n2c2/OHNLP (Open Health NLP) challenge [42]. Transformer-based models like Bidirectional Encoder Representations from Transformers (BERT), XLNet, and Robustly optimized BERT approach (RoBERTa) have been explored [43]. In their experiments on the clinical STS dataset (called MedSTS) [41], authors showed that these models achieved very good performance [43]. In [9], an experimental comparison of five deep learning-based models have been performed: Convolutional Neural Network, BioSentVec, BioBERT, BlueBERT, and ClinicalBERT. In the experiments on MedSTS dataset [41], BioSentVec and BioBERT obtained the best performance. In contrast to these works which deal with English data where resources are abundant, our study focuses on French clinical text data where resources are scarce or inaccessible.

3 Proposed Approach

In this section, we present the approach followed by CONCORDIA. Overall, it operates as follows. First, each sentence pair is represented by a set of features. Then, machine learning algorithms rely on these features to build models. For feature engineering, various text similarity measures are explored including token-based, character-based, vector-based measures, and particularly the one using word embedding. The top-performing combinations of the different measures are then adopted to build supervised models. An overview of the proposed approach is shown in Fig. 1.

3.1 Feature Extraction

Token-Based Similarity Measures. In this approach, each sentence is represented by a set of tokens/words. The degree of similarity between two sentences depends on the number of common tokens into these sentences.

The **Jaccard similarity** measure [18] of two sentences is the ratio of the number of tokens shared by the two sentences and the total number of tokens in both sentences. Given two sentences S1 and S2, X and Y respectively the sets of tokens of S1 and S2, the Jaccard similarity is defined as follows [12]:

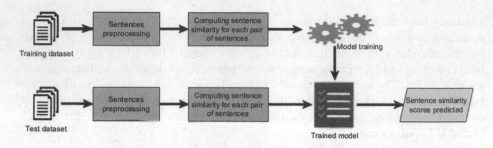

Fig. 1. Overview of the proposed approach [12].

$$sim_{Jaccard}(S1, S2) = \frac{|X \cap Y|}{|X \cup Y|} \qquad (1)$$

The **Dice similarity** measure [10] of two sentences is the ratio of two times the number of tokens shared by the two sentences and the total number of tokens in both sentences. Given two sentences S1 and S2, X and Y respectively the sets of tokens of S1 and S2, the Dice similarity is defined as [12]:

$$sim_{Dice}(S1, S2) = \frac{2 \times |X \cap Y|}{|X| + |Y|} \qquad (2)$$

The **Ochiai similarity** measure [33] of two sentences is the ratio of the number of tokens shared by the two sentences and the square root of the product of their cardinalities. Given two sentences S1 and S2, X and Y respectively the sets of tokens of S1 and S2, the Ochiai similarity is defined as [12]:

$$sim_{Ochiai}(S1, S2) = \frac{|X \cap Y|}{\sqrt{|X| \times |Y|}} \qquad (3)$$

The **Manhattan distance** measures the distance between two sentences by summing the differences of token frequencies in these sentences. Given two sentences S1 and S2, n the total number of tokens in both sentences and Xi and Yi respectively the frequencies of token i in S1 and S2, the Manhattan distance is defined as [12]:

$$d_{Manhattan}(S1, S2) = \sum_{i=1}^{n} |X_i - Y_i| \qquad (4)$$

Character-Based Similarity Measures. The **Q-gram similarity** [40] is a character-based measure widely used in approximate string matching. Each sentence is sliced into sub-strings of length Q (Q-grams). Then, the similarity between the two sentences is computed using the matches between their corresponding Q-grams. For this purpose, the Dice similarity (described above) is applied using q-grams instead of tokens.

The **Levenshtein distance** [24] is an edit distance which computes the minimal number of required operations (character edits) to convert one string into another. These operations are insertions, substitutions, and deletions.

Vector-Based Similarity Measures. The Term Frequency - Inverse Document Frequency (TD-IDF) weighting scheme [20] is commonly used in information retrieval and text mining for representing textual documents as vectors. In this model, each document is represented by a weighted real value vector. Then, the cosine measure is used to compute similarity between documents. Formally, let $C = \{d_1, d_2, \ldots, d_n\}$, a collection of n documents, $T = \{t_1, t_2, \ldots, t_m\}$, the set of terms appearing in the documents of the collection and the documents d_i and d_j being represented respectively by the weighted vectors $d_i = (w_1^i, w_2^i, \ldots, w_m^i)$ and $d_j = (w_1^j, w_2^j, \ldots, w_m^j)$, their cosine similarity is defined as [12]:

$$Sim_{COS}(d_i, d_j) = \frac{\sum_{k=1}^{m} w_k^i w_k^j}{\sqrt{\sum_{k=1}^{m} \left(w_k^i\right)^2} \sqrt{\sum_{k=1}^{m} \left(w_k^j\right)^2}} \tag{5}$$

where w_k^l is the weight (TF.IDF value) of the term t_k in the document d_l. In the context of this work, the considered documents are sentences.

The **word embedding**, specifically the word2vec model [30], on the other hand, allows to build distributed semantic vector representations of words from large unlabeled text data. It is an unsupervised and neural network-based model that requires large amount of data to construct word vectors. Two main approaches are used to training, the continuous bag of words (CBOW) and the skip gram model. The former predicts a word based on its context words while the latter predicts the context words using a word. Considering the context word, the word2vec model can effectively capture semantic relations between words. This model is extended to sentences for learning vector representations of sentences [23]. Like the TF.IDF scheme, the cosine measure is used to compute the semantic sentence similarity.

Before applying token-based, vector-based and Q-gram similarity algorithms, preprocessing consisting of converting sentences into lower cases is performed. Then, the pre-processed sentences are tokenized using the regular expression tokenizers of the Natural Language Toolkit (NLTK) [3]. Therafter, the punctuation marks (dot, comma, colon, ...) and stopwords are removed.

3.2 Models

We proposed supervised models which rely on sentence similarity measures described in the previous section. For feature selection, combinations of different similarity measures (which constitute the features) were experimented. These supervised models require a labeled training set consisting of a set of sentence pairs with their assigned similarity scores. First, each sentence pair was represented by a set of features. Then, traditional machine learning algorithms were used to build the models, which were thereafter used to determine the similarity between unlabeled sentence pairs. Several machine learning algorithms were explored: Linear Regression (LR), Support Vector Machines (SVM), Random Forest (RF), Extreme Gradient Boosting (XGBoost), Extreme Learning Machine (ELM) and Multilayer Perceptron (MLP). Based on their performance on the validation set, we retained RF and MLP which outperformed the other models. In addition, we proposed a Linear Regression (LR) model taking as inputs

Table 1. Sample annotated sentence pairs. **Vote** indicates the gold similarity score between the two sentences [12].

Sentence 1	Sentence 2	Vote
La plupart des biberons d'étain sont de type balustre à tétine vissée sur pied (ou piédouche)	On a ensuite fait des biberons en étain et en fer blanc	0
La proportion de résidents ayant des prothèses dentaires allait de 62% à 87%	Dans toutes les études, la plupart des participants avaient des dentiers (entre 62% et 87%)	1
Les essais contrôlés randomisés, les essais cas-témoins et les études de cohorte comprenant des enfants et des adultes soumis à n'importe quelle intervention pour l'hématome aigu de l'oreille	Nous avons recherché des essais portant sur des adultes ou des enfants ayant subi un hématome	2
Les agents de déplétion du fibrinogène réduisent le fibrinogène présent dans le plasma sanguin, la viscosité du sang et améliorent donc le flux sanguin	Ils réduisent également l'épaisseur du sang (ou la viscosité), ce qui permet d'améliorer le flux sanguin jusqu'au cerveau	3
Refermez le flacon immédiatement après utilisation	Refermez l'embout du flacon avec le bouchon immédiatement après utilisation	4
La dose d'entretien recommandée est également de 7,5 mg par jour	La posologie usuelle est de 7,5 mg de chlorhydrate de moexipril par jour	5

the predicted similarity scores of both models and the average score of the different similarity measures.

An extension of the models proposed in the DEFT 2020 challenge were performed using several techniques. For this, we considered this sentence similarity computation task as regression problem. Thus, we used regressors to predict real values and then converted these values into integer values in the range [0–5] rather than multi-class classifiers. Furthermore, we used grid search technique to determine the optimal values of the models hyper-parameters. In addition, the LR model, instead of taking as inputs the predicted scores of the other models, combines scores predicted by the MLP model with the word2vec semantic similarity scores. The motivation is to better take into account the meanings of the sentences. For this purpose, we created a French clinical corpus of 70 K sentences partially from previous DEFT datasets.

4   Evaluation

In order to assess the proposed semantic similarity computing approach, we used benchmarks of French clinical datasets [16,17] provided by the organizers of the DEFT 2020 challenge. The EDRM (Accuracy in relative distance to the average solution) and the Spearman correlation coefficient are used as the official evaluation metrics [5].

We additionally used the Pearson correlation coefficient and the accuracy metrics. The Pearson correlation coefficient is commonly used in semantic text similarity evaluation [6,37,42], while the accuracy measure enables to determine the correctly predicted similarity scores.

4.1 Datasets

In the DEFT 2020 challenge, the organizers provided annotated clinical texts for the different tasks [16,17]. The task 1 of this DEFT challenge aims at determining the degree of similarity between pairs of French clinical sentences. Therefore, an annotated training set of 600 pairs of sentences and a testing set of 410 are made available. In total, 1,010 pairs of sentences derived from clinical notes are provided. Each sentence pair is manually annotated with a numerical score indicating the degree of similarity between the two sentences. The clinical sentence pairs are annotated independently by five human experts that assess the similarity scores between sentences ranging from 0 (that indicates the two sentences are completely dissimilar) to 5 (that indicates the two sentences are semantically equivalent). Then, scores resulting from the majority vote are used as the gold standard. Table 1 shows examples of sentence pairs in the training set with their gold similarity scores. The distribution of the similarity scores in the training set is highlighted in Fig. 2.

During the challenge, only the similarity scores associated with the sentence pairs in the training set are provided. Thus, the training set is partitioned into two datasets: a training set of 450 and a validation set of 150 sentence pairs. This validation set was then used to select the best subset of features but also to tune and compare machine learning models.

4.2 Results

The CONCORDIA proposed approach is experimented with different combinations of similarity measures as features for building the models. For each model, the results of the best combination are reported. The results of the proposed models on the validation set (please see Sect. 4.1) are presented in Table 2. According to the Pearson correlation coefficient, the MLP-based model got the best performance with a score of 0.8132. The MLP-based model slightly outperforms the RF-based model, while the latter yielded the highest Spearman correlation coefficient with a score of 0.8117. The LR-based model using predicted scores of the two other models as inputs got the lowest performance in this validation set.

Table 2. Results of the proposed models over the validation dataset [12].

Models	Pearson correlation	Spearman correlation
Random Forest model	0.8114	**0.8117**
Multilayer Perceptron model	**0.8132**	0.8113
Linear Regression model	0.8083	0.7926

Thereafter, the models were built on the entire training set using the best combinations of features, which yielded the best results in the validation set. Table 3 shows the official `CONCORDIA` results during the DEFT 2020 challenge [5, 12]. According to the EDRM, the MLP model got significantly better results. We also note that the RF model performed better than the LR model, which combines the predicted similarity scores of the two other models. However, the latter yielded the highest Spearman correlation coefficient over the official test set.

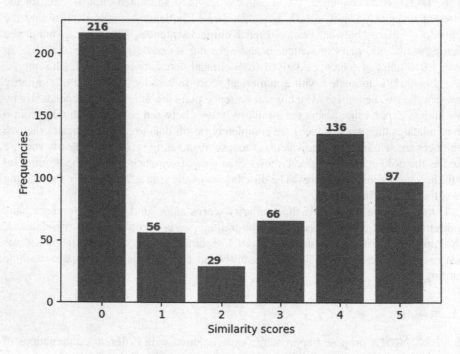

Fig. 2. Distribution of similarity scores in the training set [12].

Table 3. Results of the proposed models over the official test set of the DEFT 2020 [12].

Models	EDRM	Spearman correlation
Random Forest model	0.7947	0.7528
Multilayer Perceptron model	**0.8217**	0.7691
Linear Regression model	0.7755	**0.7769**

Compared to the other participating systems in the task 1 of the DEFT 2020 challenge, the proposed MLP model got the best performance (achieving an EDRM of 0.8217) [5]. Overall, `CONCORDIA` obtained EDRM scores higher than the average EDRM (0.7617). In addition, the two `CONCORDIA` best learning models, respectively the MLP model and the RF model, obtained EDRM scores greater than (for MLP) or equal to (for RF) the median score (0.7947). According to the Spearman correlation, the LR-based and MLP-based learning models got the best performance (respectively 0.7769 and 0.7691) out of all the other methods presented at the task 1 of the DEFT 2020 challenge.

Extension of the models proposed in the DEFT 2020 challenge are performed using several techniques. Table 4 shows the post challenge results of our improved models. The performances of the different models are significantly increased. In particular, the MLP based model now achieves a Spearman correlation of 0.80. On the other hand, the LR based model combining the predicted similarity scores of the MLP model and the word embedding similarity scores obtains the higher Spearman correlation with 0.8030.

Table 4. Results of the improved models over the official test set of the DEFT 2020.

Models	Pearson correlation	Spearman correlation
Random Forest model	0.8004	0.7948
Multilayer Perceptron model	0.8054	0.80
Linear Regression model	**0.8056**	**0.8030**

5 Discussion

5.1 Findings

The official results of the DEFT 2020 challenge showed that our approach is effective and relevant for measuring semantic similarity between sentences in the French clinical domain. Experiments performed after the challenge demonstrated also that word embedding semantic similarity can improve the performance of supervised models.

In order to estimate the importance of the different features in predicting the similarity between sentence pairs, the Pearson correlation coefficient of each feature is computed over the entire training dataset (please see Table 5). The findings show that the 3-gram and 4-gram similarity measures obtained the best correlation scores (respectively, 0.7894 and 0.7854). They slightly outperformed the semantic similarity measure based on the word embedding (0.7746) and the 5-gram similarity (0.7734). In addition, we noted that the Dice, Ochiai and TF.IDF based similarity measures performed well with correlation scores higher than 0.76. Among the explored features, the Levenshtein similarity was the less important feature (with a correlation score of 0.7283) followed by the Jaccard similarity (0.7354) and the Manhattan distance (0.7354). These results are consistent with those of the related work [8, 39] although the word embedding based measure got the highest Pearson correlation coefficient in [39].

Table 5. Importance of each feature according to the Pearson correlation coefficient over the entire training set [12].

Feature	Pearson correlation
Q-gram similarity (Q = 3)	0.7894
Q-gram similarity (Q = 4)	0.7854
Word2vec similarity	0.7746
Q-gram similarity (Q = 5)	0.7734
Dice similarity	0.7644
TF-IDF similarity	0.7639
Ochiai similarity	0.7630
Jaccard similarity	0.7354
Manhattan distance	0.7354
Levenshtein similarity	0.7283

Using of together all these various similarity measures as features to build the models did not allow to increase their performance. On the contrary, it led to a drop of their performance. Thus, combinations of several similarity measures were experimented. The top-performing combination (which yield results presented in Sect. 4.2) was achieved with the following similarity measures: Dice, Ochiai, 3-gram, 4-gram, and Levenshtein. These findings show that these similarity measures complement each other and their optimal combination in supervised models allows to improve the models performance.

5.2   Comparison with Other Participating Systems

Most of systems submitted on the task 1 of the DEFT 2020 challenge mainly used string-based similarity measures (e.g. Jaccard, Cosine) or distances (Euclidean, Manhattan, Levenshtein) between sentences. Various machine learning models (e.g. Logistic Regression, Random Forest) were trained using these features [5]. Models of multilingual word embeddings derived from BERT (Bidirectional Encoder Representations from Transformers), in particular Sentence M-BERT and MUSE (Multilingual Universal Sentence Encoder) were equally developed but their performance were limited on this task. Compared with these systems, CONCORDIA explores more advanced features (e.g. word embedding) to determine the degree of similarity between sentences. In addition, instead of combining all the explored similarity measures as features, feature selection method were used to optimize the performance of our models. Furthermore, CONCORDIA is based on traditional ML algorithms for computing semantic sentence similarity.

5.3   Analysis of CONCORDIA Performance

Evaluation of the CONCORDIA semantic similarity approach on the DEFT 2020 dataset showed its effectiveness in this task. The results also demonstrated the relevance of the features used to measure similarity between French clinical sentences. Thus, all the CONCORDIA's learning models allowed to correctly estimate the semantic similarity between most of the sentence pairs of the official dataset. However, an analysis of the prediction errors using the Mean squared error (MSE) highlight variations of the models performance according to the similarity classes. Figure 3 shows the performance of our models over the official test set of the DEFT 2020 challenge. Overall, the LR model significantly made fewer errors. Moreover, the MLP model performed slightly better than the RF model in all similarity classes except class 4. These findings are consistent with the official results (Table 3) based on the Spearman correlation coefficient. The results also show that the RF and MLP models made fewer errors in predicting classes 5 and 0 but they performed much worse in predicting classes 2 and 3. We equally note that the proposed models, especially the RF model and the MLP model, struggled in predicting the middle classes (1, 2 and 3). Indeed, in the official test set, classes 1 and 2 are respectively 37 and 28. The RF model did not predict any value in both classes, while the MLP model predicted only 9 values of the class 1. The low performance in predicting these classes may be also attributed to the fact that they are less representative in the training dataset.

5.4 Limitations and Future Work

An extensive analysis of the results reveals limitations of CONCORDIA in predicting semantic similarity of some sentence pairs. The similarity measures used (Dice, Ochiai, Q-gram, and Levenshtein) struggle to capture the semantics of sentences. Therefore, our methods failed to correctly predict similarity scores for sentences having similar terms, but which are semantically not equivalent. For example, for sentence pair 224 (id = 224 in Table 6) in the test set, all methods estimated that the two sentences are roughly equivalent (with a similarity score of 4) while they are completely dissimilar according to the human experts (with similarity score of 0). On the other hand, our methods are limited in predicting the semantic similarity of sentences that are semantically equivalent but use different terms. For example, the sentences of pair 127 (id = 127 in Table 6) are considered completely dissimilar (with a similarity score of 0) while they are roughly equivalent according to the human experts (with a similarity score of 4). To address these limitations, we proposed a semantic similarity measure based on words embedding. But the combination of this semantic measure with the other similarity measures in supervised models led to a drop in performance.

Several avenues are identified to improve the performance of the proposed approach. First, we plan to explore additional similarity measures, especially those capable to capture the meanings of sentences. A post challenge experiment performed with word embedding on medium French corpus slightly improved the performance. Using a larger corpus could enable to increase significantly the performance. Furthermore, to overcome the limitation related to semantics, we plan the use of specialized biomedical resources, such as the UMLS (Unified Medical Language System) Metathesaurus. The latter contains various semantic resources, some of which are available in French (MeSH, Snomed CT, ICD 10, etc.). Another avenue would be to investigate the use of deep learning models such as BERT in the French clinical domain.

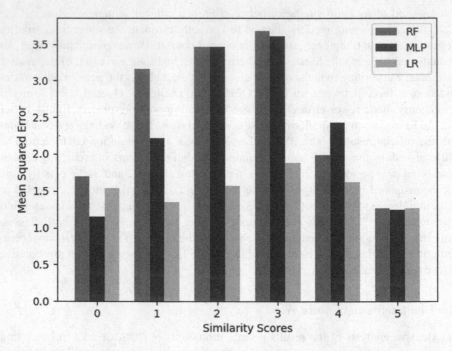

Fig. 3. The mean squared error of the proposed models according to the similarity classes over the test set [12].

Table 6. Sample similarity scores prediction of sentence pairs. **Vote** indicates the gold similarity scores while **Pred** indicates the predicted similarity scores.

Id	Sentence pair	Vote	Pred
42	Sentence 1: Ce médicament est contre-indiqué en cas d'hypersensibilité aux anesthésiques locaux ou à l'un des composants, et dans les situations suivantes Sentence 2: N'utilisez jamais Septanest 40 mg/ml adrenalinee au 1/200 000, solution injectable à usage dentaire en cas d'hypersensibilité (allergie) aux anesthésiques locaux ou à l'un des composants et dans les situations suivantes	4	4
127	Sentence 1: Eviter la prise de boissons alcoolisées et de médicaments contenant de l'alcool Sentence 2: La prise d'alcool est formellement déconseillée pendant la durée du traitement	4	0
224	Sentence 1: La persistance du canal artériel (PCA) est associée à une mortalité et une morbidité chez les nouveau-nés prématurés Sentence 2: Administration prophylactique d'indométacine intraveineuse pour prévenir la mortalité et la morbidité chez les nouveau-nés prématurés	0	4
338	Sentence 1: Nous avons évalué les bénéfices et les risques cliniques des agents stimulant l'érythropoïèse contre l'anémie dans la polyarthrite rhumatoïde Sentence 2: Qu'est-ce que l'anémie dans la polyarthrite rhumatoïde et que sont les agents stimulant l'érythropoïèse	0	4

6 Conclusion

In this paper, we presented the CONCORDIA approach which is based on supervised models for computing semantic similarity between sentences in the French clinical domain. Several machine learning algorithms have been explored and the top-performing ones (Random forest and Multilayer perceptron) retained. In addition, a Linear regression model combining the output of the MLP model with word embedding similarity were proposed. CONCORDIA achieved the best performance on a French standard dataset, provided in the context of an established international challenge, DEFT 2020 challenge. An extension of this approach after the challenge let to improve significantly the models performance. Several avenues to improve the effectiveness of the models are considered.

References

1. Agirre, E., et al.: SemEval-2015 task 2: semantic textual similarity, English, Spanish and pilot on interpretability. In: Proceedings of the 9th International Workshop on Semantic Evaluation (SemEval 2015), pp. 252–263. Association for Computational Linguistics, Denver (2015). https://doi.org/10.18653/v1/S15-2045, https://www.aclweb.org/anthology/S15-2045
2. Agirre, E., et al.: SemEval-2016 task 1: semantic textual similarity, monolingual and cross-lingual evaluation. In: Proceedings of the 10th International Workshop on Semantic Evaluation (SemEval-2016), pp. 497–511. Association for Computational Linguistics, San Diego (2016). https://doi.org/10.18653/v1/S16-1081, https://www.aclweb.org/anthology/S16-1081
3. Bird, S., Loper, E.: NLTK: the natural language toolkit. In: Proceedings of the ACL Interactive Poster and Demonstration Sessions, pp. 214–217. Association for Computational Linguistics, Barcelona (2004). https://www.aclweb.org/anthology/P04-3031
4. Bodenreider, O.: The unified medical language system (UMLS): integrating biomedical terminology. Nucleic Acids Res. **32**(Database issue), D267–D270 (2004). https://doi.org/10.1093/nar/gkh061, https://www.ncbi.nlm.nih.gov/pmc/articles/PMC308795/
5. Cardon, R., Grabar, N., Grouin, C., Hamon, T.: Presentation of the DEFT 2020 Challenge: open domain textual similarity and precise information extraction from clinical cases. In: Actes de la 6e conférence conjointe Journées d'Études sur la Parole (JEP, 33e édition), Traitement Automatique des Langues Naturelles (TALN, 27e édition), Rencontre des étudiants Chercheurs en Informatique pour le Traitement Automatique des Langues (RÉCITAL, 22e édition). Atelier DÉfi Fouille de Textes, pp. 1–13. ATALA et AFCP, Nancy (2020). https://www.aclweb.org/anthology/2020.jeptalnrecital-deft.1
6. Cer, D., Diab, M., Agirre, E., Lopez-Gazpio, I., Specia, L.: SemEval-2017 task 1: semantic textual similarity multilingual and crosslingual focused evaluation. In: Proceedings of the 11th International Workshop on Semantic Evaluation (SemEval-2017), pp. 1–14. Association for Computational Linguistics, Vancouver (2017). https://doi.org/10.18653/v1/S17-2001, https://www.aclweb.org/anthology/S17-2001
7. Chandrasekaran, D., Mago, V.: Evolution of semantic similarity-a survey. ACM Comput. Surv. 54(2) (Feb 2021). https://doi.org/10.1145/3440755, https://doi.org/10.1145/3440755, place: New York, NY, USA Publisher: Association for Computing Machinery
8. Chen, Q., Du, J., Kim, S., Wilbur, W.J., Lu, Z.: Deep learning with sentence embeddings pre-trained on biomedical corpora improves the performance of finding similar sentences in electronic medical records. BMC Med. Inform. Decis. Making **20**(1), 73 (2020). https://doi.org/10.1186/s12911-020-1044-0

9. Chen, Q., Rankine, A., Peng, Y., Aghaarabi, E., Lu, Z.: Benchmarking effectiveness and efficiency of deep learning models for semantic textual similarity in the clinical domain: validation study. JMIR Med. Inform. **9**(12), e27386 (2021). https://doi.org/10.2196/27386
10. Dice, L.R.: Measures of the amount of ecologic association between species. Ecology **26**(3), 297–302 (1945). https://doi.org/10.2307/1932409, https://app.dimensions.ai/details/publication/pub.1069656769, http://pdfs.semanticscholar.org/2304/5299013e8738bc8eff73827ef8de256aef66.pdf
11. Dramé, K., Mougin, F., Diallo, G.: Large scale biomedical texts classification: a kNN and an ESA-based approaches. J. Biomed. Semant. **7**, 40 (2016). https://doi.org/10.1186/s13326-016-0073-1
12. Dramé, K., Sambe, G., Diallo, G.: CONCORDIA: computing semantic sentences for French clinical documents similarity. In: Proceedings of the 17th International Conference on Web Information Systems and Technologies - WEBIST, pp. 77–83. INSTICC, SciTePress (2021). https://doi.org/10.5220/0010687500003058
13. Farouk, M.: Sentence semantic similarity based on word embedding and WordNet. In: 2018 13th International Conference on Computer Engineering and Systems (ICCES), pp. 33–37 (2018). https://doi.org/10.1109/ICCES.2018.8639211
14. Farouk, M.: Measuring sentences similarity: a survey. Indian J. Sci. Technol. **12**(25), 1–11 (2019). https://doi.org/10.17485/ijst/2019/v12i25/143977, http://arxiv.org/abs/1910.03940, arXiv: 1910.03940
15. Fernando, S., Stevenson, M.: A semantic similarity approach to paraphrase detection. In: Proceedings of the 11th Annual Research Colloquium of the UK Special Interest Group for Computational Linguistics, pp. 45–52. Citeseer (2008)
16. Grabar, N., Cardon, R.: CLEAR - simple corpus for medical French. In: Proceedings of the 1st Workshop on Automatic Text Adaptation (ATA), pp. 3–9. Association for Computational Linguistics, Tilburg (2018). https://doi.org/10.18653/v1/W18-7002, https://www.aclweb.org/anthology/W18-7002
17. Grabar, N., Claveau, V., Dalloux, C.: CAS: French corpus with clinical cases. In: Lavelli, A., Minard, A.L., Rinaldi, F. (eds.) Proceedings of the Ninth International Workshop on Health Text Mining and Information Analysis, Louhi@EMNLP 2018, Brussels, Belgium, 31 October 2018, pp. 122–128. Association for Computational Linguistics (2018). https://aclanthology.info/papers/W18-5614/w18-5614
18. Jaccard, P.: The distribution of the flora in the alpine zone. 1. New Phytol. **11**(2), 37–50 (1912). https://doi.org/10.1111/j.1469-8137.1912.tb05611.x, https://nph.onlinelibrary.wiley.com/doi/abs/10.1111/j.1469-8137.1912.tb05611.x, _eprint: https://nph.onlinelibrary.wiley.com/doi/pdf/10.1111/j.1469-8137.1912.tb05611.x
19. Jiang, J.J., Conrath, D.W.: Semantic similarity based on corpus statistics and lexical taxonomy. In: Proceedings of the 10th Research on Computational Linguistics International Conference, pp. 19–33. The Association for Computational Linguistics and Chinese Language Processing (ACLCLP), Taipei (1997). https://aclanthology.org/O97-1002
20. Jones, K.S.: A statistical interpretation of term specificity and its application in retrieval. J. Doc. (2004). https://doi.org/10.1108/00220410410560573, https://www.emerald.com/insight/content/doi/10.1108/00220410410560573/full/html
21. Kenter, T., de Rijke, M.: Short text similarity with word embeddings. In: Proceedings of the 24th ACM International on Conference on Information and Knowledge Management, CIKM 2015, pp. 1411–1420. Association for Computing Machinery, New York (2015). https://doi.org/10.1145/2806416.2806475
22. Landauer, T.K., Foltz, P.W., Laham, D.: An introduction to latent semantic analysis. Discour. Process. **25**(2–3), 259–284 (1998). https://doi.org/10.1080/01638539809545028, _eprint: https://doi.org/10.1080/01638539809545028

23. Le, Q.V., Mikolov, T.: Distributed representations of sentences and documents. arXiv:1405.4053 [cs] (2014)
24. Levenshtein, V.I.: Binary codes capable of correcting deletions, insertions, and reversals. Sov. phys. Dokl. **10**, 707–710 (1965)
25. Lin, D.: An information-theoretic definition of similarity. In: Proceedings of the Fifteenth International Conference on Machine Learning, ICML 1998, pp. 296–304. Morgan Kaufmann Publishers Inc., San Francisco (1998)
26. Liu, H., Wang, P.: Assessing sentence similarity using WordNet based word similarity. J. Softw. **8**(6), 1451–1458 (2013). https://doi.org/10.4304/jsw.8.6.1451-1458
27. McInnes, B.T., Pedersen, T., Pakhomov, S.V.: UMLS-interface and UMLS-similarity : open source software for measuring paths and semantic similarity. In: AMIA Annual Symposium Proceedings 2009, pp. 431–435 (2009). https://www.ncbi.nlm.nih.gov/pmc/articles/PMC2815481/
28. Mihalcea, R., Corley, C., Strapparava, C.: Corpus-based and knowledge-based measures of text semantic similarity. In: Proceedings of the 21st National Conference on Artificial Intelligence, AAAI 2006, vol. 1, pp. 775–780. AAAI Press, Boston (2006)
29. Mikolov, T., Chen, K., Corrado, G., Dean, J.: Efficient estimation of word representations in vector space. arXiv:1301.3781 [cs] (2013)
30. Mikolov, T., Sutskever, I., Chen, K., Corrado, G., Dean, J.: Distributed representations of words and phrases and their compositionality. arXiv:1310.4546 [cs, stat] (2013)
31. Miller, G.A.: WordNet: a lexical database for English. Commun. ACM **38**(11), 39–41 (1995). https://doi.org/10.1145/219717.219748
32. Niwattanakul, S., Singthongchai, J., Naenudorn, E., Wanapu, S.: Using of jaccard coefficient for keywords similarity. In: Proceedings of The International MultiConference of Engineers and Computer Scientists 2013, pp. 380–384 (2013)
33. Ochiai, A.: Zoogeographical studies on the soleoid fishes found in Japan and its neighbouring regions-II. Bull. Jpn. Soc. scient. Fish. **22**, 526–530 (1957). https://ci.nii.ac.jp/naid/10024483079
34. P, S., Shaji, A.P.: A survey on semantic similarity. In: 2019 International Conference on Advances in Computing, Communication and Control (ICAC3), pp. 1–8 (2019). https://doi.org/10.1109/ICAC347590.2019.9036843
35. Pawar, A., Mago, V.: Calculating the similarity between words and sentences using a lexical database and corpus statistics. arXiv:1802.05667 [cs] (2018)
36. Pennington, J., Socher, R., Manning, C.D.: GloVe: global vectors for word representation. In: Empirical Methods in Natural Language Processing (EMNLP), pp. 1532–1543 (2014). http://www.aclweb.org/anthology/D14-1162
37. Rastegar-Mojarad, M., et al.: BioCreative/OHNLP challenge 2018. In: Proceedings of the 2018 ACM International Conference on Bioinformatics, Computational Biology, and Health Informatics, BCB 2018, p. 575. Association for Computing Machinery, New York (2018). https://doi.org/10.1145/3233547.3233672
38. Resnik, P.: Using information content to evaluate semantic similarity in a taxonomy. In: Proceedings of the 14th International Joint Conference on Artificial Intelligence, IJCAI 1995, vol. 1, pp. 448–453. Morgan Kaufmann Publishers Inc., San Francisco (1995)
39. Soğancıoğlu, G., Öztürk, H., Özgür, A.: BIOSSES: a semantic sentence similarity estimation system for the biomedical domain. Bioinformatics **33**(14), i49–i58 (2017). https://doi.org/10.1093/bioinformatics/btx238
40. Ukkonen, E.: Approximate string-matching with q-grams and maximal matches. Theor. Comput. Sci. **92**(1), 191–211 (1992). https://doi.org/10.1016/0304-3975(92)90143-4, https://www.sciencedirect.com/science/article/pii/0304397592901434
41. Wang, Y., et al.: MedSTS: a resource for clinical semantic textual similarity. Lang. Resour. Eval. **54**(1), 57–72 (2018). https://doi.org/10.1007/s10579-018-9431-1

42. Wang, Y., Fu, S., Shen, F., Henry, S., Uzuner, O., Liu, H.: The 2019 n2c2/OHNLP track on clinical semantic textual similarity: overview. JMIR Med. Inform. **8**(11), e23375 (2020). https://doi.org/10.2196/23375, https://medinform.jmir.org/2020/11/e23375. Company: JMIR Medical Informatics Distributor: JMIR Medical Informatics Institution: JMIR Medical Informatics Label: JMIR Medical Informatics Publisher: JMIR Publications Inc., Toronto, Canada

43. Yang, X., He, X., Zhang, H., Ma, Y., Bian, J., Wu, Y.: Measurement of semantic textual similarity in clinical texts: comparison of transformer-based models. JMIR Med. Inform. **8**(11), e19735 (2020). https://doi.org/10.2196/19735, http://www.ncbi.nlm.nih.gov/pubmed/33226350

A Comparative Study of Energy Domain Ontologies

José Miguel Blanco[✉][iD], Bruno Rossi[iD], and Tomáš Pitner[iD]

Faculty of Informatics, Masaryk University, Brno, Czech Republic
{jmblanco,brossi}@mail.muni.cz, pitner@muni.cz

Abstract. The energy domain is part of Critical Infrastructures (CI), in which Smart Grids (SG) play the role of major enabler of concepts such as Smart Cities. The capability of reasoning through ontologies is of paramount importance to allow a better integration of sensors and devices part of the smart energy domain. In this paper, we provide a comprehensive evaluation of semantic reasoning in the energy domain, by evaluating the performance of ten ontologies in terms of different metrics such as load time and run-time performance, discussing how such ontologies can be applicable in case of deployment on devices with constrained resources.

Keywords: Smart grids · Ontologies · Semantic web reasoners · Performance

1 Introduction

Critical Infrastructures (CIs) are fundamental in the context of the modern society. CIs have been defined as any asset, system or composed system that are fundamental for critical functioning of the society, having impact on health, safety, security, economic or social well-being of citizens—with any disruption leading to dramatic consequences [13,24].

The energy domain is one of the key CIs categories, in which Smart Grids (SG) constitute the convergence of Cyber-Physical Systems (CPS) and communication technology to bring higher level of welfare to energy consumers. SGs led over time to an improvement of the energy sector, driven by the integration of smart technologies (like smart meters [7]), smart services, and communication technologies towards a more sustainable and secure electricity supply driven by renewable energy sources [44]. However, being the SG a representation of a CPS, there is high level of complexity in the integration of cyber resources (e.g., computing algorithms, communication and control software) with the physical parts (e.g., sensors, smart meters) [15].

The Smart Grid Architecture Model (SGAM) [5] was introduced with the aim to split the complexity of the grid into several layers and their integration: a component layer (physical devices), a communication layer (protocols), a data layer (information data models), a function layer (functionalities provided), and a business layer (the business requirements). In this paper, we focus more on the data layer, in which data quality

The research was supported from ERDF/ESF "CyberSecurity, CyberCrime and Critical Information Infrastructures Center of Excellence" (No. CZ.02.1.01/0.0/0.0/16_019/0000822).

M. Marchiori et al. (Eds.): WEBIST 2020/2021, LNBIP 469, pp. 43–58, 2023.
https://doi.org/10.1007/978-3-031-24197-0_3

management is of paramount importance, allowing to support the smart services provided to customers [17]. In this direction, the application of semantic reasoning and domain ontologies allows a better integration of the many devices and sensors involved and their integration for the energy services provided [4,6,18,38,46].

Semantic reasoners applied to resource-constrained devices such as smart meters have seen some research focused on [1,40,41]. For example, the provision of a lightweight reasoner based on OWL to be implemented in a resource-constrained platform [41], or the evaluation of real-time performance of reasoning with Linked Data for SG communication [40]. Yet, it still remains to investigate the general availability and performance of larger ontologies in the energy domain. Many ontologies have been defined over time for the energy sector with different aims, like to model the devices and components in SGs or to enable health monitoring of SG components (we will discuss the ontologies in Sect. 3). However, at the moment there is no exhaustive and extensive evaluation of the energy ontologies in terms of their availability and performance.

In this paper, we extend our previous research [3] by analyzing a wider set of energy ontologies, providing a broader view on the semantic support in the context of SGs. We focus in particular on the availability and support of the energy ontologies: their descriptive statistics (like general axioms counts), their applicability and the performance overhead (load time, run-time impact and execution time of the reasoner [25,26]) that can potentially hinder their adoption on low resources devices. Overall, the goal is to provide a comprehensive view on the ontologies available in the energy domain.

The article is structured as follows. In Sect. 2 we discuss Semantic Modelling in the Energy domain. In Sect. 3 we provide our review of existing ontologies for the Energy domain. In Sect. 4 we explain our experimental evaluation of the identified ontologies in terms of several performance metrics and the performance evaluation of the reasoners. In Sect. 5 we provide the main results from the experimental evaluation. In Sect. 6 we discuss related works related to ontologies for the energy domain. In Sect. 7 we conclude the article.

2   Energy Domain and Semantic Modelling

The Energy domain has encountered a paramount shift in the last years. The emergence of the Smart Grid has meant the modernization of several aspects connected to power provision to industry and consumers, by allowing bi-directional communication with the support of Information Technology (IT) and the provision of related smart services [14]. Overall, the adoption of Smart Grids leads to more efficient energy transmission, reduction of failures and restoration times – in general better services for customers at reduced costs [19].

However, to build such services there is the need to integrate the amount of big data generated in the energy domain [35,45], as streaming data plays a major role, as data is continuously generated from several devices, like smart meters – providing reasoning capabilities over such data streams is of paramount importance. Semantic models can be applied to create and deploy energy management services and applications for consumers and utility operators [23,46]. The benefit of a semantic data model (*ontology*) is to help in processing more efficiently the huge amount of information generated, improving data integration and exchange [23]. Thus, ontologies can provide a machine-readable and machine-understandable vocabulary for the energy domain [39].

In the energy domain, to enable exchanging information about the configuration and status of the power network, the Common Information Model (CIM) defined by IEC [8] defined a semantic model to be used as baseline for the provision of semantic services [32]. CIM is often used in the context of Smart Grids to extract the RDFs semantics from the underlying model (an example can be seen in Fig. 1 from [39], in which authors convert part of the CIM UML data model into an RDF schema defining 961 classes for the energy domain).

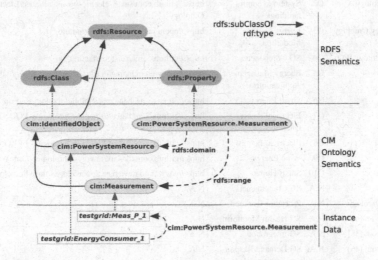

Fig. 1. Example of part of RDF schema extracted from CIM UML model semantics (from Schumilin et al. [39]).

Overall, many ontologies were proposed over time in the energy domain (e.g., [9, 20, 28, 29]). Each ontology covers different needs in the energy domain, such as energy management applications, power devices network communication, and smart home devices. Together with the needs, also the overall extent of the ontologies varies depending on the scope of the ontologies. In this research we aim at shedding light on the availability and performance of some of the main energy domain ontologies.

3 Review of Ontologies for the Energy Domain

The main aim of this section is to provide an overview of the ontologies that we will be analyzing. For that matter we have collected ontologies that are related to the energy domain. The ontologies that we have captured in this work can be seen in Table 1. This table shows all the considered ontologies, with their respective aim, the URL from where they were accessed and, also, a key to refer to them more easily and accessible all throughout the paper. It is also important to mention that some of the ontologies that we have collected are not available as of today. Nevertheless, these are still included in the table to provide a ample approach to the topic at hand and, at the same time, showcasing how the disappearance of resources hurts research and implementation. Also, let us note that not all the ontologies here are presented in research papers or other similar venues; some of them are extracted from industry standards and have yet to appear in the aforementioned mediums.

Table 1. Smart grids ontologies.

Name	Key	Aim	URL
OEMA Ontology network	O1	Whole Network Ontology	http://www.purl.org/oema/ontologynetwork
SEPA's Ontology	O2	System to control buildings	https://github.com/smart-electric-power-alliance/Electric-Grid-Ontology
Open Energy Ontology (OEO)	O3	Energy System Modelling	https://openenergy-platform.org/ontology/
Facility Ontology (FO)	O4	SG Components	https://github.com/usnistgov/facility
DABGEO	O5	Energy Management Applications	https://innoweb.mondragon.edu/ontologies/dabgeo/index-en.html
SARGON	O6	Smart Energy	https://git.rwth-aachen.de/acs/public/ontology/sargon
PQONT	O7	Electrical Power Quality	https://github.com/dkucuk/Energy-Ontologies-PQONT
FEONT	O8	Electrical Energy	https://github.com/dkucuk/Energy-Ontologies-FEEONT
OntoWind	O9	Wind Energy	https://github.com/dkucuk/Energy-Ontologies-OntoWind
ThinkHome	O10	Smart Home	https://www.auto.tuwien.ac.at/downloads/thinkhome/ontology
SSG	N.A.	SG Components	N.A.
Prosumer Ontology	N.A.	Prosumer Oriented	N.A.
Ontology from [6]	N.A.	SG Health Monitoring	N.A.
Ontology from [38]	N.A.	SG Integration	N.A.
Ontology from [46]	N.A.	SG Demand/Response Applications	N.A.

The ontology (O1) that appears in [9], named OEMA, focuses on having a modular approach, so it can be applied to different parts of the energy domain with ease. For our work we are considering all the modules as a whole so the ontology can be described as a "whole network" ontology. The Smart Electic Power Alliance (SEPA) developed an ontology (O2) whose focus is the control of buildings and its energy; in particular it focuses on the energy usage which is relevant for our investigation. Another ontology (O3) considered is the Open Energy Ontology, whose purpose is the modellization of the energy system as a whole; in particular it focuses on providing it from the perspective of the open source model. An ontology (O4) named as Facility Ontology was devised to consider the functioning of a facility and, in particular, considering the energy consumption of the machinery and the facility as an independent entity. A continuation of the work of O1 can be found in the ontology (O5) DABGEO [10], that focuses on allocating complete control of the energy from a perspective of managing the different applications.

The ontology (O6) known as SARGON [20] was developed as to take care of the smart energy domain, in particular with the usage of IoT devices and its intrinsic verticality of deployment. The PQONT ontology (O7) [27] is introduced as the ontology to be in charge of the quality of the energy, so it provides a common framework for any problems regarding the quality of electrical power. By FEONT [28] we find an ontology (O8) whose responsibility is to cover the terrain of electrical energy and counts with weighted attributes so it is possible for it to deal with the fuzziness of the textual representation of its concepts. The ontology (O9) that has been developed to deal with the energy generated by wind generators can be found under the name of OntoWind [29] and proposes a solid foundation for semantic management of energy from renewable sources. Finally, the last ontology available (O10) goes by the name of ThinkHome [34] focusing on the domain of Smart Homes and aiming at reducing their energy consumption by the means of optimization; it also provides a structure for some additional autonomous agents.

Finally, there are some ontologies that, while related, are no longer available. These ontologies correspond to the ones described in [6,18,36,38], and [46]. Going into detail, the unnamed ontology of [6] focuses on monitoring the health of the components of a SG, in particular, that of any given transformer. The Prosumer ontology introduced by [18] offers support for grids that are prosumer-oriented; i.e., that have a high number of users that act both as consumers and producers. The ontology SSG, introduced in [36], aims at modeling the SG components, their features and properties, allowing the achievement of the SG objectives. In [38] an ontology is defined so it is able to enable the communication and integration between buildings and SG energy management. Finally, [46] defines a new ontology that focuses on dealing with the demand and response of the SG energy.

4 Experimental Evaluation

This section is to establish the process that we follow to obtain and measure the metrics of the ontologies that we have collected in Table 1. The tools that have been used for this task include Protégé[1] *5.0.0* Linux version, and the reasoners HermiT *1.4.3.456* and Pellet *2.2.0*.

The process can be seen as whole in Fig. 2. This process, therefore, begins by the download of the ontology from the corresponding repository listed in the aforementioned Table 1. After the ontology has been acquired, it is loaded into Protégé. One of the benefits that working with Protégé provides is that, if the ontology might try to load some additional and accessory ontologies, it will try to load them automatically or, if that is not possible, it will notify us. In the case that there is such request, we will proceed to load the missing ontologies manually. After the main ontology and all the accessories ones that have been requested are loaded, we proceed to merge them into one final ontology that comes out as the ontology that we will be measuring. The fact that we will be using an ontology with all its request allows us to be as close as possible to a real-world ontology and, therefore, a real-world situation.

Once the merged ontology has been loaded into Protégé, we proceed to note down all the metrics of the ontology. In this instance we are acquiring the metrics labelled as Axiom, Logical Axiom Count, Declaration Axiom Count, Class Count, Object Property Count, Data Property Count, Individual Count, and Annotation Property Count. Additionally we also use the log available from Protégé to annotate how much time it has taken to load the ontology.

---

[1] https://protege.stanford.edu/products.php.

Finally, we can start the associated reasoner of Protégé and obtain the reasoning time thanks again to its log. Once we have finished with all this, we are finally able to extract conclusions from the data that we have collected.

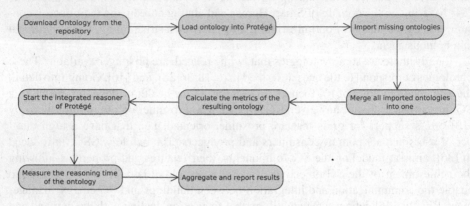

Fig. 2. Analysis process flow.

4.1 Metrics

The results obtained from analyzing the ontologies of the energy domain, and collected in Table 1, have been displayed in Table 2. All the metrics that appear here have been obtained in accord to the aforementioned process. The machine used to obtain these data was an Intel i7-3537U CPU @ 2.00 GHz, with 8 GB of RAM, running Ubuntu 20.04.2 LTS. The metrics regarding time were extracted performing the same benchmark five times in new instances of Protégé and finding the average.

Another measurement was to calculate the memory and CPU usage for each of the ten ontologies considered. These data have been captured and can be seen in Figs. 5 and 6. The method used for this consisted in using Python's libraries `psrecord` and `matplotlib` to create the following script:

```
psrecord $(pgrep process_name)
--interval 1 --plot file_name.png
```

As a final note, the times of each ontology have been collected in the comparative Figs. 3 and 4. Let us note that the missing bars represent a time that is not available because, for some or other reason, the reasoner was not able to process said ontology. Additionally, the scale of both figures is different. As a final note, let us point out that the ontologies have been assigned to one or another figure according to their magnitude, not according to their numbering.

4.2 Issues

The work required to obtain all the ontologies and perform the benchmarks has been a challenging endeavour. And despite our best efforts, some issues have permeated the

Table 2. Descriptive statistics of energy domain ontologies.

	O1	O2	O3	O4	O5	O6	O7	O8	O9	O10
Axiom	24251	5491	8563	4449	11678	2322	1144	897	1143	4206
Logical Axiom Count	9710	2426	1614	2217	4349	739	378	120	254	1958
Declaration Axioms Count	5835	111	1215	745	2590	393	206	128	170	747
Class Count	3544	250	928	388	1964	172	62	114	94	545
Object Property Count	963	70	83	339	270	88	5	N.A. (0)	13	105
Data Property Count	728	28	N.A. (0)	7	204	86	136	1	28	65
Individual Count	70	234	104	18	69	55	N.A. (0)	6	25	31
Annotation Property Count	50	117	95	7	43	28	5	13	12	22
Loading time [in ms]	3651.4	12284.6	1296.2	3735.6	1973.2	1273.2	436.8	383	446.6	1626
Reasoning time (HermiT) [in ms]	N.A.	1106	331.8	N.A.	56051.2	981544.3	481.8	315.8	435.2	9375.2
Reasoning time (Pellet) [in ms]	27145.2	788.2	N.A.	N.A.	N.A.	16737	343.4	290.6	357.8	13252.4

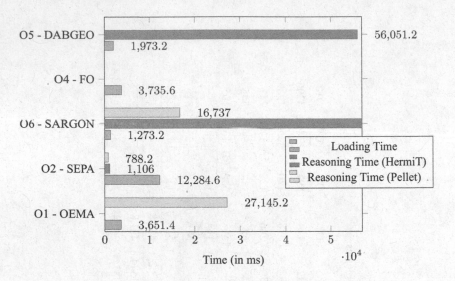

Fig. 3. Performance comparison of ontologies (1).

results. We list these issues below. Let us also note that these issues, while not making impossible to work with any of the ontologies, hinder their application and, therefore, should be carefully considered when deploying them into real-world situations.

The issues that have been found when performing the analysis of the ontologies are:

- O1 is not able to be processed by the reasoner HermiT because it, the reasoner, does not support built-in atoms, something that O1 has.
- O3 is not processed by Pellet because of a problem with the transitive rules.
- O4 is not processed by HermiT nor Pellet. It only reasons with ELK (with an average time of 1784.4 ms) but in a suboptimal manner.
- For O5 an error happens while running the Pellet reasoner and Protégé crashes. This issue is due to trying to use a literal as an individual.
- O6 reasons really slow with HermiT for unspecified reasons.

5 Experimental Results

The figures and tables that are available come to show that the biggest ontology, in terms of Axioms, is O1, with a number that is more than double the one of the closest ontology, O5. On the other hand, the title of smallest ontology in terms of axioms corresponds, by a close margin, to O8. The number of axioms that O8 has is less than 1/25th of that of O1. It would be easy to assume that there is a trend between these two ontologies, one might come to expect the biggest to perform also the worst. And at the same time for the smallest to have the fastest times. Nevertheless, this is simply not true. On the one hand, there are two different ontologies whose loading time is bigger than the one of O1: O2 and O4. It is particularly interesting for O4 has no characteristic that might be associated with these, as all its metrics are lower than those of O1, except for

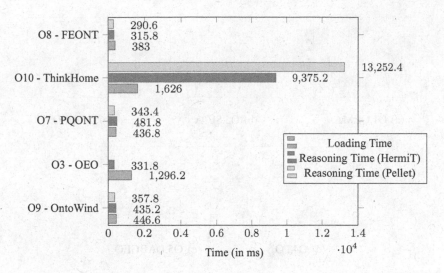

Fig. 4. Performance comparison of ontologies (2).

the Individual Count and the Annotation Property Count, that are slightly bigger. This trend follows through with the case of O2, whose Individual Count and Annotation Property Count are the biggest of all ontologies (at least doubling O1 in that regard), and it is also the ontology that performs the worst with respect to loading time; i.e., it has the biggest loading time. On the other hand, the case for O8 seems a bit clearer as its metrics can be seen as the smallest overall, which seems to point us towards the idea that the lower the metrics, the fastest the ontology will load. We could conclude that a lower number for the metrics helps to load the ontology faster, but having a high one does not imply automatically a high loading time, as it seems to be rather linked to some specific metrics.

Another metric to be considered is the reasoning. In particular, the reasoning with HermiT takes the longest with O6 by a very wide margin. We can only assume that is due to some unspecified problem with the ontology as the time is of a higher order of magnitude than any of the other times. Going into detail, the metrics of O6 are not particularly high nor low, so it is difficult to track this issue, one could argue that it is might be due to the inner structure of the ontology and the behaviour of the reasoners, but there are no data to support such statement. Outside of O6, the second highest reasoning time with HermiT is the one of O5 which is the ontology that is able to be processed by this reasoner with the highest metrics; therefore we can assume that the higher metrics do hinder the reasoning capabilities of HermiT. On the other hand, the lowest reasoning time corresponds to O8. This comes to reinforce our general idea that the smaller the ontology, the better it performs, including reasoning with HermiT, as also O7 and O9 perform in a similar manner while being rather small. Finally, it is interesting to look at the behaviour of O2, that despite having a high loading time, presumably linked to a high Annotation Property Count, has an acceptable reasoning time. In particular, its performance is better than the one from O5, with a lower Annotation Property Count, further strengthening this point.

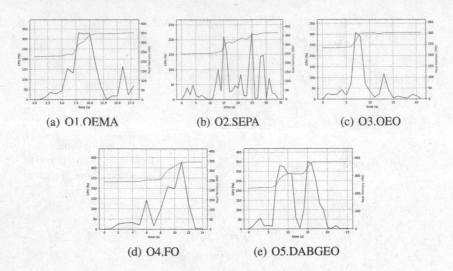

(a) O1.OEMA   (b) O2.SEPA   (c) O3.OEO

(d) O4.FO   (e) O5.DABGEO

Fig. 5. Performance of the ontologies (I) Source: [3].

If we look at the time it takes to reason using Pellet we find that the trend between smallest and biggest ontology metrics and reasoning time seems to be true. O1 takes the longest to be processed while also being the largest ontology as we have established before, while O8 takes the least time and also being the smallest ontology. This should come to show that size of an ontology is crucial when using Pellet if it is intended to be used in a time-constrained situation. It is even more important if we take into account that the difference in size is almost of 100 times.

The last of the metrics to be considered for the analysis is the memory and CPU usage, which seems to keep on the same pace as the previous results: O1 is the most demanding ontology because it also happens to be the largest. And yet again, the performance of O8 seems to be the most optimal, also being the smallest. We could easily reach for the conclusion that the smaller the ontology is, the better it will perform, but that is not entirely true, as within the remaining ontologies, some like O9 perform poorly than O6, despite the former being smaller than the latter, regarding the memory and CPU usage. It is also worth mentioning that, despite this, O9 is faster than O6 in all the benchmarks performed, so choosing one over the other might boil down to what the constraints are, if one has more time or more memory/CPU.

As a final point to be noted, it is important to state that O7, O8 and O9 are developed by the same main author. In particular, these ontologies have some of the best performances out of all the ones compared, making them one of the best choices if one is in need of finding the right ontology to reason about a specific domain in a resource-constrained situation.

6   Related Works

There are several research works that deal with the evaluation of the performance of ontologies. However, to our knowledge, there are no prior studies that deal with perfor-

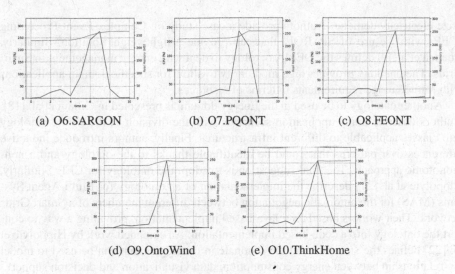

(a) O6.SARGON　　　　　(b) O7.PQONT　　　　　(c) O8.FEONT

(d) O9.OntoWind　　　　　(e) O10.ThinkHome

Fig. 6. Performance of the ontologies (II).

mance evaluation of ontologies in the energy domain. One first study addressed the measurement of performance of 350 real-world ontologies and four OWL2 reasoners [25]. This is one of the largest study available, in which the goal is to identify a set of metrics that can predict the performance of semantic web reasoners. As the method, authors use machine learning models to see which metrics could be the best predictors of performance of the ontologies. In the evaluation, eight ontology-level metrics are considered to be good predictors for ontologies performance. More recently, in an extension paper, authors adopt an even larger number of 450 ontologies, with the same goal as in the previous paper [26]. In this extension paper, authors also focus more on the identification of performance hotspots, defining what could be the bottlenecks when designing an ontology [26]. Similarly to the other papers, Wang et al. [42] identifies the bottlenecks in semantic web reasoners in terms of impact for performance. Four case studies based on generated and real-world ontologies are included in the article. Furthermore, authors identify challenges for the engineering aspects of ontologies and implement a tool to support statistical analysis of the performance of ontologies.

Recently, Peña et al. [33] show an enriched ontological model to improve the effectiveness of a recommender system. Authors go through all the characteristics that make an ontology effective, adapting them to the current task. Also, Maarala et al. [31] introduces a new semantic technology reasoner to be applied to the Internet of Things (IoT) domain. Their intention is to make the reasoner and data collection as scalable as possible in the context of real-life scenarios. Also here, the focus is on evaluating performance data highlighting out possible bottlenecks.

Regarding ontologies in the Energy domain, there are several studies that report the design and evaluation of ontologies for this domain [2,9,11,12,18,21,22,30,37,38,43, 46].

Zhout et al. [46] propose to use ontologies to model Smart Grid information exchanged at various levels in the context of Demand and Response programs to optimize electricity demand. Authors provide a case study on Complex Event Processing (CEP) with the use of SPARQL, that can provide a lightweight solution. Similarly, Cuenca et al. [9] defines the OEMA ontology to deal with energy management in Smart Grids. The ontology provides high modularity to allow for specific domain applications with limited usage requirements in terms of resources.

Another ontology to be used in the Energy domain is presented in Gillani et al. [18]. Authors describe many application scenarios with the division of the whole ontology into classes applicable to different infrastructures. Finally, authors introduce inductive inferences over patterns that could be identifiable thanks to the ontology and a non-monotonic approach. The final suggestion is to adopt the ontology for CEP. Similarly, Hippolyte et al. [21] describe the implementation of an ontology for Multi Agent Systems (MAS) for the automatic negotiation between different members of a Smart Grids network. Their work is based on a Java-based implementation, providing a way to convert the ontology into a code-based implementation. An extended work by Hippolyte et al. [22] defines the structure and the rationale in ontologies that can be used to model the relationship between energy consumption, data visualization and decision support.

Another ontology for energy management is introduced in Schachinger et al. [38]. Authors focus on providing an abstraction layer for the integration of building energy management systems and Smart Grids. They provide theoretical testing of the ontology to showcase all the relations between classes and instances of the ontology. Finally, Li et al. [30] present an ontology focused on key performance indicators to show the elements that require more energy given their power consumption patterns. The authors intend to use the ontology as a way to interchange data between different stakeholders of the Smart Grids network, thus supporting Big Data scenarios.

Describing the provided ontologies in the Energy domain is not enough if there are no supporting semantic tools. With this goal, Atanasov et al. [2] propose a semantic model for prepaid smart metering devices. Based on all the data generated from smart meters, they define semantic labels required for the data to be processed. The main research result is that from time and volume of power consumption we can derive effective semantics. The work of Santodomingo et al. [37] is focused on the standardization of the different data types that are present in the Smart Grids context. The approach can be useful if the same ontology has not been deployed to all the devices or if not in presence of Web of Things (WoT).

Dogdu et al. [11] reflect on the state of the art for the implementation of semantic technologies in the Energy domain, giving a precise overview of their applicability and their benefits over data models. The work done is based on a real-world implementation of semantic technologies in Smart Grids. Similarly, Donohoe et al. [12] presents a survey about the technologies available when dealing with the data produced from Smart Grids, focusing on context-aware technologies.

Wemlinger et al. [43] focus on smart environments and the provision of a semantic framework. The benefit is to integrate all data generated by the smart devices into the semantic web reasoner – that can help to trace the patterns of malfunctioning appliances. Also Flores-Martin et al. [16] represent a unifying method for different smart devices, but with the focus on smart devices. The goal is the integration of wearables to be adopted for the detection of malfunctions in smart meters.

7   Conclusions

This work has served the purpose of showcasing the state of the art of the main ontologies of the energy domain and how they interact with different reasoners. We have tracked down these ontologies and have analyzed them thanks to the use of Protégé. This analysis has lead us to point some of the strengths of these ontologies, as well as some of their disadvantages. We have been able to establish a relationship between a smaller ontology and a more optimal performance, although the converse does not always follow, with some larger ontologies performing better than some comparably smaller ones. This conclusion is specially important in the domain because of their intended implementation in resource-constrained platforms such as smart meters.

From all of the ontologies that we have described in the paper we have found that O1 - OEMA comes across as the one with a highest toll on the system, with the most demanding memory and CPU usage. It is also the ontology with the highest values for metrics overall. On the other end, we have O8 - FEONT as the ontology with more limited demands on the system. We suggest that O8 - FEONT is the most fit ontology for any resource-constrained task as long as its expressivity is enough. In that regard, any of the other related ontologies, O7 - PQONT and O9 - OntoWind, can be considered similar, as their performance is good with a relatively small footprint.

Furthermore, it is worth noting that, despite an almost overflowing amount of references on the semantic web technologies in the domain of energy, there are some ontologies that are not available. And while the situation improves if we expand the domain from SG to Energy domain [3], it is still far from perfect: There are broken URLs, ontologies that are no longer available, outdated platforms, and even non-reachable authors. There are also a few available ontologies that will not work properly with some staples of the semantic web reasoning, such as Protégé, without the involvement of the designers. In that regard we can conclude that one of the most important works to be done regarding ontologies is their genesis, making sure that the author puts in the necessary amount of work so it withstands the test of time.

Some future lines of work include providing a solid common platform, based on Apache Jena[2] framework, to extend the comparison beyond the readily available tools. We also want to provide approaches to improve the loading and reasoning times as well as the resource load of the available ontologies. Finally, it is our intention to also provide a comparison of the performance of the ontologies and reasoning methods in a real-world environment such as a resource-constrained device.

Acknowledgements. The research was supported from ERDF/ESF "CyberSecurity, Cyber-Crime and Critical Information Infrastructures Center of Excellence" (No. CZ.02.1.01/0.0 /0.0/16_019/0000822).

References

1. Ali, S., Kiefer, S.: μOR – a micro OWL DL reasoner for ambient intelligent devices. In: Abdennadher, N., Petcu, D. (eds.) GPC 2009. LNCS, vol. 5529, pp. 305–316. Springer, Heidelberg (2009). https://doi.org/10.1007/978-3-642-01671-4_28

---

[2] https://jena.apache.org/index.html.

2. Atanasov, I.I.: Structure of semantic information for prepaid smart metering. In: 2015 12th International Conference on Telecommunication in Modern Satellite, Cable and Broadcasting Services (SIKS), pp. 293–296 (2015)
3. Blanco, J.M., Rossi, B., Pitner, T.: A comparison of smart grids domain ontologies. In: The 17th International Conference on Web Information Systems and Technologies (WEBIST). SciTePress (2021)
4. Blanco, J.M., Rossi, B., Pitner, T.: A time-sensitive model for data tampering detection for the advanced metering Infrastructure. In: 2021 16th Conference on Computer Science and Intelligence Systems (FedCSIS), pp. 511–519. IEEE (2021)
5. Bruinenberg, J., et al.: CEN-CENELEC-ETSI smart grid co-ordination group smart grid reference architecture. CEN, CENELEC, ETSI, Technical report, pp. 98–107 (2012)
6. Catterson, V.M., Davidson, E.M., McArthur, S.D.: Issues in integrating existing multi-agent systems for power engineering applications. In: Proceedings of the 13th International Conference on, Intelligent Systems Application to Power Systems, pp. 6-pp. IEEE (2005)
7. Chren, S., Rossi, B., Pitner, T.: Smart grids deployments within EU projects: the role of smart meters. In: 2016 Smart Cities Symposium Prague (SCSP), pp. 1–5. IEEE (2016)
8. Commission, I.E., et al.: Energy management system application program interface (EMS-API)-part 301: common information model (CIM) base. Electric Power Industry Standard of the PRC, ed, p. 196 (2003)
9. Cuenca, J., Larrinaga, F., Curry, E.: A unified semantic ontology for energy management applications. In: WSP/WOMoCoE@ISWC (2017)
10. Cuenca, J., Larrinaga, F., Curry, E.: DABGEO: a reusable and usable global energy ontology for the energy domain. J. Web Semant. **61–62**, 100550 (2020). https://doi.org/10.1016/j.websem.2020.100550
11. Dogdu, E., et al.: Ontology-centric data modelling and decision support in smart grid applications a distribution service operator perspective. In: 2014 IEEE International Conference on Intelligent Energy and Power Systems (IEPS), pp. 198–204 (2014). https://doi.org/10.1109/IEPS.2014.6874179
12. Donohoe, M., Jennings, B., Balasubramaniam, S.: Context-awareness and the smart grid: requirements and challenges. Comput. Netw. **79**, 263–282 (2015). https://doi.org/10.1016/j.comnet.2015.01.007
13. EU: Council directive 2008/114/EC on the identification and designation of European critical infrastructures and the assessment of the need to improve their protection. L345 3, 0075-0082 (2008)
14. Fang, X., Misra, S., Xue, G., Yang, D.: Smart grid-the new and improved power grid: a survey. IEEE Commun. Surv. Tutor. **14**(4), 944–980 (2011)
15. Farhangi, H.: The path of the smart grid. IEEE Power Energ. Mag. **8**(1), 18–28 (2009)
16. Flores-Martin, D., Berrocal, J., García-Alonso, J., Canal, C., Murillo, J.M.: Enabling the interconnection of smart devices through semantic web techniques. In: Bakaev, M., Frasincar, F., Ko, I.-Y. (eds.) ICWE 2019. LNCS, vol. 11496, pp. 534–537. Springer, Cham (2019). https://doi.org/10.1007/978-3-030-19274-7_41
17. Ge, M., Chren, S., Rossi, B., Pitner, T.: Data quality management framework for smart grid systems. In: Abramowicz, W., Corchuelo, R. (eds.) BIS 2019. LNBIP, vol. 354, pp. 299–310. Springer, Cham (2019). https://doi.org/10.1007/978-3-030-20482-2_24
18. Gillani, S., Laforest, F., Picard, G.: A generic ontology for prosumer-oriented smart grid. In: CEUR Workshop Proceedings, vol. 1133 (2014)
19. Goel, S., Hong, Y., Papakonstantinou, V., Kloza, D.: Smart Grid Security. Springer, London (2015). https://doi.org/10.1007/978-1-4471-6663-4
20. Haghgoo, M., Sychev, I., Monti, A., Fitzek, F.H.: SARGON - smart energy domain ontology. IET Smart Cities **2**(4), 191–198 (2020)

21. Hippolyte, J.L., et al.: Ontology-based demand-side flexibility management in smart grids using a multi-agent system. In: 2016 IEEE International Smart Cities Conference (ISC2), Trento, Italy, pp. 1–7. IEEE (2016). https://doi.org/10.1109/ISC2.2016.7580828
22. Hippolyte, J.L., Rezgui, Y., Li, H., Jayan, B., Howell, S.: Ontology-driven development of web services to support district energy applications. Autom. Constr. **86**, 210–225 (2018). https://doi.org/10.1016/j.autcon.2017.10.004
23. Janev, V., Popadić, D., Pujić, D., Vidal, M.E., Endris, K.: Reuse of semantic models for emerging smart grids applications. arXiv preprint arXiv:2107.06999 (2021)
24. Jarmon, J.A.: The New Era in US National Security: Challenges of the Information Age. Rowman & Littlefield Publishers, Lanham (2019)
25. Kang, Y.-B., Li, Y.-F., Krishnaswamy, S.: Predicting reasoning performance using ontology metrics. In: Cudré-Mauroux, P., et al. (eds.) ISWC 2012. LNCS, vol. 7649, pp. 198–214. Springer, Heidelberg (2012). https://doi.org/10.1007/978-3-642-35176-1_13
26. Kang, Y.B., Pan, J.Z., Krishnaswamy, S., Sawangphol, W., Li, Y.F.: How long will it take? accurate prediction of ontology reasoning performance. In: Proceedings of the Twenty-Eighth AAAI Conference on Artificial Intelligence, AAAI 2014, Québec City, Québec, Canada, pp. 80–86. AAAI Press (2014)
27. Küçük, D., Salor-Durna, Ö., Inan, T., Çadirci, I., Ermis, M.: PQONT: a domain ontology for electrical power quality. Adv. Eng. Inform. **24**, 84–95 (2010)
28. Küçük, D.: A high-level electrical energy ontology with weighted attributes. Adv. Eng. Inform. **29**(3), 513–522 (2015). https://doi.org/10.1016/j.aei.2015.04.002
29. Küçük, D., Küçük, D.: OntoWind: An Improved and Extended Wind Energy Ontology. arXiv:1803.02808 (2018)
30. Li, Y., García-Castro, R., Mihindukulasooriya, N., O'Donnell, J., Vega-Sánchez, S.: Enhancing energy management at district and building levels via an EM-KPI ontology. Autom. Constr. **99**, 152–167 (2019). https://doi.org/10.1016/j.autcon.2018.12.010
31. Maarala, A.I., Su, X., Riekki, J.: Semantic reasoning for context-aware internet of things applications. IEEE Internet Things J. **4**(2), 461–473 (2017). https://doi.org/10.1109/JIOT.2016.2587060
32. Nieves, J.C., Espinoza, A., Penya, Y.K., De Mues, M.O., Pena, A.: Intelligence distribution for data processing in smart grids: a semantic approach. Eng. Appl. Artif. Intell. **26**(8), 1841–1853 (2013)
33. Peña, P., Trillo-Lado, R., Hoyo, R., Rodríguez-Hernández, M., Abadía, D.: Ontology-quality evaluation methodology for enhancing semantic searches and recommendations: a case study. In: Proceedings of the 16th International Conference on Web Information Systems and Technologies, Budapest, Hungary, pp. 277–284. SCITEPRESS - Science and Technology Publications (2020). https://doi.org/10.5220/0010143602770284
34. Reinisch, C., Kofler, M.J., Kastner, W.: ThinkHome: a smart home as digital ecosystem. In: 4th IEEE International Conference on Digital Ecosystems and Technologies, pp. 256–261 (2010). https://doi.org/10.1109/DEST.2010.5610636. ISSN 2150-4946
35. Rossi, B., Chren, S.: Smart grids data analysis: a systematic mapping study. IEEE Trans. Industr. Inf. **16**(6), 3619–3639 (2019)
36. Salameh, K., Chbeir, R., Camblong, H.: *SSG*: an ontology-based information model for smart grids. In: Hameurlain, A., Wagner, R., Morvan, F., Tamine, L. (eds.) Transactions on Large-Scale Data- and Knowledge-Centered Systems XL. LNCS, vol. 11360, pp. 94–124. Springer, Heidelberg (2019). https://doi.org/10.1007/978-3-662-58664-8_4
37. Santodomingo, R., Uslar, M., Rodríguez-Mondéjar, J.A., Sanz-Bobi, M.A.: Rule-based data transformations in electricity smart grids. In: Bassiliades, N., Gottlob, G., Sadri, F., Paschke, A., Roman, D. (eds.) RuleML 2015. LNCS, vol. 9202, pp. 447–455. Springer, Cham (2015). https://doi.org/10.1007/978-3-319-21542-6_29

38. Schachinger, D., Kastner, W., Gaida, S.: Ontology-based abstraction layer for smart grid interaction in building energy management systems. In: 2016 IEEE International Energy Conference (ENERGYCON), pp. 1–6 (2016). https://doi.org/10.1109/ENERGYCON.2016.7513991

39. Schumilin, A., Stucky, K.U., Sinn, F., Hagenmeyer, V.: Towards ontology-based network model management and data integration for smart grids. In: 2017 Workshop on Modeling and Simulation of Cyber-Physical Energy Systems (MSCPES), pp. 1–6. IEEE (2017)

40. Speiser, S., Wagner, A., Raabe, O., Harth, A.: Web technologies and privacy policies for the smart grid. In: IECON 2013–39th Annual Conference of the IEEE Industrial Electronics Society, pp. 4809–4814 (2013). https://doi.org/10.1109/IECON.2013.6699913. ISSN 1553-572X

41. Tai, W., Keeney, J., O'Sullivan, D.: COROR: a composable rule-entailment owl reasoner for resource-constrained devices. In: Bassiliades, N., Governatori, G., Paschke, A. (eds.) RuleML 2011. LNCS, vol. 6826, pp. 212–226. Springer, Heidelberg (2011). https://doi.org/10.1007/978-3-642-22546-8_17

42. Wang, T.D., Parsia, B.: Ontology performance profiling and model examination: first steps. In: Aberer, K., et al. (eds.) ASWC/ISWC -2007. LNCS, vol. 4825, pp. 595–608. Springer, Heidelberg (2007). https://doi.org/10.1007/978-3-540-76298-0_43

43. Wemlinger, Z., Holder, L.: The COSE ontology: bringing the semantic web to smart environments. In: Abdulrazak, B., Giroux, S., Bouchard, B., Pigot, H., Mokhtari, M. (eds.) ICOST 2011. LNCS, vol. 6719, pp. 205–209. Springer, Heidelberg (2011). https://doi.org/10.1007/978-3-642-21535-3_27

44. Yu, X., Cecati, C., Dillon, T., Simoes, M.G.: The new frontier of smart grids. IEEE Ind. Electron. Mag. 5(3), 49–63 (2011)

45. Zhang, Y., Huang, T., Bompard, E.F.: Big data analytics in smart grids: a review. Energy Inform. 1(1), 1–24 (2018). https://doi.org/10.1186/s42162-018-0007-5

46. Zhou, Q., Natarajan, S., Simmhan, Y., Prasanna, V.: Semantic information modeling for emerging applications in smart grid. In: 2012 Ninth International Conference on Information Technology - New Generations, pp. 775–782 (2012). https://doi.org/10.1109/ITNG.2012.150

Semantic Label Representations with Lbl2Vec: A Similarity-Based Approach for Unsupervised Text Classification

Tim Schopf[1](✉)(iD), Daniel Braun[2](iD), and Florian Matthes[1](iD)

[1] Department of Computer Science, Technical University of Munich, Boltzmannstrasse 3, Garching, Germany
{tim.schopf,matthes}@tum.de
[2] Department of High-tech Business and Entrepreneurship, University of Twente, Drienerlolaan 5, Enschede, The Netherlands
d.braun@utwente.nl

Abstract. In this paper, we evaluate the Lbl2Vec approach for unsupervised text document classification. Lbl2Vec requires only a small number of keywords describing the respective classes to create semantic label representations. For classification, Lbl2Vec uses cosine similarities between label and document representations, but no annotation information. We show that Lbl2Vec significantly outperforms common unsupervised text classification approaches and a widely used zero-shot text classification approach. Furthermore, we show that using more precise keywords can significantly improve the classification results of similarity-based text classification approaches.

Keywords: Natural language processing · Unsupervised text classification · Text representations · Text similarity · Semantic label representations

1 Introduction

Supervised text classification has gained a lot of attention recently, due to the succes of Pretrained Language Models (PLMs). Training supervised classification algorithms or even fine-tuning PLMs requires a large amount of labeled data. However, high-quality annotated datasets often do not exist, particularly in industrial settings. Annotating datasets usually requires a lot of manual effort and causes high expenses. Unsupervised text classification approaches, however, can significantly reduce annotation costs since they can be trained on unlabeled datasets. Despite this opportunity, supervised text classification approaches based on transformer models such as BERT [6] or XLNet [28] are significantly more studied than unsupervised text classification approaches. In this work, we contribute to the less researched field of unsupervised text classification by evaluating the Lbl2Vec [18] approach.

The general approach for unsupervised text classification is to map text to labels based on their textual description. Thereby, classification is based on semantic similarities of text representations and thus avoids the need for annotated training data. Usually, this kind of approach is applied when dealing with a large corpus of unlabeled text documents that need to be classified into topics of interest. These types of tasks

© Springer Nature Switzerland AG 2023
M. Marchiori et al. (Eds.): WEBIST 2020/2021, LNBIP 469, pp. 59–73, 2023.
https://doi.org/10.1007/978-3-031-24197-0_4

are becoming increasingly common, considering the ever growing amount of unlabeled text data. To illustrate the problem, we assume the following scenario as an example: we collected a large number of tech-related text articles from various websites. From this corpus, we want to classify articles based on their relatedness to certain companies such as Apple, Google or Microsoft. Since we do not possess any metadata about the text articles, we can only rely on the texts themselves for this purpose. What appears to be a simple text classification task initially, may actually turn out to be more complex than expected. To use a conventional supervised classification approach, we would need to annotate the text articles first, since they require a large amount of labeled training data [33]. As already mentioned, this likely involves high annotation expenses.

In this work, we evaluate the similarity-based Lbl2Vec approach, which is able to perform unsupervised classification on a large corpus of unlabeled text documents. This approach enables us to classify a text document corpus without having to annotate any data. For classification, Lbl2Vec uses semantic similarities between documents and keywords describing a certain class only. Intuitively, using semantic meanings matches the approach of a human being. In addition, this approach can significantly reduce annotation costs since only a small number of keywords are needed instead of a large number of labeled documents.

Lbl2Vec creates jointly embedded word, document and label representations. The label representations are obtained from the manually predefined keywords. Because vector representations of documents and labels share the same embedding space, their semantic relationship can be measured using cosine similarity. Eventually this similarity can be used to assign a certain class to a text document.

The contributions of our work can be summarized as follows:

– We provide a comprehensive explanation of Lbl2Vec, based on the original paper [18] and additional illustrations.
– We evaluate Lbl2Vec against commonly used unsupervised text classification approaches and against a state-of-the-art zero-shot learning (ZSL) approach.
– We conduct experiments with different Lbl2Vec hyperparameter settings and examine which hyperparameter values yield good label vectors.
– We examine the role of keywords used to describe classes for similarity-based text classification.

2 Lbl2Vec

Lbl2Vec [18] is a similarity-based approach for unsupervised text classification. It creates jointly embedded label, document, and word vector representations from a given text document corpus. The semantic label representations are derived from predefined keywords for each class and used to classify text documents. The intuition of this approach is that many semantically similar keywords can represent a class. First, Lbl2Vec generates jointly embedded document and word vector representations. Then, the algorithm learns label vectors from the predefined keywords. Finally, Lbl2Vec classifies documents based on similarities between the document and label representations. Since label and document representations share the same embedding space, their cosine similarities can be used as a classification indicator. The authors made Lbl2Vec publicly available as a ready-to-use tool under the 3-Clause BSD license[1].

In addition to the text document corpus, Lbl2Vec requires manually predefined keywords as input. For each class, a set of semantically coherent keywords will be used to create the label vector representation later. Table 1 shows example keywords representing different classes.

Table 1. Manually predefined example keywords for different sports classes.

Class	Keywords
Basketball	NBA, Basketball, LeBron
Soccer	FIFA, Soccer, Messi
Baseball	MLB, Baseball, Ruth

Given the predefined keywords and the unlabeled text document corpus as input, Lbl2Vec initially learns jointly embedded word and document vector representations using Doc2Vec [10]. Specifically, Lbl2Vec uses the distributed bag of words version of paragraph vector (PV-DBOW) and interleaves it with Skip-gram [13] training to learn jointly embedded document and word representations. After learning jointly embedded vectors, representations of semantically similar documents are located close to each other in embedding space and also close to representations of the most distinguishing words. Figure 1 illustrates the jointly embedded document and word representations.

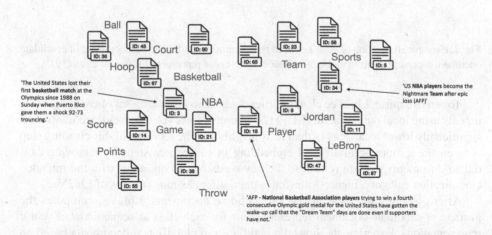

Fig. 1. Example illustration of jointly embedded document and word vector representations, learned by Lbl2Vec [19].

Following the learning of jointly embedded document and word representations, Lbl2Vec uses the class keywords to train semantic label representations. For each class, Lbl2Vec uses the cosine similarities between the average of the keyword vector representations and the document vector representations to find a set of most similar

---

[1] https://github.com/sebischair/Lbl2Vec.

candidate documents. To include only the document representations most similar to the predefined keywords in the set of candidate documents, Lbl2Vec requires the following parameters:

- s as cosine similarity threshold between the average of the keyword vector representations and the document vector representations. Only documents that exceed s are included in the candidate documents.
- d_{min} as the minimum number of documents for each set of candidate documents. This parameter prevents the selection of an insufficient number of documents in case s is chosen too restrictive.
- d_{max} as the maximum number of documents for each set of candidate documents.

Figure 2 illustrates candidate documents for some example classes.

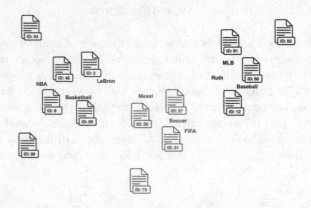

Fig. 2. Example illustration of class keyword representations with their respective set of candidate document representations in embedding space. Each color represents a different class [19].

To remove noise, Lbl2Vec cleans outlier documents from each set of candidate documents using local outlier factor (LOF) [2]. Thereby, Lbl2Vec removes documents with significantly lower local density than their neighbors. The intuition of this cleaning step is to ensure a more accurate label embedding in subsequent steps by removing candidate documents that are related to the keywords but do not align with the intended classification category. Figure 3 illustrates the outlier cleaning process of Lbl2Vec.

After obtaining the cleaned sets of candidate documents, Lbl2Vec computes the average of candidate document representations for each class as semantic label vector representations. Experiments showed it is difficult to classify text documents based on similarities to keywords, even if their representations share the same embedding space [18]. Therefore, Lbl2Vec computes the label vectors as averages of document representations rather than averages of keyword representations. Figure 4 illustrates examples of label vector representations.

For classification, Lbl2Vec uses the cosine similarities between the label vector representations and document vector representations. Text documents are assigned to the class where their vector representations are most similar to the respective semantic label representation. Figure 5 illustrates an example classification result.

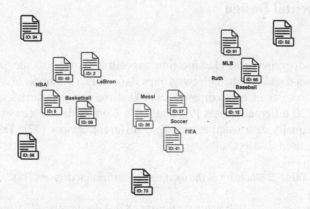

Fig. 3. Example illustration of the Lbl2Vec outlier cleaning step. Red documents are outliers that are removed from the candidate documents [19] (Color figure online).

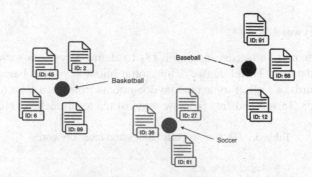

Fig. 4. Example illustration of the label vector representations, calculated as the average of the respective set of cleaned candidate document representations [19].

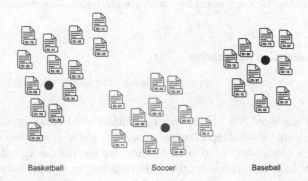

Fig. 5. Example illustration of a Lbl2Vec classification result. Circles represent the label vectors of classes. Colors represent the classes [19].

3 Experimental Design

3.1 Datasets

To conduct unsupervised text classification experiments, we use the 20Newsgroups and AG's Corpus datasets. The 20Newsgroups dataset is a common text classification dataset which consists of approximately 20,000 different news articles, equally distributed across 20 different classes [9]. The AG's Corpus dataset consists of 127,600 news articles, equally distributed among four different classes [32]. Table 2 shows a summary of the used datasets.

Table 2. Summary of the used text classification datasets [18].

Datasets	#Training documents	#Test documents	#Classes
20Newsgroups	11,314	7,532	20
AG's Corpus	120,000	7,600	4

3.2 Label Keywords

We adopt the expert knowledge approach [8] to define keywords for each class in the respective datasets. Therefore, we define some initial keywords based on the class names. Afterwards, we select some random documents from each class to derive more salient keywords. Table 3 and Table 4 show some of the resulting keywords.

Table 3. AG's Corpus class names and label keywords.

Class name	Label keywords
World	government, election, state, president, politics, democracy, war, ...
Sports	sports, football, baseball, rugby, basketball, championship, ...
Business	business, company, market, oil, consumers, price, products, ...
Science/Technology	science, technology, web, google, microsoft, software, laboratory,

3.3 Text Classification Approaches

For evaluation, we conduct experiments with the following text classification approaches:

Word2Vec: We use Word2Vec [13] to create semantic word vector representations for each dataset. To learn the word representations, we use a Skip-gram model with a vector size of 300 and a surrounding window of 5. Then, we use the average of word vectors as document and label representations. For classification, we use the cosine similarities between the resulting document and label representations. Documents are assigned to the class where the cosine similarity to the class label representation is the highest.

SBERT: Sentence-BERT (SBERT) is a modification of BERT [6] that uses siamese and triplet network structures to derive semantically meaningful sentence embeddings [15].

Table 4. 20Newsgroups class names and label keywords.

Class name	Label keywords
alt.atheism	atheism, god, atheists, religion, atheist, belief, believe, jesus, ...
comp.graphics	image, graphics, jpeg, images, gif, tiff, quicktime, animation, ...
comp.os.ms-windows.misc	windows, microsoft, win, driver, computer, ...
comp.sys.ibm.pc.hardware	bus, drives, bios, disk, dos, motherboard, floppy, cpu, port, ...
comp.sys.mac.hardware	mac, apple, hardware, monitor, powerbook, macintosh, ...
comp.windows.x	computer, windows, program, openwindows, application, ...
misc.forsale	sale, shipping, forsale, price, sell, offer, trade, ...
rec.autos	cars, engine, ford, dealer, oil, toyota, driver, tires, ...
rec.motorcycles	motorcycles, bike, ride, bmw, helmet, honda, harley, ...
rec.sport.baseball	sport, baseball, game , team, hit, pitcher, hitter, sox, ...
rec.sport.hockey	sport, hockey, season, nhl, cup, playoffs, ...
sci.crypt	encryption, key, privacy, algorithm, nsa, security, ...
sci.electronics	electronics, wire , battery, voltage, power, amp, ...
sci.med	medical, disease, cancer, patients, health, doctor, medicine, ...
sci.space	space, nasa, orbit, moon, earth, solar, satellite, mars, ...
soc.religion.christian	religion, christians, god , church, bible, jesus, christ, believe, ...
talk.politics.guns	guns, fbi, firearms, weapons, militia, crime, violence, ...
talk.politics.mideast	israel, armenia, turkey, arab, muslim, ...
talk.politics.misc	president, government, clinton, jobs, tax, insurance, state, ...
talk.religion.misc	religion, jesus, god, bible, lord, moral, judas,

We use the average of SBERT sentence embeddings as document representations and the average of SBERT keyword embeddings as class representations. Then, we classify the text documents according to the highest cosine similarity of the resulting SBERT representations of documents and classes. For our experiments, we use the pretrained general purpose *all-mpnet-base-v2* SBERT model.

Zero-Shot Text Classification: In general, zero-shot text classification (0SHOT-TC) approaches use labeled training instances of seen classes to predict testing instances of unseen classes [26]. Although 0SHOT-TC approaches use annotated data for training, they do not use label information about the target classes and generalize their learned knowledge to classify instances of unseen classes. Because pretrained 0SHOT-TC models do not require training or fine-tuning on labeled instances from target classes, they can be classified as a type of unsupervised text classification strategy. Traditional text classifiers usually struggle to understand the underlying classification problem because class names are converted to simple indices [30]. This makes it difficult for them to generalize to unseen classes. Therefore, a 0SHOT-TC approach similar to that of humans is required, which classifies instances based on semantic class meanings. This is precisely the intuition behind the idea of modeling 0SHOT-TC as an entailment problem [30]. The zero-shot entailment model uses the class label descriptions as hypotheses and is therefore able to understand the semantic meanings of classes [30]. This approach allows the classifier to generalize to unseen classes and currently produces state-of-the-art results in the *label-fully-unseen* 0SHOT-TC setting. In the *label-fully-unseen* setting, 0SHOT-TC aims at learning a classifier $f(\cdot) : X \rightarrow Y$, where classifier $f(\cdot)$ never sees Y-specific labeled data in its model development [30].

For our experiments, we choose a DistilBART zero-shot entailment model, trained on the MultiNLI dataset [27] to classify the respective whole document corpora. As hypotheses we use the respective keywords lists concatenated with "and".

KE + LSA: This refers to an approach that uses keyword enrichment (KE) and subsequent unsupervised classification based on Latent Semantic Analysis (LSA) [5] vector cosine similarities [8]. For this approach, we do not conduct any experiment ourselves, but use the results reported in the original paper [8] for evaluation.

Lbl2Vec: We train Lbl2Vec [18] models, using the respective datasets described in Sect. 3.1. We conduct experiments with different d_{min} values, while $s = 1$, and $d_{max} =$ *the maximum number of documents in the respective dataset*. The detailed results of the experiments using different d_{min} values are shown in Sect. 4.2. The respective best F1-scores on both data sets obtained with Lbl2Vec are shown in Table 5.

For each approach, we conduct experiments with two different keywords sets. First, we use the manually predefined keywords described in Sect. 3.2. Then, we use the respective class names as keywords. For the 20Newsgroups dataset, we separate the class names at the dots and replace the abbreviations with their full names. Section 4.1 shows the results of the experiments that use the manually predefined keywords. The results of the experiments that use the class names as keywords are shown in Sect. 4.3.

4   Evaluation

4.1   Classification Results

We classify the documents from the datasets described in Sect. 3.1 using the keywords described in Sect. 3.2 and the approaches described in Sect. 3.3. Since we do not need label information to train the classifiers, we use the entire concatenated datasets for training and testing respectively. Table 5 shows the classification results of our experiments.

Table 5. F1-scores (micro) of text classification approaches on different datasets. For all experiments, the keywords described in Sect. 3.2 are used. The best results on the respective dataset are displayed in bold. Since we use micro-averaging to calculate our classification results, we realize equal F1, Precision, and Recall scores respectively.

	20Newsgroups	AG's corpus
Word2Vec	22.68	34.52
SBERT (all-mpnet-base-v2)	63.42	79.39
Zero-shot Entailment (DistilBART)	12.42	32.54
KE + LSA	61.0	76.6
Lbl2Vec	**77.03**	**82.96**

We observe that Lbl2Vec yields best F1-scores among all approaches by a large margin on both datasets. It even outperforms the SBERT approach, although SBERT currently generates sentence embeddings that achieve state-of-the-art results in text similarity tasks. Although the SBERT approach performs worse than Lbl2Vec, it nevertheless shows that the more advanced SBERT embeddings perform significantly better than Word2Vec embeddings in this similarity-based classification task. Surprisingly, the zero-shot entailment approach performs significantly worse than the Word2Vec approach and even worst of all approaches examined. The KE + LSA approach, which uses basic LSA embeddings, performs comparatively well and only slightly worse than the SBERT approach, which uses more sophisticated transformer-based embeddings.

4.2   Lbl2Vec Hyperparameter Analysis

To examine the effect of the number of documents used to compute the label vectors on the Lbl2Vec classification results, we conduct experiments with different d_{min} parameter values. The higher the d_{min} parameter values, the more document representations are used for calculating the label vector as their average. To conduct the experiments, we use the datasets described in Sect. 3.1 and the keywords described in Sect. 3.2. The results are shown in Fig. 6 and Fig. 7.

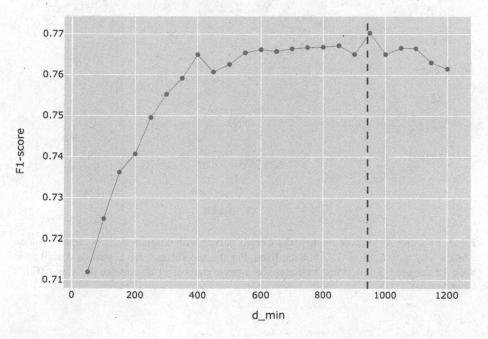

Fig. 6. F1-scores of Lbl2Vec on the 20Newsgroups dataset with different d_{min} parameter values, while $s = 1$ and $d_{max} = 18,846$ are fixed. For the experiments, the keywords described in Sect. 3.2 are used. The red line indicates the average number of documents per class. (Color figure online)

On both datasets, we observe that F1-scores improve with increasing d_{min} parameter values until a peak is reached. After the peak, the F1-scores get worse with increasing d_{min} parameter values. For the 20Newsgroup dataset, the peak occurs after d_{min} is higher than the average number of documents per class. However, the F1-scores already reach a high plateau after d_{min} is about 60% of the average number of documents per class. For the AG's Corpus dataset, the peak occurs at $d_{min} = 22,000$. This is about 69% of the average number of documents per class. However, almost similar F1-scores are achieved at $d_{min} = 18,000$, which is about 56% of the average number of documents per class.

The results show, that a sufficiency amount of candidate document representations are needed to compute good label vectors. Furthermore, the results indicate that a minimum d_{min} value of approximately 60% of the average number of documents per class yields good label vectors for classification.

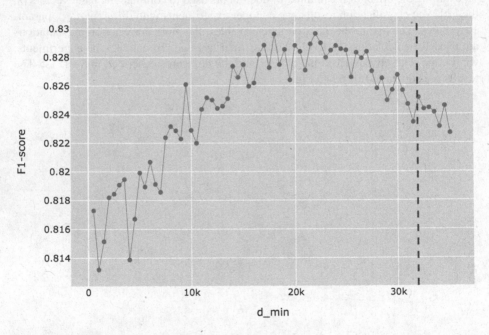

Fig. 7. F1-scores of Lbl2Vec on the AG's Corpus dataset with different d_{min} parameter values, while $s = 1$ and $d_{max} = 127,600$ are fixed. For the experiments, the keywords described in Sect. 3.2 are used. The red line indicates the average number of documents per class. (Color figure online)

4.3 Keywords Analysis

Table 6. F1-scores (micro) of text classification approaches on different datasets. For all experiments, the class names are used as keywords. The best results on the respective dataset are displayed in bold. Since we use micro-averaging to calculate our classification results, we realize equal F1, Precision, and Recall scores respectively.

	20Newsgroups	AG's Corpus
Word2Vec	11.71	26.61
SBERT (all-mpnet-base-v2)	52.98	62.75
Zero-shot Entailment (DistilBART)	43.29	64.70
Lbl2Vec	**67.64**	**66.02**

To examine how the use of different keywords affects the classification results, we conduct experiments using the class names as label keywords instead of the manually predefined ones. For the 20Newsgroups dataset, we separate the class names at the dots and replace the abbreviations with their full names. The results of these experiments are shown in Table 6.

Overall, Lbl2Vec outperforms all other text classification approaches examined. Furthermore, we observe that in comparison to the experiments using the manually predefined keywords in Sect. 4.1, the F1-scores for the Word2Vec, SBERT, and Lbl2Vec approaches decrease significantly. The pure class names, in comparison to the manually predefined keywords, contain fewer and less precise class descriptions, which affects the label vectors and the classification results negatively. However, this only applies to the similarity-based text classification approaches. In contrast, the zero-shot entailment approach yields significantly improved classification results using the class names as hypotheses instead of the manually predefined keywords. The experiments show that the simultaneous use of many keywords as hypothesis confuses the zero-shot entailment approach. As a result, this affects the 0SHOT-TC performance negatively.

5 Related Work

Most unsupervised text classification approaches leverage semantic text similarities. Thereby, these approaches generate semantic representations of texts as well as of label descriptions, and then aim to align the texts with the labels using similarity metrics. In one of the earlier works, this approach was described as "Dataless Classification" [3]. Thereby, text and label descriptions were embedded in a common semantic space using Explicit Semantic Analysis (ESA) [7] and the label with the highest matching score was selected for classification [3]. Further, ESA was applied in a dataless hierarchical classification approach that exploited the hierarchical structure of labels [23]. The general idea of "Dataless Classification" is based on the assumption that, for text classification, label representations are equally important as text representations and already was studied extensively [4,11,24].

Eventually, the term "Dateless Classification" became less common and currently rather fits into the general concept of similarity-based text classification approaches. A very common similarity-based approach, which is also often used as a baseline for unsupervised text classification, embeds texts and labels with Word2Vec [13] and tries to predict the correct class with cosine similarities [16]. Word2Vec [13] creates semantic word embeddings based on their surrounding context and can be trained specifically for different languages and domains [1,22]. Instead of Word2Vec vectors, similarities between LSA [5] representations were also used for unsupervised text classification. Furthermore, DocSCAN uses Semantic Clustering by Adopting Nearest-Neighbors of text representations for unsupervised text classification [25].

Similar to unsupervised text classification approaches, ZSL approaches also aim to classify instances of unseen classes. Unlike unsupervised approaches, however, ZSL approaches use annotated training data from seen classes to predict instances of unseen classes [26]. Although ZSL models are partly trained on annotated data, they do not require label information about the unseen target classes for prediction and are therefore often considered equivalent to unsupervised approaches [20]. Jointly embedded document, label and word representations were also used in 0SHOT-TC to learn a ranking function for multi-label classification [14]. Additionally, different kinds of semantic knowledge (word embeddings, class descriptions, class hierarchy, and a general knowledge graph) were used for 0SHOT-TC [31], while other approaches tackle the task in a semi-supervised self-training approach [29] or treat 0SHOT-TC as entailment problem [30].

6 Conclusion

In this work, we showed how to effectively use Lbl2Vec for unsupervised text classification. Our experiments demonstrated that Lbl2Vec performs significantly better than other approaches in classifying text documents of unseen classes. Furthermore, our Lbl2Vec hyperparameter analysis indicates, that a minimum d_{min} value of approximately 60% of the average number of documents per class yields good label vectors for classification. In addition, using more accurate keywords can improve the classification performance of similarity-based text classification approaches such as Lbl2Vec. Future work can examine the use of keyphrase extraction approaches [21], knowledge graphs [17], or Masked Language Models (MLMs) for keyword generation. Thereby, a pretrained MLMs predicts what words can replace the class names under most contexts [12]. Usually, the top-50 predicted words have a similar meaning to the masked class name [12]. Therefore, using the top-50 predicted words as label keywords holds the potential to automate the keyword definition process and further improve F1-scores of similarity-based text classification approaches.

References

1. Braun, D., Klymenko, O., Schopf, T., Kaan Akan, Y., Matthes, F.: The language of engineering: training a domain-specific word embedding model for engineering. In: 2021 3rd International Conference on Management Science and Industrial Engineering, MSIE 2021,

pp. 8–12. Association for Computing Machinery, New York (2021). https://doi.org/10.1145/3460824.3460826

2. Breunig, M.M., Kriegel, H.P., Ng, R.T., Sander, J.: LoF: identifying density-based local outliers. In: Proceedings of the 2000 ACM SIGMOD International Conference on Management of Data, SIGMOD 2000, pp. 93–104. Association for Computing Machinery, New York (2000). https://doi.org/10.1145/342009.335388

3. Chang, M.W., Ratinov, L.A., Roth, D., Srikumar, V.: Importance of semantic representation: dataless classification. In: AAAI, pp. 830–835 (2008). https://www.aaai.org/Library/AAAI/2008/aaai08-132.php

4. Chen, X., Xia, Y., Jin, P., Carroll, J.: Dataless text classification with descriptive LDA. In: Proceedings of the Twenty-Ninth AAAI Conference on Artificial Intelligence, AAAI 2015, pp. 2224–2231. AAAI Press (2015). https://www.aaai.org/ocs/index.php/AAAI/AAAI15/paper/view/9524

5. Deerwester, S.C., Dumais, S.T., Landauer, T.K., Furnas, G.W., Harshman, R.A.: Indexing by latent semantic analysis. J. Am. Soc. Inf. Sci. **41**, 391–407 (1990). https://cis.temple.edu/vasilis/Courses/CIS750/Papers/deerwester90indexing_9.pdf

6. Devlin, J., Chang, M.W., Lee, K., Toutanova, K.: BERT: pre-training of deep bidirectional transformers for language understanding. In: Proceedings of the 2019 Conference of the North American Chapter of the Association for Computational Linguistics: Human Language Technologies, Volume 1 (Long and Short Papers), Minneapolis, Minnesota, pp. 4171–4186. Association for Computational Linguistics (2019). https://doi.org/10.18653/v1/N19-1423

7. Gabrilovich, E., Markovitch, S.: Computing semantic relatedness using Wikipedia-based explicit semantic analysis. In: Proceedings of the 20th International Joint Conference on Artifical Intelligence, IJCAI 2007, San Francisco, CA, USA, pp. 1606–1611. Morgan Kaufmann Publishers Inc. (2007). https://www.ijcai.org/Proceedings/07/Papers/259.pdf

8. Haj-Yahia, Z., Sieg, A., Deleris, L.A.: Towards unsupervised text classification leveraging experts and word embeddings. In: Proceedings of the 57th Annual Meeting of the Association for Computational Linguistics, Florence, Italy, pp. 371–379. Association for Computational Linguistics (2019). https://doi.org/10.18653/v1/P19-1036. https://aclanthology.org/P19-1036

9. Lang, K.: Newsweeder: learning to filter netnews. In: Proceedings of the 12th International Machine Learning Conference (ML 1995) (1995)

10. Le, Q., Mikolov, T.: Distributed representations of sentences and documents. In: Xing, E.P., Jebara, T. (eds.) Proceedings of the 31st International Conference on Machine Learning. Proceedings of Machine Learning Research, Bejing, China, vol. 32, pp. 1188–1196. PMLR (2014). https://proceedings.mlr.press/v32/le14.html

11. Li, Y., Zheng, R., Tian, T., Hu, Z., Iyer, R., Sycara, K.: Joint embedding of hierarchical categories and entities for concept categorization and dataless classification. In: Proceedings of COLING 2016, the 26th International Conference on Computational Linguistics: Technical Papers, Osaka, Japan, pp. 2678–2688. The COLING 2016 Organizing Committee (2016). https://aclanthology.org/C16-1252

12. Meng, Y., et al.: Text classification using label names only: a language model self-training approach. In: Proceedings of the 2020 Conference on Empirical Methods in Natural Language Processing (EMNLP), pp. 9006–9017. Association for Computational Linguistics (2020). https://doi.org/10.18653/v1/2020.emnlp-main.724

13. Mikolov, T., Sutskever, I., Chen, K., Corrado, G.S., Dean, J.: Distributed representations of words and phrases and their compositionality. In: Burges, C.J.C., Bottou, L., Welling, M., Ghahramani, Z., Weinberger, K.Q. (eds.) Advances in Neural Information Processing Systems, vol. 26. Curran Associates, Inc. (2013). https://proceedings.neurips.cc/paper/2013/file/9aa42b31882ec039965f3c4923ce901b-Paper.pdf

14. Nam, J., Mencía, E.L., Fürnkranz, J.: All-in text: learning document, label, and word representations jointly. In: AAAI Conference on Artificial Intelligence (2016). https://www.aaai.org/ocs/index.php/AAAI/AAAI16/paper/view/12058

15. Reimers, N., Gurevych, I.: Sentence-BERT: sentence embeddings using Siamese BERT-networks. In: Proceedings of the 2019 Conference on Empirical Methods in Natural Language Processing and the 9th International Joint Conference on Natural Language Processing (EMNLP-IJCNLP), Hong Kong, China, pp. 3982–3992. Association for Computational Linguistics (2019). https://doi.org/10.18653/v1/D19-1410. https://aclanthology.org/D19-1410

16. Sappadla, P.V., Nam, J., Mencia, E.L., Fürnkranz, J.: Using semantic similarity for multi-label zero-shot classification of text documents. In: Proceedings of European Symposium on Artificial Neural Networks, Computational Intelligence and Machine Learning (2016). https://www.esann.org/sites/default/files/proceedings/legacy/es2016-174.pdf

17. Schneider, P., Schopf, T., Vladika, J., Galkin, M., Simperl, E., Matthes, F.: A decade of knowledge graphs in natural language processing: a survey. In: Proceedings of the 2nd Conference of the Asia-Pacific Chapter of the Association for Computational Linguistics and the 12th International Joint Conference on Natural Language Processing, pp. 601–614. Association for Computational Linguistics (2022). https://aclanthology.org/2022.aacl-main.46

18. Schopf, T., Braun, D., Matthes, F.: Lbl2Vec: an embedding-based approach for unsupervised document retrieval on predefined topics. In: Proceedings of the 17th International Conference on Web Information Systems and Technologies - WEBIST, pp. 124–132. INSTICC, SciTePress (2021). https://doi.org/10.5220/0010710300003058

19. Schopf, T., Braun, D., Matthes, F.: Lbl2Vec github repository (2021). https://github.com/sebischair/Lbl2Vec

20. Schopf, T., Braun, D., Matthes, F.: Evaluating unsupervised text classification: zero-shot and similarity-based approaches. In: 2022 6th International Conference on Natural Language Processing and Information Retrieval (NLPIR), NLPIR 2022. Association for Computing Machinery, New York (2023)

21. Schopf, T., Klimek, S., Matthes, F.: Patternrank: leveraging pretrained language models and part of speech for unsupervised keyphrase extraction. In: Proceedings of the 14th International Joint Conference on Knowledge Discovery, Knowledge Engineering and Knowledge Management - KDIR, pp. 243–248. INSTICC, SciTePress (2022). https://doi.org/10.5220/0011546600003335

22. Schopf, T., Weinberger, P., Kinkeldei, T., Matthes, F.: Towards bilingual word embedding models for engineering. In: 2022 4th International Conference on Management Science and Industrial Engineering, MSIE 2022. Association for Computing Machinery, New York (2022). https://doi.org/10.1145/3535782.3535835

23. Song, Y., Roth, D.: On dataless hierarchical text classification. In: Proceedings of the AAAI Conference on Artificial Intelligence, vol. 28, no. 1 (2014). https://ojs.aaai.org/index.php/AAAI/article/view/8938

24. Song, Y., Upadhyay, S., Peng, H., Roth, D.: Cross-lingual dataless classification for many languages. In: Proceedings of the Twenty-Fifth International Joint Conference on Artificial Intelligence, IJCAI 2016, pp. 2901–2907. AAAI Press (2016). https://www.ijcai.org/Proceedings/16/Papers/412.pdf

25. Stammbach, D., Ash, E.: DocSCAN: unsupervised text classification via learning from neighbors. arXiv abs/2105.04024 (2021). https://arxiv.org/abs/2105.04024

26. Wang, W., Zheng, V.W., Yu, H., Miao, C.: A survey of zero-shot learning: settings, methods, and applications. ACM Trans. Intell. Syst. Technol. **10**(2) (2019). https://doi.org/10.1145/3293318

27. Williams, A., Nangia, N., Bowman, S.: A broad-coverage challenge corpus for sentence understanding through inference. In: Proceedings of the 2018 Conference of the North

American Chapter of the Association for Computational Linguistics: Human Language Technologies, Volume 1 (Long Papers), New Orleans, Louisiana, pp. 1112–1122. Association for Computational Linguistics (2018). https://doi.org/10.18653/v1/N18-1101. https://aclanthology.org/N18-1101

28. Yang, Z., Dai, Z., Yang, Y., Carbonell, J., Salakhutdinov, R., Le, Q.V.: XLNet: Generalized Autoregressive Pretraining for Language Understanding. Curran Associates Inc., Red Hook (2019)

29. Ye, Z., et al.: Zero-shot text classification via reinforced self-training. In: Proceedings of the 58th Annual Meeting of the Association for Computational Linguistics, pp. 3014–3024. Association for Computational Linguistics (2020). https://doi.org/10.18653/v1/2020.acl-main.272. https://aclanthology.org/2020.acl-main.272

30. Yin, W., Hay, J., Roth, D.: Benchmarking zero-shot text classification: datasets, evaluation and entailment approach. In: Proceedings of the 2019 Conference on Empirical Methods in Natural Language Processing and the 9th International Joint Conference on Natural Language Processing (EMNLP-IJCNLP), Hong Kong, China, pp. 3914–3923. Association for Computational Linguistics (2019). https://doi.org/10.18653/v1/D19-1404. https://aclanthology.org/D19-1404

31. Zhang, J., Lertvittayakumjorn, P., Guo, Y.: Integrating semantic knowledge to tackle zero-shot text classification. In: Proceedings of the 2019 Conference of the North American Chapter of the Association for Computational Linguistics: Human Language Technologies, Volume 1 (Long and Short Papers), Minneapolis, Minnesota, pp. 1031–1040. Association for Computational Linguistics (2019). https://doi.org/10.18653/v1/N19-1108. https://aclanthology.org/N19-1108

32. Zhang, X., Zhao, J., LeCun, Y.: Character-level convolutional networks for text classification. In: Cortes, C., Lawrence, N., Lee, D., Sugiyama, M., Garnett, R. (eds.) Advances in Neural Information Processing Systems, vol. 28. Curran Associates, Inc. (2015). https://proceedings.neurips.cc/paper/2015/file/250cf8b51c773f3f8dc8b4be867a9a02-Paper.pdf

33. Zhang, Y., Meng, Y., Huang, J., Xu, F.F., Wang, X., Han, J.: Minimally Supervised Categorization of Text with Metadata, pp. 1231–1240. Association for Computing Machinery, New York (2020). https://doi.org/10.1145/3397271.3401168

Towards Intelligent Processing of Electronic Invoices: The General Framework and Case Study of Short Text Deep Learning in Brazil

Diego Santos Kieckbusch[✉], Geraldo Pereira Rocha Filho[ID], Vinicius Di Oliveira[ID], and Li Weigang[ID]

TransLab/CIC, University of Brasilia, Brasilia, DF 70910-900, Brazil
diego.kieckbusch@aluno.unb.br, {geraldof,weigang}@unb.br

Abstract. An electronic invoice (E-invoice) is a kind of document that records the transactions of goods or services and then stores and exchanges them electronically. E-invoice is an emerging practice and presents a valuable source of information for many areas. Dealing with these invoices is usually a very challenging task. Information reported is often incomplete or presents mistakes. Before any meaningful treatment of these invoices, it is necessary to evaluate the product represented in each file. This research puts forward a conceptual framework to explain how to apply machine learning technology to extract meaningful information from invoices at different levels of aggregation. Related work in the field is contextualized within a given framework. A study case based on real data from Electronic invoice (NF-e) and Electronic Consumer Invoice (NFC-e) documents in Brazil, related to B2B and retail transactions. We compared traditional term frequency models with the Convolutions sentence classification models. Our experiments show that even if invoice text descriptions are short and there are a lot of errors and typos, simple term frequency models can achieve high baseline results on product code assignment.

Keywords: CNN · Electronic invoice · Short-text classification

1 Introduction

The purpose of an invoice is to record the transactions of goods and services between buyers and sellers. Invoicing is very important in daily commercial and financial operations. It is also a rich source of information for financial analysis, fraud detection [10], value chain analysis, product tracking, and hazard alarms [3]. Even though local regulations may differ, the overall structure of these documents is similar in many countries. In Brazil, this process started in 2008, first Electronic invoice (NF-e), then Electronic Consumer Invoice (NFC-e), which is a nationwide B2B transaction reporting integrated system. Similar measures have also been taken in Italy [2] and China [27,30]. Invoices exist in various forms, from physical documents to semi-structured data, and each form has its challenges. Knowing how to deal with this type of document can bring many valuable applications. This scenario leads us to the problem of how to extract meaningful information from invoice documents.

© Springer Nature Switzerland AG 2023
M. Marchiori et al. (Eds.): WEBIST 2020/2021, LNBIP 469, pp. 74–92, 2023.
https://doi.org/10.1007/978-3-031-24197-0_5

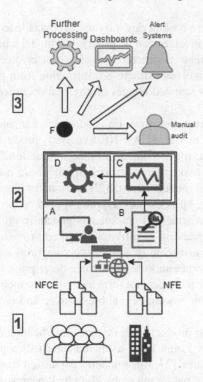

Fig. 1. Invoice processing in a nutshell.

Figure 1 presents an overview of invoice processing in three phases. At the bottom, Label 1, we have both retail and larger companies that issue invoices as part of their day-to-day activities. In Fig. 1, these invoices are represented by the NF-e and Electronic Consumer Invoice (NFC-e) documents, the Brazilian document for retail, and B2B invoices. These invoices are reported to a centralized system through web applications. Once reported, these invoices are processed to aid in a particular task. This process is depicted in Label 2, as an analyst selects relevant data to the core problem(A), data is then cleaned(B), explored(C), and used as the input to train a task-specific model, Label D. The trained model and analyzed data set (F) is then used as input for other applications and to aid manual auditing of other invoices, Label 3.

Due to a large amount of data, our first answer was to look at the problem through the lens of machine learning. Invoices are semi-structured documents with both tabular data and short text. Our previous work [11] focused on using the product description field to predict the universal code of each product. By further reading the existing literature on invoice processing, we step back and try to organize different stages, tasks, challenges, and techniques used in the process. We try to organize these topics in a conceptual framework to guide researchers and developers by creating a common thinking landscape to share knowledge and promote discussion.

This framework presents a layered structure for invoice processing. The three levels above represent different levels of abstraction: the more granular product transaction level, in which invoices are broken down by the products listed, the invoice level, and the issuer level, in which invoices can be grouped to model a business or sector behavior. There is a need to create a structured database of invoice data at the base level. This type of task often involves extracting information from physical documents and user-oriented files such as scanned images of physical documents to a more computer-oriented representation.

We also expand our previous work on product-level invoice classification. In our last work, we presented a model, SCAN-NF, to classify products transactions based on the short-text product description contained in the transaction. We validated our model through a study case on two different Brazilian electronic invoice models: the NF-e and NFC-e models. These models report B2B and retail transactions, respectively. As mentioned by [6], short text processing has some special properties: 1) the contribution of the individual author is small; 2) grammar is generally informal and unstructured, and 3) the sending and receiving of information in real-time and mass; 4) large-scale data is the unbalanced distribution of interesting categories and presents the labeling bottleneck. Compared to other short texts, invoice description is very short, containing only a few words, which usually can not form a complete sentence. This exacerbates the problem of domain-specific vocabulary, abbreviations, and typos because the authors use their own logic.

Some related works on product-level invoice classification are mainly concentrated in China. Their solutions range from using hashing techniques to dealing with an unknown number of features [27,30], semantic expansion trough external knowledge bases [27], classification of paragraph embedding by k-nearest-neighbors [23] to different artificial neural network architectures [26,31]. Semantic expansion is prevalent not only on invoice classification but also on short-text classification [14,24]. These works are not suited for the Brazilian case either due to language differences or reliance on knowledge bases only available in English and Chinese [9]. In the literature, there are gaps in the models suitable for classifying languages other than Chinese.

We focus on the Brazilian electronic invoice model due to its maturity. Standardization of electronic invoices was initiated in 2008 in Brazil and has evolved since then. Currently, every business transaction must report a standardized electronic invoice to a centralized system. Brazil utilizes two types of electronic invoices: Electronic Invoice (NF-e), which records B2B transactions, and Consumer Electronic Invoices (NFC-e), which records retail transactions. Mandatory reports of the NFC-e only began in 2017, and audition processes performed on NF-e documents are not performed in NFC-e data. Manual auditing of these invoices is expensive and time-consuming, especially for NFC-e data, due to a more significant number of issuers and the low quality of reported data. Since tax auditing is a fundamental activity for the Treasury Office, autonomous or semi-autonomous tools for processing large invoice datasets are of great value [15].

While fields are audited for fulfillment and type, there are breaches for exploits and errors. One fundamental vulnerability is in the reported product code, called MERCOSUR Common Nomenclature (NCM), which is a standardized nomenclature for products and services in MERCOSUR. It defines the correct taxation and if the product is eligible for tax exemption. One could miss-classify products to benefit from lower taxation.

As the main contribution of this research, we present both a contextual framework for invoice processing and present a study case on product level classification of invoices based on Brazilian data. We expand the points presented in our last article [11], in which we proposed a system to aid fiscal auditors to recognize product transactions. We present experiments using character-level CNN and support vector machines. Character level representation may be used to tackle typos and abbreviations, such tokens would not be correctly represented when using pre-trained word embedding. Support Vector machines trained over TF-IDF representation act as an example of a term count model. Our case study focuses on invoices in Brazil because the relevant data can be obtained through cooperation with the Treasury Office. Although the case study in this article is aimed at Brazil's data, we have briefly outlined the resources in other languages that could help to process invoices.

This article is organized as follows. In Sect. 2, we give a context framework, which provides the prospect of e-invoice processing. In the third part, we introduce the related work on invoice and short text classification. Section 4 describes the architecture of the SCAN-NF system and classification model. In Sect. 5, we show a case study on real NF-e and NFC-e data. Results are presented in Sect. 6. We present closing remarks and future works in the final section.

2   Contextual Framework

In this section, we present a contextual framework to understand the landscape of invoice processing. The framework is organized in a layered structure, with each layer representing a sequential step in invoice processing. Figure 2 presents a visual representation of the proposed framework. At the base level, there is the data structuring layer.

Although electronic invoices have become more and more popular in recent years, in many cases, useful documents only exist in physical forms or user-oriented digital files, such as document pictures and PDFs. Before processing any meaningful information, we need to extract data from these documents and store it in some semi-structured mode. Related works have shown that computer vision solutions are useful for extracting useful information from physical documents directly [8,17,22,28,28]. These methods can greatly reduce the costs and workload for generating invoice data sets. This task is especially important in auditing, because it is necessary to cross the information reported in invoices with sales records in other systems.

The remaining steps in our framework relate to different levels of abstraction that can be applied to invoice modeling. These steps include product transaction processing, invoice processing and issuer processing. Each level serves as the stepping stone for the next. Product transaction is the first layer of processing, representing each individual product or service transaction represented on every invoice in the data. At this level, we are interested in extracting granular information such as product description, product price, due taxes as well as other task-oriented attributes. The main form of input at this level is the product description. Our work, both in this chapter as well as in our last article, is situated at this level, as we treat product description as a short-text classification problem to predict the correct product code for each transaction. This exemplifies

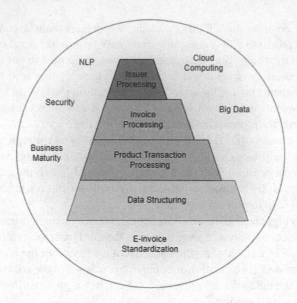

Fig. 2. E-invoice processing framework.

the main concern at this stage: we are interested in creating a good representation for each product transaction in order to produce the input for later tasks. It is much easier to analyze products transactions from a standardized product taxonomy than processing text descriptions [13].

At the invoice processing level, individual product transactions are aggregated and used to represent each invoice in conjunction to other meta-data. It is possible to track the relationship between multiple products in the same invoice. For example, Paalman [16] utilized two-step clustering to track fraudulent invoices. Auto-encoders have also been employed in fraud detection by measuring the distance between the reported text and the expected text produced by the model [20]. At this level, we can also model consumer behavior by utilizing association rules based on common product transactions. Another example is the usage of invoices issued by healthcare centers to extract association rules between commonly used medication [1].

At the higher level of abstraction, the behavior of parties involved in transactions is taken into account. One approach is to utilize previously known troubled issuers as a flag in processing invoices. An example of this kind of procedure is Chang's work [3], in which information about companies involved in violations is used to select and mark invoices to create an alarm system for safe edible oil. Another way to include issuer analysis in invoice processing is through graph analysis. It would be possible to model an oriented graph, each node representing an issuer with invoices being used to create the links between issuers. From this structure, it would be possible to look for communities, cycles, and other graph-oriented sub-structures and correlate them to real-world issues. At the time of this work, we have not been able to find works that model invoice processing utilizing graphs. We hope to address this tackle this problem in the future.

2.1 Larger Context

Invoice processing is also related to other concerns that are not directly related to extracting information from invoice documents. Due to a large amount of data, invoice-based systems require Big data architecture [5]. This may lead to solutions in distributed computing paradigm as storing and processing are more feasible in clusters than in single machines. The adoption of e-invoicing from the get-go is also a key factor, as it streamlines the data structuring layer, doing away with the need of using expensive image processing techniques to create digital representations of invoices. A maturity model for e-invoicing from the business perspective was provided by Cuylen [4].

3 Short Text Processing

In this section, we take a closer look at works related to invoice product transactions. We model product transaction processing as a short text classification problem, in which the main input is the short text snippet present in transaction descriptions. We present related work on traditional term-count-based methods and Neural Networks, as well as other product transaction processing models.

3.1 Traditional Methods

A Common representation technique in text classification is to create a term frequency vector to represent each document. Matrix factorization techniques can then be applied to engineer features in a smaller dimensional space. Due to the low word count in short text documents, there is lower co-occurrence of terms across the document-term matrix, which may hinder matrix factorization methods.

A possible solution to this problem is to directly address the brevity of short text by expanding on it. Document expansion utilizes the original text as the query to a secondary system. This system is then responsible to return similar documents to the query provided. The representation of the original text document is then calculated based on the collection of returned documents. This expansion can also be done term-wise by using lexical databases to extract terms with a strong semantic relationship to important terms in the documents. Early works attempted to address this problem by expanding available information through auxiliary databases [19,25]. Phan [18] proposed a framework for short text classification that used an external "universal dataset" to discover a set of hidden topics through Latent Semantic Analysis. Other work proposed to utilize web search engines as the query system [19].

For several reasons, document extension technology may not be suitable for invoice classification. Primarily there is an overhead mainly in processing and communication. The query of auxiliary documents increases the processing cost, which requires a good similarity function to identify related documents, and processing more documents than the initial data set also increases the cost. Communication with the auxiliary system may also bring bottleneck to the system. Finally, there is the additional cost of setting up and maintaining the auxiliary system in languages other than English. This is particularly important because these resources may not be easily available.

3.2 Neural Network Based Methods

Artificial neural networks (ANN) have become popular in many data-driven methods, because they allow better representation learning of problems with high dimensions (such as text and image classification). In Short-text classification, both Convolutions Neural networks (CNN) and Recurrent Neural Networks (RNN) have been used to create sentence embedding that could be classified. The general method follows two main steps: each item in the sentence is replaced by a vector with a fixed length, and input into the neural networks. These vectors can either be randomly initialized or trained independently to solve a self-supervised problem. These vectors generally incorporate underlying semantics of the corpus they were trained upon, demonstrated by the composition of vectors with similar meanings: the distance of the vector for the terms "King" and "man" is very similar to the distance between "Queen" and "woman".

The neural network will then perform sequential transformations of the input vectors representing a final output vector that will represent the whole input sentence. The classification itself is done on the final layer in which the learned vector is used to generate the classification label. The architecture proposed by Kim [12] serves as the basis for most CNN-based solutions. In CNN models, sliding windows of different sizes move through the input vectors learning to filter sub-structures throughout the training process. One common problem in short text is typos and abbreviations. Because of the training method of word vectors, typos and abbreviations are completely different from the original term. Zhang [29] utilized a 12-layer CNN to learn features from character embedding. On Character level CNN models, terms are created by forming sets of characters. This solves the problem of lack of vocabulary, misspellings and abbreviations, because words with similar structures will have similar embedding vectors. Wang [24] combined the word and character CNN with knowledge extension to classify short texts. The model used knowledge bases to return related concepts and included them in the text before the embedding layer. Knowledge bases included: YAGO, Probase, FreeBase, and DBpedia. A character-based CNN was used in parallel to the word concept CNN. Representations learned by both networks were concatenated before the final fully connected layer.

Naseem [14] proposed an expanded meta-embedding approach for sentiment analysis of short-text that combined features provided by word embedding, part of speech tagging, and sentiment lexicons. The resulting compound vector was fed to a Bidirectional long-short term memory (BiLSTM) with an attention network. The rationale behind the choice for an expanded meta-embedding is that language is a complex system, and each vector provides only a limited understanding of the language.

3.3 Invoice Classification

Invoice classification techniques have ranged from traditional count-based methods to neural-based architectures. In 2017, Chinese invoice data was made public for Chinese researchers, which motivated research in the area. This leads to the prevalence of works dealing with the Chinese invoice system.

Some works aimed to address the data sparsity problem by utilizing a hash trick for dimensionality reduction [30]. Yue [27] performed semantic expansion of features through external knowledge bases before using the hash trick for dimensionality reduction. Tang [23] utilized paragraph embedding to create a reduced representation and then applied the K-NN classifier. Yu [26] utilized a parallel RNN-CNN architecture, with the resulting vectors being combined in a fully connected layer. Zhu [31] combined features selected through filtering with representation learned through the LSTM model.

Different from most western languages, in western languages, text is expressed through words with spaces as separators, while in Chinese, there is no separator and no clear word boundary. Words are constructed based on the context. Chinese invoice classification words leaned towards RNN-based architectures in a way to mitigate errors produced in the word segmentation step.

Chinese works aside, Paalman et al. [16] worked on the reduction of feature space through 2-step clustering. The first step was to reduce the number of terms through filtering and then cluster the distributed semantic vector provided by different pre-trained word embeddings. This method was compared to traditional representation schemes and matrix factorization techniques. In the experiments, simple term frequency and TF-IDF normalization performed better than the models of Latent Dirichlet Allocation (LDA) and Latent Semantic Analysis (LSA).

3.4 Discussion of Related Work

Term count-based methods mainly address short-text processing through filtering and knowledge expansion. The problem with filtering is that there is information loss in a context where information is already poor. Semantic expansion is mainly done through knowledge bases. Communication with knowledge base becomes the bottleneck of the system, and because of the amount of invoice data, it is not suitable for invoice processing. Furthermore, knowledge bases may not be available in languages other than English and Chinese [9].

The limitation of pre-trained word embeddings comes down to vocabulary coverage and word sense [7]. These are significant to invoice classification. Words in invoices are often misspelled and abbreviated. Also, taxpayers often mix words of multiple languages depending on the kind of product being reported. Finally, invoices have little or no context to eliminate the ambiguity of word meaning.

Most invoice classification models did not utilize traditional ANN. The research of Yu and others [26] is the only one to combine both CNN and BiLSTM. However, CNN and BiLSTM were used in parallel over different fields. Zhu [31] combined a LSTM network with traditional methods using filtered features. While effective for the Chinese language, these architectures are not suitable for Brazilian invoice model. We propose a CNN-based model to solve these shortcomings, which does not depend on pre-trained word embedding and external knowledge base.

There is a gap between the general task of invoice text classification and similar tasks of Sentence and Short-Text classification in Natural Language Processing (NLP). Sentences are modeled as the components of a larger document. It is important to understand the context before and after the sentence, as well as the processing of the sentence itself. Even though we may draw parallels of the sentence role in a document being similar to that of an individual product transaction in an invoice, there is little meaning to the product transaction order in an invoice. Invoices is just a simple report, and there is no potential intention to tell anything beyond the product transactions itself. The words on the invoices often doesn't even have complete sentences.

Another thing worth studying about invoice classification is that it's a very different use case from the traditional short text. The main object of study of short-text works addresses news snippets, review comments, and tweets. The task is generally either to identify a general very broad category, such as news topics or to identify sentiment-related attributes from the text. These tasks require a deeper understating of the text and need to address different challenges from Invoice Processing. In sentiment analysis, it is necessary to take into account not only sarcasm but negations, conjunctions, and adverbs as these change the meaning of the sentence.

We believe that although the invoice product descriptions is similar to other short text problems, the classification of invoice text is obviously different and solutions may be different. The NLP field has been moving towards language understanding through large self-supervised models such as Transformer models. The task of classifying an invoice is less dependent on understanding the meaning of the text fragments, but more dependent on finding key terms that allow us to assign the correct code. The problem then becomes the large shifting vocabulary used by issuers to describe their products.

4   Architecture of SCAN-NF

In this section, we present an overview of the architecture of the SCAN-NF system and inner models, Fig. 3. The system's goal is to assign the proper NCM product code to each product transaction based on the product description. The labeled transaction is then used as inputs for other analyses by Tax Auditors and Specialists. The system works in two phases: a training phase and a prediction phase. During the training phase, the system is fed audited data from the tax office server of the Department of Economy of the Federal District (SEFAZ) in Brasilia to train a supervised model. Two models are trained, one for the classification of NF-e Documents and another for NFC-e Documents. After training, these models are used on new data during the prediction phase.

The system works as follows: Data is extracted from the tax office server (Label 1 in Fig. 3). Product description and corresponding NCM code for each product in each invoice are then extracted (Label 2 in Fig. 3). Text is then cleaned from irregularities (Label 3 in Fig. 3). A training dataset is constructed by balancing target classes samples and dropping duplicates (Label 4 in Fig. 3). The training set is then fed to a CNN model that learns to classify product descriptions (Label 5 in Fig. 3). Outputs at the training phase of the system are used to validate models before being put into production (Label 6 in Fig. 3). During the Prediction Phase, trained models are utilized to classify new data. These datasets may be composed of invoices issued by a suspected party or a large, broad dataset used for exploratory analysis (Label 7 in Fig. 3). Models trained in the training phase are then employed for the task at hand (Label 8 in Fig. 3). The final output of the model is the classified set of products inputs (Label 9 in Fig. 3). This set of classified product transactions is then used in manual auditing by tax auditors (Label 10 in Fig. 3).

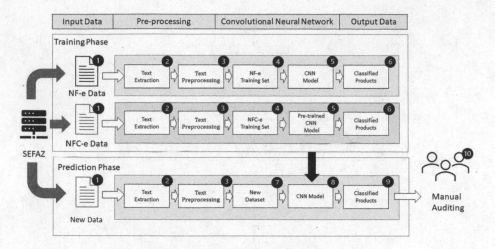

Fig. 3. Architecture of SCAN-NF. Extracted from [11].

The system is intended to aid tax auditors in auditioning invoices issued by already suspicious parties to pinpoint inconsistencies and irregularities. Currently, NFC-e documents are not audited due to the amount of data, a more significant number of issuers, and the nature of the data. Our solution helps auditors pinpoint inconsistencies in documents reported by an already suspicious party and allows for the automatic processing of more data. We hope that this solution will improve the productivity of tax auditors regarding NF-e processing and be the first step towards NFC-e processing.

There are different possibilities for the classification model used in the system. The sentence classification model proposed by Kim [12] can be used as a single multi-label classification model. However, due to the high number of possible NCM codes and high invoice data, we propose an ensemble model built from binary classifiers. Binary classifiers trained on individual classes can be pre-trained, stored, and then combined in multi-label classifiers on demand. This allows individual models to be updated and added without re-training other models.

Figure 4 presents architecture used in single models. The input layer takes the indexed word tokens. Each word index is replaced by a randomly initiated word vector representation in the embedding layer. The resulting vector is then reshaped to fit one-dimensional convolutions layers. Each convolution layer applies different sized filters to the encoded sentence. Max pooling is applied to the learned filters to extract the most useful features. Each convolution is applied in parallel, and they are then concatenated in a single vector, flattened, and fed to a Fully connected layer that will output the final classification. Soft-max was used as the activation function of the model, with the loss being determined by the categorical cross-entropy function.

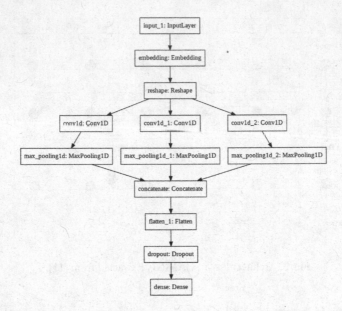

Fig. 4. Flowchart of single CNN word based model. Extracted from [11].

4.1   NF-e and NFC-e

The NF-e is the Brazilian national electronic fiscal document, created to substitute physical invoices, providing judicial validity to the transaction and real-time tracking for the tax office [21]. It contains detailed information about invoice identification, issuer identification, recipient identification, product, transportation, tax information, and total values. In our work, we utilize data present in product transactions, namely product description and NCM code. Data regarding issuer and recipient is kept hidden. NFC-e is a simplified version of the NFC-e used in retail services.

There are validations rules for the NCM field in the NF-e manual [21]. According to the experts engaged in tax audit and the schedule published in NF-e annual, although the verification procedures of NF-e documents have been implemented, NFC-e documents have not planned these verification procedures in the next few years. This leads to poor data quality.

5   Case Study of Brazilian E-Invoices

To validate our model, we conducted a case study based on real NFC-e and NF-e documents from SEFAZ. Data were separated into training and test sets, and different models were trained. Models were validated through cross-validation. Hyper-parameter optimization was conducted based on the average performance through all folders of cross-validations.

5.1 Dataset

In our experiments, we utilized data provided by the estate tax office of SEFAZ. Data provided included both NFC-e and NF-e documents. NF-e data consisted of invoices for cosmetics. NFC-e data consisted of a larger dataset of products from multiple sectors. We selected NCM codes present in the NF-e dataset and created a curated dataset with balanced classes. Due to disparity in market share, preserving product frequency would bias the models toward larger issuers and the most popular products. This could lead models to better classify invoices from large companies or learn their representation as to the norm. Our design decision was to drop duplicate product descriptions for each target class. While there is a significant vocabulary overlap between NF-e and NFC-e documents regarding NF-e data, NFC-e presents a much more vast vocabulary. Table 1 presents detailed information on the number of samples used in the experiment.

Table 1. Number of samples and datasets used in experiments. Extracted from [11].

	NF-E	NFC-E
Number of raw product samples	198882	99637515
Number of samples in balanced dataset	36234	49536
Number of balanced classes	18	18
Vocabulary Size	3646	15312
Shared Terms	2342	

5.2 Baseline Models

Besides the single and ensemble models presented in the SCAN-NF section, We utilize other classification models to create a baseline of comparison to our proposed model. We utilize SVM trained on the TF-IDF representation and Convolutional Neural Network trained on character representation.

SVM represents frequentist models and challenges the idea that traditional term count-based models fail at short text classification due to a sparse attribute matrix and low term count. We argue that while dimensionality reduction is particularly difficult due to low term co-occurrence, each product class will be defined by a handful of highly important terms. We expect these models to perform similarly to our CNN approach. Character-based Neural network is supposed to address typos and abbreviations.

5.3 Experiments

We conducted two experiments with different model sets. In the first one, we compare the single model and the ensemble model approaches. The single model is composed of a single CNN model trained on multi-label classification. The ensemble model is composed of a set of binary models. Each binary model is trained on a distinct class in a binary classification problem. The ensemble model takes the list of binary models and is then fine-tuned as a multi-label classification problem. Callbacks are set to stop training based on validation error loss.

In the second experiment, we investigated models based on different representations. We trained a character-based convolutions neural network and an SVM classifier based on the TF-IDF representation of text. This experiment aims to address whether or not the points made by related work on the effectiveness of these representations hold for Invoice classification. We expect character-based representation to have a higher complexity than a word-based model due to the need to construct words from the ground up. We expect the TF-IDF-based SVM classifier to perform significantly worse than the CNN models based on related work on both invoice and short-text processing.

Data were separated into training and test sets. We utilized the validation accuracy score to set an early stop on the training of the CNN models. Hyper-parameter optimization was conducted based on the average performance through all folders of cross-validations.

5.4 Metrics

We evaluate models based on the following metrics: accuracy, precision, recall, and top k Accuracy. Metrics are calculated based on True Positives, True Negatives, False Negatives, and False Positives.

Accuracy is given by the rate of correct predictions overall predictions: $(TP + TN)/(TP + TN + FP + FN)$. Top k Accuracy represents how often the correct answer will be in the top k outputs of the model. Accuracy is useful for getting an overall idea of model performance. In unbalanced datasets, recall and precision can paint a better picture of how the model behaves.

The recall represents the recovery rate of positive samples and is given by $TP/(TP + FN)$. Precision evaluates the correct set of retrieved samples and is given by $TP/(TP+FP)$. We utilize the F1-score, the harmonic mean of precision and recall, to get a balanced assessment of model performance on imbalanced classification.

In our experiments, we first set up a CNN architecture. We defined hyper-parameters through optimization using the hyper-opt library. Table 2 presents the parameters and values used in optimization, final parameters are highlighted in bold.

6   Results

In this section, we present the results of the experiments. We separate reports between the two experiments and datasets.

6.1   Single vs Ensemble CNN Approach

Figure 5 presents single and ensemble model performance on both the NF-e dataset e NFC-e datasets. We present results side by side. The key points of interest are that while both datasets model presented little deviation in the accuracy, there was a larger gap between precision and recall. In both datasets, the single model presented better

Table 2. Parameters used in CNN models optimization.

Parameter	Word CNN values	CHAR CNN values
Number of filters on 1D convolution #1	{0,100,200,300, 400,500,600}	{0,100,200,300, 400,500,**600**}
1D convolution kernel size #1	{**3**,5,7,9}	{**3**,5,7,9}
Number of filters on 1D convolution #2	{**50**,100,200,300, 400,500,600}	{50,100,200,300,400,500,**600**}
1D convolution kernel size #2	{3,5,7,**9**}	{3,5,7,**9**}
Number of filters on 1D convolution #3	{0,100,200,300, 400,500,**600**}	{0,100,200,300,400,500,**600**}
1D convolution kernel size #3	{**3**,5,7,9}	{3,5,7,**9**}
Dropout rate	[0, **0.29**, 0.5]	[0, **0.26**, 0.5]
Optimizer	{dam, Adagrad, Adadelta, **Nadam**}	{dam, **Adagrad**, Adadelta, Nadam}

recall at the cost of precision when compared to the ensemble model. We can see that while model accuracy deviated sightly, differences in recall and precision were more evident.

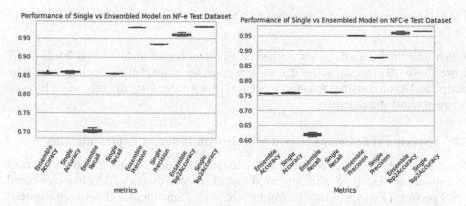

Fig. 5. Results of Experiment 1: single and ensemble models on NF-e and NFC-e datasets. Adapted from [11].

Singular models and binary models were trained through 5 epochs, while the fine tune of the ensemble model was done through 12 epochs. Each epoch took 4sec/10.000 samples to be performed. In practice, the ensemble model takes 20 times longer to be trained than the single model due to the training of binary models and fine-tuning of the ensemble model.

Individual class performance of the ensemble model is shown in Fig. 6. Due to the unbalanced nature of the problem, all classes presented high accuracy scores, scoring

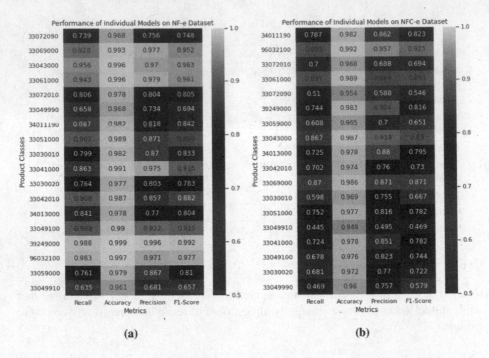

Fig. 6. Individual binary model performance on NF-e and NFC-e datasets. Extracted from [11].

higher than 96%. Of all models, 15 had an F1 score higher than 0.8, and 7 had an F1 score above 0.9. This signalizes that some classes are more challenging to predict than others, and some classification models are less trustworthy. Overall, there was a balance between recall and precision.

6.2   Experiment 2: Comparison of Models with Different Representations

Table 3 presents the mean accuracy and standard deviation of each based on ten runs of training and testing of each optimized model on both datasets. The character-based CNN performed very similarly to Word CNN, with a small trade-off between datasets. The character-based CNN performed better on the more unstructured retail invoices of the NFC-e dataset. The SVM model performed worse than the other models on both datasets. The Char took 13 epochs to train, significantly more than the single word CNN model.

Table 3. Accuracy metric of models on Experiment 2.

Accuracy	Word CNN	Char CNN	TF-IDF SVM
NF-e	0.869 ± 0,001	0.865 ± 0,001	0.776 ± 0,001
NFC-e	0.779 ± 0,001	0.784 ± 0,001	0.661 ± 0,001

6.3   Comparison of Approaches

From both experiments, it is clear that NFC-e product classification is a more complex problem than NF-e classification. Results also varied between different product classes. Regarding the comparison between single and ensemble approaches to word CNN models, we can see a trade-off between recall and precision, with the ensemble model presenting higher precision at the cost of the recall. This indicates that one approach may overcome the other based on the particular task. The single model will return a higher rate of classes of interest but may require more effort in the manual audit due to filtering out false positives. Models consistently achieved around 95% top2 accuracy on both datasets. This means that models can be used as recommendation systems to classify product descriptions.

There are also differences in the maintainability of approaches. The ensemble approach allows individual models to be updated without the need for all models to be updated. This also impacts the system's scalability, as additional classes can be added to the model without retraining the whole model at each addition.

Regarding text representation, word-based and character-based convolutional neural networks presented similar results. While the character-based model performed better on the NFC-e dataset, it is not clear if this resulted from handling typos and abbreviations. We could raise the question that the different results between word and character-based were the trade-off of handling typos at the cost of having to build word filters from the sum of character filters. In future work, this property of modeling typos can be better measured by introducing typos and abbreviations in a controlled dataset. Overall, CNN models managed to map product descriptions to the corresponding NCM code, while the SVM model struggled in both classes. This is in line with related work on short text processing findings.

7   Conclusion and Future Work

This work presented a general framework for invoice classification and expanded our previous work on invoice classification through a study case on Brazilian electronic invoices. Our experiments confirmed previous works on short-text classification, as the term-count model performed worse than text vector models. In our experimental datasets, both word and character-based CNN managed to map product descriptions to product code.

As a summary of this work, the main contributions include: 1) review the literature from the principle research and systems related to the studies of electronic invoices; 2) identify the characteristics and differences between short text processing and electronic invoice processing, especially using NCM code; 3) use machine learning to establish conceptual framework and SCAN-NF system for invoice classification; 4) experiments and analysis of NF-e and NFC-e data sets by SCAN-NF. Even though the invoice classification models are developed for E-invoicing in Brazil, it is easily extended for other countries by some reasonable adjusting.

We hope to improve the presented model by inserting it into real-world applications that can aid tax auditors, researchers, and public administrators in decision-making and day-to-day operations. Following our framework, the next step is to utilize the output of the studied methods to engineer invoice-level attributes. One such attribute is the expected tax return for misreported invoices based on the expected tax return of individual product transactions.

On the computational side, we will focus on transfer learning. Transformers have emerged as the go-to method for transfer learning in NLP. We will focus on comparing the performance of models trained on the representation provided by pre-trained transformers and previously studied models and the need to fine-tune existing models.

Acknowledgements. This work has been partially supported by the Brazilian National Council for Scientific and Technological Development (CNPq) under grant number 309545/2021-8. Thanks to Mr. Sergio Neto and other colleagues from the Department of Economy of the Federal District in Brasilia.

References

1. Agapito, G., Calabrese, B., Guzzi, P.H., Graziano, S., Cannataro, M.: Association rule mining from large datasets of clinical invoices document. In: Proceedings - 2019 IEEE International Conference on Bioinformatics and Biomedicine, BIBM 2019, pp. 2232–2238 (2019). https://doi.org/10.1109/BIBM47256.2019.8982934
2. Bardelli, C., Rondinelli, A., Vecchio, R., Figini, S.: Automatic electronic invoice classification using machine learning models. Mach. Learn. Knowl. Extr. **2**(4), 617–629 (2020). https://doi.org/10.3390/make2040033, https://www.mdpi.com/2504-4990/2/4/33
3. Chang, W.T., Yeh, Y.P., Wu, H.Y., Lin, Y.F., Dinh, T.S., Lian, I.: An automated alarm system for food safety by using electronic invoices. PLoS ONE **15**(1), e0228035 (2020). https://doi.org/10.1371/journal.pone.0228035
4. Cuylen, A., Kosch, L., Breitner, M.H.: Development of a maturity model for electronic invoice processes. Electron. Mark. **26**(2), 115–127 (2015). https://doi.org/10.1007/s12525-015-0206-x
5. Da Rocha, C.C., et al.: SQL query performance on Hadoop: an analysis focused on large databases of Brazilian electronic invoices. In: ICEIS 2018 - Proceedings of the 20th International Conference on Enterprise Information Systems 1(ICEIS), pp. 29–37 (2018). https://doi.org/10.5220/0006690400290037
6. Enamoto, L., Weigang, L., Filho, G.P.R.: Generic framework for multilingual short text categorization using convolutional neural network. Multimedia Tools Appl. **80**(9), 13475–13490 (2021). https://doi.org/10.1007/s11042-020-10314-9
7. Faruqui, M., Tsvetkov, Y., Rastogi, P., Dyer, C.: Problems with evaluation of word embeddings using word similarity tasks, pp. 30–35 (2016). https://doi.org/10.18653/v1/w16-2506
8. Feng, Y., Jiang, P., Gu, Z., Dai, Y.: Study of recognition of electronic invoice image. In: 2021 IEEE Information Technology, Networking, Electronic and Automation Control Conference, ITNEC, vol. 5, pp. 1582–1586 (2021). https://doi.org/10.1109/ITNEC52019.2021.9586969
9. Grida, M., Soliman, H., Hassan, M.: Short text mining: state of the art and research opportunities. J. Comput. Sci. **15**(10), 1450–1460 (2019). https://doi.org/10.3844/jcssp.2019.1450.1460
10. He, Y., Wang, C., Li, N., Zeng, Z.: Attention and memory-augmented networks for dual-view sequential learning. In: Proceedings of the ACM SIGKDD International Conference on Knowledge Discovery and Data Mining, pp. 125–134 (2020). https://doi.org/10.1145/3394486.3403055

11. Kieckbusch, D.S., Filho, G.P.R., Oliveira, V.D., Weigang, L.: SCAN-NF: a CNN-based system for the classification of electronic invoices through short-text product description. In: Mayo, F.J.D., Marchiori, M., Filipe, J. (eds.) Proceedings of the 17th International Conference on Web Information Systems and Technologies, WEBIST 2021, 26–28 October 2021, pp. 501–508. SCITEPRESS (2021). https://doi.org/10.5220/0010715200003058

12. Kim, Y.: Convolutional neural networks for sentence classification. In: EMNLP 2014 Conference on Empirical Methods in Natural Language Processing, Proceedings of the Conference (2011), pp. 1746–1751 (2014). https://doi.org/10.3115/v1/d14-1181

13. Marinho, M.C., Di Oliveira, V., Neto, S.A.P.B., Weigang, L., Borges, V.R.P.: Visual analysis of electronic invoices to identify suspicious cases of tax frauds. In: Rocha, Á., Ferrás, C., Méndez Porras, A., Jimenez Delgado, E. (eds.) ICITS 2022. LNNS, vol. 414, pp. 185–195. Springer, Cham (2022). https://doi.org/10.1007/978-3-030-96293-7_18

14. Naseem, U., Razzak, I., Musial, K., Imran, M.: Transformer based deep intelligent contextual embedding for Twitter sentiment analysis. Future Gen. Comput. Syst. **113**, 58–69 (2020). https://doi.org/10.1016/j.future.2020.06.050

15. Oliveira, V.D., Chaim, R.M., Weigang, L., Neto, S.A.P.B., Filho, G.P.R.: Towards a smart identification of tax default risk with machine learning. In: Mayo, F.J.D., Marchiori, M., Filipe, J. (eds.) Proceedings of the 17th International Conference on Web Information Systems and Technologies, WEBIST 2021, 26–28 October 2021, pp. 422–429. SCITEPRESS (2021). https://doi.org/10.5220/0010712200003058

16. Paalman, J., Mullick, S., Zervanou, K., Zhang, Y.: Term based semantic clusters for very short text classification. In: International Conference Recent Advances in Natural Language Processing, RANLP, vol. 2019, pp. 878–887 (2019). https://doi.org/10.26615/978-954-452-056-4_102

17. Palm, R.B., Laws, F., Winther, O.: Attend, copy, parse end-to-end information extraction from documents. In: Proceedings of the International Conference on Document Analysis and Recognition, ICDAR, pp. 329–336 (2019). https://doi.org/10.1109/ICDAR.2019.00060, https://www.scopus.com/inward/record.uri?eid=2-s2.0-85079851980&doi=10.1109%2FICDAR.2019.00060&partnerID=40&md5=29b092a6c8a3c0caf86779867d63d202

18. Phan, X.H., Nguyen, L.M., Horiguchi, S.: Learning to classify short and sparse text & web with hidden topics from large-scale data collections. In: 2008 Proceeding of the 17th International Conference on World Wide Web, WWW 2008, pp. 91–99 (2008). https://doi.org/10.1145/1367497.1367510

19. Sahami, M., Heilman, T.D.: A web-based kernel function for measuring the similarity of short text snippets. In: Proceedings of the 15th International Conference on World Wide Web, pp. 377–386 (2006). https://doi.org/10.1145/1135777.1135834

20. Schulte, J., et al.: ELINAC: autoencoder approach for electronic invoices data clustering. Appl. Sci. **12**, 3008 (2022). https://doi.org/10.3390/app12063008

21. SEFAZ: Manual de Orientação do Contribuinte - Padrões Técnicos de Comunicação. ENCAT (2015)

22. Tang, P., et al.: Anomaly detection in electronic invoice systems based on machine learning. Inf. Sci. **535**, 172–186 (2020). https://doi.org/10.1016/j.ins.2020.03.089

23. Tang, X., Zhu, Y., Hu, X., Li, P.: An integrated classification model for massive short texts with few words. In: ACM International Conference Proceeding Series, pp. 14–20 (2019). https://doi.org/10.1145/3366715.3366734

24. Wang, J., Wang, Z., Zhang, D., Yan, J.: Combining knowledge with deep convolutional neural networks for short text classification. In: IJCAI International Joint Conference on Artificial Intelligence, pp. 2915–2921 (2017). https://doi.org/10.24963/ijcai.2017/406

25. Yih, W.T., Meek, C.: Improving similarity measures for short segments of text. In: Proceedings of the National Conference on Artificial Intelligence, vol. 2, pp. 1489–1494 (2007)

26. Yu, J., Qiao, Y., Shu, N., Sun, K., Zhou, S., Yang, J.: Neural network based transaction classification system for chinese transaction behavior analysis. In: Proceedings - 2019 IEEE International Congress on Big Data, BigData Congress 2019 - Part of the 2019 IEEE World Congress on Services, pp. 64–71 (2019). https://doi.org/10.1109/BigDataCongress.2019. 00021

27. Yue, Y., Zhang, Y., Hu, X., Li, P.: Extremely short Chinese text classification method based on bidirectional semantic extension. In: Journal of Physics: Conference Series. vol. 1437 (2020). https://doi.org/10.1088/1742-6596/1437/1/012026

28. Zhang, H., Dong, B., Feng, B., Yang, F., Xu, B.: Classification of financial tickets using weakly supervised fine-grained networks. IEEE Access **8**, 129469–129477 (2020). https:// doi.org/10.1109/ACCESS.2020.3007528,   https://www.scopus.com/inward/record.uri? eid=2-s2.0-85089215581&doi=10.1109%2FACCESS.2020.3007528&partnerID=40& md5=9fffb4e8a98ac64be2fa28de21f4e632

29. Zhang, X., LeCun, Y.: Text understanding from scratch (2016). http://arxiv.org/abs/1502. 01710

30. Zhou, M., Hu, X., Zhu, Y., Li, P.: A novel classification method for short texts with few words. In: Proceedings of 2019 IEEE 3rd Information Technology, Networking, Electronic and Automation Control Conference, ITNEC 2019, pp. 861–865 (2019). https://doi.org/10. 1109/ITNEC.2019.8729520

31. Zhu, Y., Li, Y., Yue, Y., Qiang, J., Yuan, Y.: A hybrid classification method via character embedding in Chinese short text with few words. IEEE Access **8**, 92120–92128 (2020). https://doi.org/10.1109/ACCESS.2020.2994450

Indonesia Government and Social Networks: Response Analysis About Food Security During COVID-19 Pandemic

Dimas Subekti[1](✉) and Eko Priyo Purnomo[2,3]

[1] Department of Government Affairs and Administration, Universitas Muhammadiyah
Yogyakarta, Yogyakarta, Indonesia
dsubekti05@gmail.com
[2] Department of Government Affairs and Administration, Jusuf Kalla School of Government,
Universitas Muhammadiyah Yogyakarta, Yogyakarta, Indonesia
[3] E-Governance and Sustainability Institute, Yogyakarta, Indonesia

Abstract. This study aims to explain how does the Indonesian government's response to the COVID-19 pandemic in terms of food security through Twitter. This type of research is qualitative, using a literature study approach. Finding in this study, the food security agency dominates the response content on Twitter compared to the logistics affairs agency. This answers that the food security agency has a fairly broad scope of duties compared to the logistics affairs agency which only focuses on rice. As well as in the narration on the Twitter accounts of the two institutions that focus on the issue of food security conditions in the Indonesia public. Therefore, if you look at their duties and responsibilities, the two institutions have succeeded in responding to the state of Indonesia's food security during the COVID-19 pandemic via Twitter. However, there are several notes that must be paid attention to by the two institutions that the response content regarding agricultural conditions is quite minimal.

Keywords: Food security · Response · Government institutions · Twitter · COVID-19 pandemic

1 Background

The Food Security Agency, which is part of the Ministry of Agriculture, and the Logistics Affairs Agency are the two institutions in charge of national food security in Indonesia. The Food Security Agency is an entity that studies, develops, and coordinates food security [1]. Meanwhile, the Logistics Affairs Agency is an Indonesian food authority that oversees the rice trade system [2]. as public institutions, these two institutions should be responsible for handling Indonesian food security in the midst of the COVID-19 pandemic. Because, there are many things that limit people's activities, Indonesia's food security is to a certain extent very disturbed. The response from the Indonesian government in this case through these two institutions is very much needed by the community. Starting from how the condition of the food to the distribution of the food.

© Springer Nature Switzerland AG 2023
M. Marchiori et al. (Eds.): WEBIST 2020/2021, LNBIP 469, pp. 93–106, 2023.
https://doi.org/10.1007/978-3-031-24197-0_6

Therefore, this study aims to explain how does the Indonesian government's response to the COVID-19 pandemic in terms of food security through Twitter.

Indonesia's food security is managed by the Food Security Agency (BKP) and the Logistics Affairs Agency (Bulog), both of which are state agencies. Therefore, a quick response from the institutions responsible for dealing with food security during the COVID-19 pandemic is a must for the benefit of the public. Because Twitter permits communication and involvement with the public, it is one of the government's tools. Twitter is a platform that allows for much more interaction. Efficient information can be activated through Twitter interaction [3]. Twitter, like chat rooms, allows users to connect with one another by utilizing the at-sign. Twitter's goal was to create worldwide social networks where people could send and receive short messages in real time [4, 5].

The community's economic existence was disrupted by the COVID-19 pandemic. People try to fulfill their basic needs to survive. As a result, the government, through the Food Security Agency (BKP) and the Logistics Affairs Agency (Bulog), must secure sufficient food supplies and inform the Indonesian people about the situation during the Covid-19 pandemic. Indonesia's economy has been impacted by the Covid-19 pandemic, as indicated by Indonesia's economic growth being to be just 2.5% over usual, despite the fact that it is capable of up to 5.02% [6]. The Indonesian people felt the effects of the COVID-19 pandemic because the closure of numerous businesses made it difficult to make ends meet, increasing unemployment, and scarcity of goods [7]. COVID-19 has an effect on people's income by causing them to engage in less economic activities [8]. Because of the COVID-19 pandemic, economic activity is in jeopardy. Covid-19 has raised concerns about survival. Thousands of employees have been laid off, and many service providers have been forced to resign [9].

At the end of 2020, the LIPI Economic Research Center (P2E LIPI) performed an online household survey of Indonesians to determine the COVID-19's influence on food security This survey identified groups of persons who work in the informal sector and have inconsistent wages, as well as poor families who are food insecure. A total of 23.84% were food insecure but not hungry, 10.14% were food insecure but not hungry, and 1.95% were food insecure but not hungry [10]. The COVID-19 pandemic has the potential to generate food insecurity in several developing and even poor countries. In 2020, the COVID-19 pandemic will have a significant influence on food availability and access. This will cause a downturn in the economy and a rise in poverty [11]. The COVID-19 pandemic has created widespread disruptions, putting the food security of billions of people in jeopardy. Food shortages caused by the pandemic might treble world hunger, particularly in Africa and developing countries like Indonesia [12].

Some previous research on the COVID-19 pandemic, food security is a major concern. Research from [13], describes food access in American cities and villages, particularly during the COVID-19 pandemic. The COVID-19 pandemic has intensified food insecurity sensitivity to food supply systems. Then, research from [14], During the COVID-19 in Addis Ababa, the focus was on food consumption and food security. Furthermore, research from [15], focus on COVID19 poses a threat to food security and Canada's agricultural sector. Research from [16, 17], present scientific perspectives on the COVID-19 pandemic's impact on global food security. While, research from [18] investigate and debate the concept of resilience of the local food system in the face of interruptions that the 2020 COVID-19 pandemic will bring to such systems. The topic, which is centered on poor and middle-income nations, also takes into account a variety of shocks and pressures affecting. In such countries, local food systems and actors are important (weather-related, economic, political or social disturbances). As well as research from [19], the focus of his research is government communication about food security during the COVID-19 Pandemic in Indonesia.

Based on several previous studies that have been described, each of which discusses access to food during COVID-19, food consumption, communication government about food security and food system in state during COVID-19. This shows that there is still no research that discusses comprehensively about government response about food security. Therefore, this study will focus on discussing the response of the Indonesian government through the two institutions responsible about food security during the COVID-19 pandemic via Twitter. The response in question is the reaction of the Indonesian government due to the disruption of Indonesian food security during the COVID-19 pandemic. so that the response is manifested in the form of behavior that appears on Twitter to explain this.

2 Framework #1: Use of Social Networks in Government

Conceptually, it can be said that the Internet can affect the practice of democracy, the use of the Internet for the government will promote its activities. Likewise, the relationship between the government and its citizens expands more interactively through communication channels [20]. The arrival of web 2.0 has heightened the debate around government 2.0, often known as social government (s-government). Government 2.0 emphasizes the interactive aspect of the government's online activities. As a result, government 2.0 demands the development of online platforms and procedures that effectively facilitate interactions between the government and citizens, with social media sites like Twitter and Facebook seen as meeting this need [21].

In the field of e-government, the focus has been on facilitating interactions between governments and citizens, as well as between government departments. Social networking and other web 2.0 technologies are examples of such intermediaries, as they constitute a relatively new but rapidly expanding platform for interactions between governments and its clients, such as citizen, businesses, and government agencies [22]. The word "social network" refers to web sites, social media, and online tools that make it easier for people to engage by allowing them to exchange information, ideas, and interests. Social network like twitter and Facebook have facilities to comunnication and interaction with other people [23]. In today's society, Twitter-facilitated exchanges have become a significant part of people's daily lives, and they're slowly penetrating the public sector [24].

The use of social network to promote relationships between governments and citizens is a valuable tool [25]. Social network power resides in its ability to connect users with one another and so establish user communities. For the government, this implies that how social media is integrated into citizen networks and how they communicate with people about activities to stimulate their participation in public services and administration is critical. Such that, how can communication and interaction structures be nurtured and established inside social networks through government-citizen relationships, as well as collaboration amongst government agencies to facilitate the government's online activities for the general public [26].

3   Framework #2: COVID-19 Pandemic Disrupts Food Security

Over 900 million people throughout the world do not have enough or food that is safe to eat on a frequent basis. The population appears to be persistently high, with no sign of a big decrease in sight [27]. The two most important drivers of food security are availability and access to food. Food availability, on the other hand, does not guarantee food access. Food may be available internationally (i.e., if everyone had equitable access, a sufficient diet could be provided for everyone), However, not all countries, households, or individuals within households in need of food have it [28]. To this end, while food supply is important, it is not the only necessity for food security. Aside from food availability, there are some crucial components of food security to consider. Other critical considerations are diet quality, supply consistency through access to the food produced, as well as time and space [29].

In a way that our global civilization has never seen before, the COVID-19 is wreaking havoc on food supply networks at all levels, from local to global. COVID-19's impact lead to long-term food insecurity and a food crisis [30]. The COVID-19 pandemic has resulted in a tremendous spread of the virus surge in hunger and food poverty in the Global South. The FAO has dubbed the food security implications While the World Food Program has labeled it a hunger pandemic, it is a crisis within a crisis, claiming that 30 million people could perish from hunger [31]. Another tragedy associated with the COVID-19 pandemic is worldwide hunger. In April 2020, the World Food Program's head warned that the coronavirus could push another 130 million people to famine by the end of the year. This amount will increase the number of people in the globe who are food insecure, which presently stands at 821 million [32].

4   Research Methods

This type of research is qualitative, using a literature study approach. Then this study also focuses on analyzing Twitter accounts, the results are elaborated with some literature, both credible online news sources and relevant journal articles. NVIVO 12 plus is used to analyze data in this research. The Food Security Agency and the Logistics Affairs Agency's Twitter accounts provided the data for this study. Because these two entities are in charge of food security in Indonesia, The Twitter accounts of the Food Security Agency and the Logistics Affairs Agency were chosen for this investigation. From March 2020 through January 2022, data will be collected through the Twitter accounts of the two institutions. The reason for this is because during that time, Indonesia was afflicted by the COVID-19 outbreak, which wreaked havoc on the country's economy.

Followers, following, tweets, retweets, response content, response narratives, and actors involved were all obtained from the Twitter accounts of the Food Security Agency and the Logistics Affairs Agency. 971 tweets have sent from the Food Security Agency's Twitter account. Furthermore, the Food Security Agency's Twitter account received 2211 retweets. Meanwhile, the Logistics Affairs Agency's Twitter accounts had 2698 tweets. Furthermore, the Logistics Affairs Agency's pages re-ceived only 542 retweets. The Food Security Agency's Twitter account has 4,391 followers and 80 following. Meanwhile, the Twitter Logistics Affairs Agency account has 7,386 and 312 following, respectively. The Food Security Agency and Logistics Affairs Agency Twitter accounts have a large number of tweets, retweets, followers, and following, indicating that they are active.

5   The Content of the Response of Food Security Institutions

Governments all across the world are increasingly use Twitter as well as other social media platforms to respond to citizens and engage them. The use of Twitter by government agencies, in particular, has become a commonly used technique for making announcements and gauging public reaction. Offer the findings as inputs to policy- and decision-making processes as government-citizen interactions grow more interactive [33]. In the context of food security during the COVID-19 pandemic, the Indonesian government through the Food Security Agency and the Logistics Affairs Agency is responsible for ensuring that the state's food is safe for the community. One of the efforts made is to respond via Twitter as one of the largest social networks used by the Indonesian people. This helps the two institutions to respond to issues that develop in the community and then provide appropriate information responses.

Figure 1 is the result of the NVIVO 12 plus from the twitter account of the food security agency and the logistics affairs agency trying to display the response to the content that has been distributed so far. It aims to compare, which institution is more dominant in one or more content. The aim is to describe the activeness of two the institution in carrying out its work responsibilities to the Indonesian public. The data in Fig. 1 is obtained by auto-code data taken from the Twitter account of the two institutions. Then, use chart analysis to display the data.

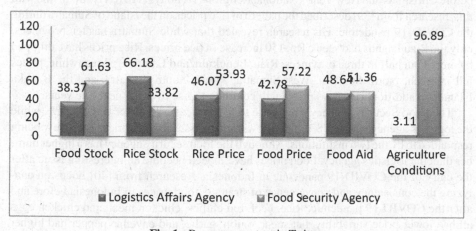

Fig. 1. Response content in Twitter.

Based on Fig. 1, the content of the response of the food security agency in discussing food stock is 61.63%. While the content of the response of the logistics affairs agency related to food stock was only 38.37%. Food security agency is dominant in response to food availability compared to logistics affairs agency. as the sector responsible for food supply, the food security agency under the ministry of agriculture has a strategy in preparing food availability in the COVID-19 pandemic situation. One of the strategies is to increase food production and keep farmers producing, provide stimulus including relaxation of people's business credit (KUR) in the agricultural sector, and accelerate assistance for agricultural facilities and infrastructure [34]. In fact, the Ministry of Agriculture ensures that food availability is maintained. Head of the Center for Food Distribution and Reserves, the Food Security Agency of the Ministry of Agriculture, Risfaheri said that the food needs of the community must still be met. This includes the Jabodetabek (Jakarta, Bogor, Depok, Tanggerang dan Bekasi) area, which is currently a red zone for the spread of the Corona virus. Risfaheri emphasized that the Ministry of Agriculture always ensures that stock and production are always in the upstream sector. While the smooth distribution is in the main task of the Ministry of Trade [35].

Furthermore, the content of the response of the food security agency which discusses rice stock is 33.82%, while the logistics affairs agency has 66.18%. The logistics affairs agency has realized the absorption of domestic rice of 1.2 million tons until the end of 2021. The president director of the logistics affairs agency, Budi Waseso, ensures that this absorption is adequate to ensure stock security during the COVID-19 pandemic [36]. This shows that the logistics agency dominates in discussing the availability of rice rather than the logistics affairs agency. This finding is in line with the results of research from [37] that the role of the logistical affairs agency has a significant positive effect on rice stabilization during the COVID-19 pandemic.

Then, the food security agency also discussed the contents of the response about rice prices on Twitter which was 53.93%, as well as the logistics affairs agency at 46.07%. According to him, the Ministry of Trade always strives to maintain rice price stability through the Availability of Supply and Price Stabilization (KPSH) policy, especially before Christmas and New Year's National Religious Holidays (HBKN) [38]. In line with this, research from [39] described the pattern of rice prices on the island of Sumatra during the COVID-19 pandemic. His research revealed that while Sumatra has ten provinces, only the Riau Islands had seen a Rp. 150 increase in rice prices. Rice prices have dropped by more than half in three provinces: Riau, Bengkulu, and Lampung. Meanwhile, prices fell in Aceh, North Sumatra, West Sumatra, Jambi, South Sumatra, and the Bangka Islands. In addition, rice food prices will continue to rise over the next five years.

The Food Security Agency's response to food prices on Twitter was 57.22%, while the logistics agency was 42.78%. This shows that the issue of food prices is actively being responded to by the two institutions. Although the food security agency has a higher number than the logistics agency. Food prices have indeed become an interesting issue after the entry of the COVID-19 pandemic in Indonesia. Research from [40] Focus on analyzing the consistency and convergence of strategic food prices in Indonesia before and after the COVID-19 pandemic. Rice, beef, red chilies, chicken meat, and chicken eggs all had lower price variability, but sugar, onion, garlic, and cayenne pepper had higher price variability. Price movements between regions show price variability that tends to increase, except for the price of chicken eggs. Several things that can be done to stabilize food prices are supply management through inter-time production arrangements and inter-regional distribution efficiency. In addition, the marketing contract system, ware-house receipt system, and strengthening of Regional Owned Enterprises for food supply management are very important. While the results of research from [41], explain that the price of food commodities at the consumer level has fluctuations at the beginning of the COVID-19 pandemic. Food commodities that experienced price increases during the COVID-19 pandemic were caused by supply constraints in the market due to distribution disruptions. Meanwhile, food commodities that experienced a decline in prices during the COVID-19 pandemic could be due to oversupply at the time of the main harvest and a decrease in demand.

Then, the content of the response of the food security agency regarding food aid on Twitter is 51.36%, while the logistics agency is 48.64%. During the COVID-19 pandemic, both are practically identical in their response to the question of food help. During the pandemic, the government provided a variety of social safety net aid to inhabitants. Regular social aid such as the Family Hope Program (PKH), Non-Cash Food Assistance (BPNT), and non-regular social support such as Cash Social Assistance (BST), Village Fund Direct Cash Assistance (BLT-DD), and rice assistance 10 kg are among the numerous types of assistance available [42]. To prepare for the impact of COVID-19 on food availability and price stability in Indonesia, the government must ensure that all food-related facilities and services, from production to consumption, are operational. The key to the effectiveness of implementing this food policy strategy is coordination across Ministries and State Agencies (K/L) [43].

Lastly, the content of the response of the food security agency regarding agricultural conditions on Twitter is 96.89, while the logistics agency is only 3.11%. This shows that the food security agency is very dominant in responding to the issue of agricultural conditions. This cannot be separated from, the food security agency has a responsibility in agriculture. The impact of COVID-19 cannot be underestimated, because it also has a very large impact on the agricultural sector, one of the effects of which is the disruption of farmers' production in all regions. There are at least 6 impacts affecting the agricultural sector: first, market and agricultural prices, when seeing the increasing level of concern, recommendations for "social distancing" reducing travel, reducing crowds, closings and further precautionary measures to halt the spread of COVID-19, consumers will create difficulties so that it will affect the stability of supply and demand for goods and services as well as prices that are likely to increase. Second, the Food Supply Chain is Slowing and Lacking because the distribution of agricultural logistics is disrupted. Third, Farmer's Health, Farmers are the relative population of the elderly compared to the general working population. The 2017 population census shows that the average age of farmers is almost 58 years. Major agricultural operators aged 65 years and over 11.7%. If COVID-19 is not contained until it penetrates the farmers, the impact will cause panic among the lower classes which will increase the slump in food production. Fourth, Agricultural Workforce, Farmers will be vulnerable if the infection is unstoppable. Fifth, Worker Safety and Personal Protective Equipment (PPE). The breeders were likely very nervous about mixing with the dung. Sixth, damage to food resources, because vegetables and fruits will be susceptible to viruses, this is because fruits easily rot [44].

The content of the response on Twitter during COVID-19 Pandemic about food stock, rice stock, food price, rice price, food aid and agriculture conditions. Response content has a relationship with each other. Table results from the Cluster Analysis which shows the connectivity between the content of the response. Connectivity between the content of the response means that one another has adjacent issues. The greater the connectivity number, the higher the proximity of the issue, and vice versa.

Based on Table 1, the highest connectivity lies in the content of rice price response with food aid. As well as the second position, the connectivity between food prices and food aid this is also not surprising, as food prices have become unstable during the COVID-19 pandemic. Therefore, the people who are affected because there are several policies that make it difficult for them to carry out their activities need food aid. Research from [45] explain in Demand shocks and supply chain concerns contributed to the months following the outbreak of the COVID-19 pandemic, there was a spike in import, export, producer, and consumer price volatility. Meat, fish, dairy, and eggs were particularly hard hit by the pandemic's shifting economy. Meanwhile, rice stock and agricultural circumstances are the answer content with the least connectedness.

Table 1. Correlation response content.

Content A	Content B	Pearson correlation coefficient
Rice price	Food aid	0.901782
Food price	Food aid	0.875209
Rice price	Food price	0.866565
Rice stock	Food price	0.78617
Rice stock	Rice price	0.656632
Rice stock	Food aid	0.644047
Food stock	Food price	0.633249
Food stock	Food aid	0.616124
Rice price	Food stock	0.514757
Food aid	Agricultural conditions	0.485846
Rice price	Agricultural conditions	0.435832
Food price	Agricultural conditions	0.394564
Rice stock	Food stock	0.370721
Food stock	Agricultural conditions	0.237446
Rice stock	Agricultural conditions	0.158669

Table 1 shows that rice price with food aid has the highest level of connection, with a value of 0.901782. Following that, there is a high 0.875209 correlation between food price and food aid. Meanwhile, the content of the response with the weakest connectivity strength, 0.158669, is rice stock with agricultural conditions.

6   The Narrative of the Response of Food Security Institutions

The narrative of the logistics affairs agency's answer is derived from the findings of NVIVO's word cloud analysis on the word frequency characteristic. The results of the word cloud analysis were obtained from the logistics affairs agency's Twitter account. The results of the data in Fig. 2 show that the logistical affairs agency intensively and consistently discusses its responsibility, namely regulating rice in Indonesia during the COVID-19 pandemic. The emergence of the word "rice", followed by several related words such as "price", "stock", "warehouse", "market", and several other words. This narrative illustrates that the logistics agency is serious in responding to food security, especially the availability of rice during the COVID-19 pandemic.

Fig. 2. Response narrative of logistics affairs agency in Twitter.

Based on Fig. 2, the logistics affairs agency responded to the availability of rice during the COVID-19 pandemic via Twitter, this was seen consistently because it was illustrated in the words "stock" and "warehouse". The government and the parliament appreciate the swiftness of the logistics affairs agency in maintaining rice stocks in the face of the COVID-19 pandemic [46]. Then, the logistical affairs agency is also very concerned about the issue of rice prices in the market, as the words "price" and "market" appear. This is indeed important, considering the Indonesian economy has been disrupted due to the COVID-19 pandemic. Rice price stability become one of the responsibilities of the logistics agency.

Research from [47], found that the price of rice has increased in various countries that produce it. This is inseparable from the entry of the COVID-19 pandemic. The causes are activity restrictions, transportation restrictions, layoffs of employees and reduction of operational hours for milling grain into rice. As well as findings from research [48], shows that a 25% rise in the global rice price would reduce total rice consumption as well as rice consumption by the poor. When the effects of a possible 12% loss in household income owing to the COVID-19-related economic slowdown are taken into account, rice consumption among the urban and rural poor reduces by 20% and 17%, respectively.

Meanwhile, the food security agency also has a narrative of its response to the food situation in Indonesia during the COVID-19 pandemic. This response narration was obtained from the Twitter account of the food security agency which was then processed through NVIVO 12 plus with the word frequency feature. Figure 3 shows the results of the narrative analysis of the response of the Food Security Agency on Twitter. Some of the words that emerged were #petanisejahtera (#prosperousfarmer), #lumbungpangandunia (#worldfoodbarn), #kedaulatangangan (#foodsovereignty), " #hargasembako (#foodofgroceries)" and many other words.

Fig. 3. Response narrative of food security agency in Twitter.

Based on Fig. 3, the Food Security Agency looks focused on the condition of Indonesian farmers, this is illustrated in #Petanisejahtera. The COVID-19 pandemic has indeed disrupted the welfare of farmers, starting from restrictive policies and also unstable prices. Whereas, when a number of economic sectors experienced a contraction or a decline in growth during the pandemic, the agricultural sector recorded different things. Minister of Agriculture Syahrul Yasin Limpo said the agricultural sector was actually able to grow in the midst of the Covid-19 pandemic. Syahrul said that the agricultural sector was recorded to be able to grow by 16.4%. This is because products from the agricultural sector are very much needed by the community. However, despite excellent statistical results, farmers in the field face a variety of challenges. Some of the causes are falling prices, distribution problems and low purchasing power in the market due to the COVID-19 pandemic [49]. Therefore, the food security agency pays more attention to farmers in its response narrative on Twitter. This is an effort to find solutions and policies that are in accordance with farmers' complaints.

Furthermore, the Food Security Agency understands that the COVID-19 pandemic that has hit Indonesia has largely disrupted food security. So that the food security agency has the idea to make Indonesia a country that has the strength to maintain its food security. This is illustrated in #lumbungpangandunia and #kedaulatanganngan. Food security is an important part of a country's national security since it ensures that the populace has access to nutritious and secure food. The stability of domestic production, as well as the availability of sufficient reserves, are both prerequisites for reaching this goal [50].

However, there are problems that must be faced in order to prepare good food security in a country, including Indonesia as a developing country. Such as research from [51], Due to improper and overly intensive use of natural resources, rising demand for livestock products, rising per capita food consumption, and other factors, food security is a threat in developing countries, as well as for the poorest segments of the population in both developed and developing countries. Therefore, the food security agency has its own challenges in order to realize Indonesia as the world's food barn and create food sovereignty, both in terms of the COVID-19 pandemic which has not ended or other challenges that will arise.

Furthermore, the logistics agency also has concerns about food prices during the COVID-19 pandemic. This was conveyed on Twitter in #hargasembako. The COVID-19 pandemic has indeed disrupted the stability of food prices in Indonesia. This is inseparable from the declining purchasing power and limited mobility of goods. Research from [52] explain how the COVID19 pandemic caused food prices to rise. Following COVID19, restrictions on movement or lockdowns were linked to an increase in the price of maize alone. Food prices were also affected by the currency rate, inflation, and crude oil prices, according to the study. In Asia and the Pacific, the coronavirus disease (COVID-19) pandemic has raised food security concerns. Border closures and export restrictions on a global scale could result in limited availability and affordability of particular food goods for countries that rely on imports [53].

7 Summing Up

The conclusion in this study is that the Food Security Agency and the Logistics Affairs Agency were very active in responding on Twitter about the state of Indonesia's food security during the COVID-19 pandemic. However, when compared, the food security agency dominates the response content on Twitter compared to the logistics affairs agency. This answers that the food security agency has a fairly broad scope of duties compared to the logistics agency which only focuses on rice. The food security agency has duties and responsibilities for Indonesian food in general, including a focus on agricultural conditions. As well as in the narration on the Twitter accounts of the logistics affairs agency and the food security agency that focus on the issue of food security conditions in the community. The food security agency even campaigned for the idea of Indonesia being a food sovereign country and as a world food producer. This is an interesting idea in the midst of the COVID-19 pandemic situation.

Therefore, if you look at their duties and responsibilities, the Food Security Agency and the Logistics Affairs Agency have succeeded in responding to the state of Indonesia's food security during the COVID-19 pandemic via Twitter. However, there are several notes that must be paid attention to by the two institutions that the response content regarding agricultural conditions is quite minimal. Even though agriculture is the advantage of Indonesia as a tropical country, this sector should be the focus of the government in creating food security. This also includes the absorption of agricultural crops by farmers, be it rice to become rice or other food ingredients.

The limitation of this research is that the data is only from one social network, namely Twitter. Therefore, the recommendation for further research is to use the two largest social networks in Indonesia, namely Facebook and Twitter. It aims to get the maximum data comparison perspective.

References

1. Bkp.pertanian.go.id, "Sejarah Pembentukan," *bkp.pertanian.go.id*. http://bkp.pertanian.go.id/sejarah. Accessed 05 Mar 2021
2. Bulog.co.id, "Pengertian Ketahanan Pangan," *Bulog.co.id* (2014). http://www.bulog.co.id/beraspangan/ketahanan-pangan/
3. Fischer, E., Reuber, A.R.: Social interaction via new social media: (How) can interactions on Twitter affect effectual thinking and behavior? J. Bus. Ventur. **26**(1), 1–18 (2011)
4. Murthy, D.: Towards a sociological understanding of social media: theorizing Twitter. Sociology **46**(6), 1059–1073 (2012)
5. Latonero, M., Shklovski, I.: Emergency management, Twitter, and social media evangelism. Int. J. Inf. Syst. Cris. Response Manag. **3**(4), 1–16 (2011)
6. Fahrika, A.I., Roy, J.: Dampak Pandemi Covid-19 Terhadap Perkembangan Makro Ekonomi di Indonesia dan Respon Kebijakan yang Ditempuh. Inovasi **16**(2), 206–213 (2020)
7. Maimunah, S.: Masalah Ekonomi Masyarakat Yang Terdampak Covid-19, *Frenxiv Pap.*, pp. 1–6 (2020)
8. Prawoto, N., Purnomo, E.P., Zahra, A.A.: The impacts of Covid-19 pandemic on socio-economic mobility in Indonesia. Int. J. Econ. Bus. Adm. **8**(3), 57–71 (2020)
9. Hossain, M.: The effect of the Covid-19 on sharing economy activities. J. Clean. Prod. **280**, 124782 (2021)
10. Purwanto, E.L.: Ketahanan Pangan Indonesia selama Pandemi: Apa yang Bisa Dilakukan untuk Memperbaikinya? *Kompas.com* (2021). https://money.kompas.com/read/2021/01/20/060800826/ketahanan-pangan-indonesia-selama-pandemi--apa-yang-bisa-dilakukan-untuk?page=all. Accessed 09 Mar 2021
11. Udmale, P., Pal, I., Szabo, S., Pramanik, M., Large, A.: Global food security in the context of COVID-19: a scenario-based exploratory analysis. Prog. Disaster Sci. **7**, 100120 (2020)
12. Zurayk, R.: Pandemic and food security: a view from the Global South. J. Agric. Food Syst. Community Dev. **9**(3), 1–5 (2020)
13. O'Hara, S., Toussaint, E.C.: Food access in crisis: food security and COVID-19. Ecol. Econ. **180**, 106859 (2021)
14. Hirvonen, K., de Brauw, A., Abate, G.T.: Food consumption and food security during the COVID-19 pandemic in Addis Ababa. Am. J. Agric. Econ. **103**(3), 772–789 (2021)
15. Deaton, B.J., Deaton, B.J.: Food security and Canada's agricultural system challenged by COVID-19. Can. J. Agric. Econ. Can. d'agroeconomie **68**(2), 143–149 (2020)
16. Mardones, F.O., et al.: The COVID-19 pandemic and global food security. Front. Vet. Sci. **7**, 928 (2020)

17. Swinnen, J., McDermott, J.: COVID-19 and global food security. EuroChoices **19**(3), 26–33 (2020)
18. Béné, C.: Resilience of local food systems and links to food security–a review of some important concepts in the context of COVID-19 and other shocks. Food Secur. **12**, 1–18 (2020). https://doi.org/10.1007/s12571-020-01076-1
19. Subekti, D., Purnomo, E., Salsabila, L., Fathani, A.: How does the Indonesian government communicate food security during COVID-19 pandemic: a social media analysis on Indonesia Official Twitter account. In: Proceedings of the 17th International Conference on Web Information Systems and Technologies (WEBIST2021), pp. 219–226 (2021)
20. Halpern, D., Katz, J.E.: From e-government to social network government: towards a transition model. In: Proceedings of the 4th Annual ACM Web Science Conference, pp. 119–127 (2012)
21. Khan, G.F., Yoon, H.Y., Park, H.W.: Social media use in public sector: a comparative study of the Korean & US government. In: ATHS panel during the 8th International Conference on Webometrics, Informatics and Scientometrics & 13th COLLNET Meeting, pp. 23–26 (2012)
22. Sandoval-Almazan, R., Gil-Garcia, J.R.: Are government internet portals evolving towards more interaction, participation, and collaboration? Revisiting the rhetoric of e-government among municipalities. Gov. Inf. Q. **29**, S72–S81 (2012)
23. Criado, J.I., Sandoval-Almazan, R., Gil-Garcia, J.R.: Government innovation through social media. Gov. Inf. Q. **30**(4), 319–326 (2013)
24. Nurmandi, A., et al.: To what extent is social media used in city government policy making? Case studies in three asean cities. Public Policy Adm. **17**(4), 600–618 (2018)
25. Khan, G.F., Yoon, H.Y., Kim, J., Park, H.W.: From e-government to social government: Twitter use by Korea's central government. Online Inf. Rev. **38**(1), 95–113 (2014)
26. Chen, H.M., Franks, P.C., Evans, L.: Exploring government uses of social media through Twitter sentiment analysis. J. Digit. Inf. Manag. **14**(5) (2016)
27. Osundahunsi, O.F., Abu, T.F.A., Enujiugha, V.N.: Effects of food safety and food security on the economic transformation of Nigeria. J. Agric. Crop. **2**(7), 62–82 (2016)
28. Stamoulis, K.G., Zezza, A.: Socioeconomic policies and food security. Interdiscip. Sustain. Issues Food Agric. **I**, 271 (2010)
29. Inegbedion, H.E.: COVID-19 lockdown: implication for food security. J. Agribus. Dev. Emerg. Econ. **11**(5), 437–451 (2021)
30. Workie, E., Mackolil, J., Nyika, J., Ramadas, S.: Deciphering the impact of COVID-19 pandemic on food security, agriculture, and livelihoods: A review of the evidence from developing countries. Curr. Res. Environ. Sustain. **2**, 100014 (2020)
31. Arndt, C., et al.: Covid-19 lockdowns, income distribution, and food security: an analysis for South Africa. Glob. Food Sec. **26**, 100410 (2020)
32. Moseley, W.G., Battersby, J.: The vulnerability and resilience of African food systems, food security, and nutrition in the context of the COVID-19 pandemic. Afr. Stud. Rev. **63**(3), 449–461 (2020)
33. Hubert, R.B., Estevez, E., Maguitman, A., Janowski, T.: Examining government-citizen interactions on Twitter using visual and sentiment analysis. In: Proceedings of the 19th Annual International Conference on Digital Government Research: Governance in the Data Age, pp. 1–10 (2018)
34. Bkp.pertanian.go.id, "Kementan Siapkan Strategi Ketahanan Pangan di Tengah Pandemi Covid-19," *bkp.pertanian.go.id* (2020). http://bkp.pertanian.go.id/blog/post/kementan-sia pkan-strategi-ketahanan-pangan-di-tengah-pandemi-covid-19. Accessed 02 Feb 2022
35. Catriana, E.: Pandemi Corona, Kementan Pastikan Ketersediaan Pangan Terjaga, *Kompas.com* (2020). https://money.kompas.com/read/2020/03/28/203600626/pandemi-corona-kementan-pastikan-ketersediaan-pangan-terjaga. Accessed 02 Feb 2022

36. Timorria, I.F.: Serap 1, 2 Juta Ton Beras selama 2021, Bulog Jamin Tak Ada Impor, *Ekonomi.bisnis.com* (2021). https://ekonomi.bisnis.com/read/20211228/12/1482487/serap-12-juta-ton-beras-selama-2021-bulog-jamin-tak-ada-impor. Accessed 02 Feb 2022

37. Mardah, S., Alfisah, E., Efrianti, K.: Peran Perum Bulog Dalam Stabilisasi Beras Masa Pandemi Covid-19 Di Banjarmasin. In: Prosiding hasil-hasil penelitian dosen-dosen universitas islam kalimantan (2021)

38. Jatnika, A.: Pemerintah akan jaga stabilitas harga beras jelang Nataru, *nasional.kontan.co.id* (2021). https://nasional.kontan.co.id/news/pemerintah-akan-jaga-stabilitas-harga-beras-jel ang-nataru. Accessed 02 Feb 2022

39. Pusvita, E.: Komparatif Trend Harga Pangan Beras Saat Pandemi Covid 19 Di Pulau Sumatera. J. Agribisnis Sos. Ekon. Pertan. **7**(1), 1–11 (2021)

40. Firdaus, M.: Disparitas Harga Pangan Strategis Sebelum dan Saat Pandemi COVID-19. J. Ekon. Indones. **10**(2), 107–120 (2021)

41. Agustian, A.: Strategi Stabilisasi Harga Pangan Pokok Pada Era Pandemi Covid-19. Pus. Sos. Ekon. dan Kebijak. Pertan. (3), 389–390 (2020)

42. Novrizaldi, Menko PMK: Pemerintah Terus Bantu Warga Miskin dan Rentan Miskin di Masa Pandemi Covid-19, *Kemenkopmk.go.id* (2021). https://www.kemenkopmk.go.id/menko-pmk-pemerintah-terus-bantu-warga-miskin-dan-rentan-miskin-di-masa-pandemi-covid-19. Accessed 02 Feb 2022

43. Hirawan, F.B., Verselita, A.A.: Kebijakan Pangan di Masa Pandemi Covid-19, Csis Comment., vol. april, no. CSIS Commentaries DMRU-048-ID, pp. 1–7 (2020)

44. A'dani, F., Sukayat, Y., Setiawan, I., Judawinata, M.G.: Pandemi Covid-19: Keterpurukan Dan Kebangkitan Pertanian Strategi Mempertahankan Ketersediaan Pangan Pokok Rumah Tangga Petani Padi Pada Masa Pandemi Covid-19 (Studi Kasus: Desa Pelem, Kecamatan Gabus, Kabupaten Grobogan, Jawa Tengah). Mimb. Agribisnis J. Pemikir. Masy. Ilm. Berwawasan Agribisnis **7**(1), 309–319 (2021)

45. Mead, D., Ransom, K., Reed, S.B., Sager, S.: The impact of the COVID-19 pandemic on food price indexes and data collection. Mon. Labor Rev. **2020**(Aug), 1–13 (2020)

46. Gareta, S.P.: Hadapi COVID-19, DPR apresiasi Bulog jaga stok beras, *Antaranews.com* (2020). https://www.antaranews.com/berita/1363022/hadapi-covid-19-dpr-apresiasi-bulog-jaga-stok-beras. Accessed 03 Feb 2022

47. Goeb, J., Zone, P.P., Kham Synt, N.L., Zu, A.M., Tang, Y., Minten, B.: Food prices, processing, and shocks: evidence from rice and COVID-19. J. Agric. Econ. **73**, 1–18 (2021)

48. Schmidt, E., Dorosh, P., Gilbert, R.: Impacts of COVID-19 induced income and rice price shocks on household welfare in Papua New Guinea: Household model estimates. Agric. Econ. **52**(3), 391–406 (2021)

49. Rizal, J.G.: Petani Merugi Saat Sektor Pertanian Tumbuh di Tengah Pandemi Corona, Apa Masalahnya? *Kompas.com* (2020). https://www.kompas.com/tren/read/2020/09/12/160500 965/petani-merugi-saat-sektor-pertanian-tumbuh-di-tengah-pandemi-corona-apa?page=all. Accessed 06 Feb 2022

50. Kaletnik, G., et al.: Features of food security of the country in conditions of economic instability (2019)

51. Abdulkadyrova, M.A., Dikinov, A.H., Tajmashanov, H.È., Shidaev, L.A., Shidaeva, E.A.: Global food security problems in the modern world economy. Int. J. Environ. Sci. Educ. **11**(12), 5320–5330 (2016)

52. Agyei, S.K., Isshaq, Z., Frimpong, S., Adam, A.M., Bossman, A., Asiamah, O.: COVID-19 and food prices in sub-Saharan Africa. African Dev. Rev. **33**, S102–S113 (2021)

53. Kim, K., Kim, S., Park, C.-Y.: Food Security in Asia and the Pacific amid the COVID-19 Pandemic (2020)

An Adaptive Filter for Preference Fine-Tuning in Recommender Systems

José Miguel Blanco[1]([envelope]) [iD], Mouzhi Ge[2] [iD], and Tomáš Pitner[1] [iD]

[1] Faculty of Informatics, Masaryk University, Brno, Czech Republic
jmblanco@mail.muni.cz, pitner@muni.cz
[2] Deggendorf Institute of Technology, Deggendorf, Germany
mouzhi.ge@th-deg.de

Abstract. A recommender system may recommend certain items that the users would not prefer. This can be caused by either the imperfection of the recommender system or the change of user preferences. When those failed recommendations appear often in the system, the users may consider that the recommender system is not able to capture the user preference. This can result in abandoning to further use the recommender system. However, given the possible failed recommendations, most recommender systems will ignore the non-preferred recommendations. Therefore, this paper proposes failure recovery solution for recommender systems with an adaptive filter. On the one hand, the proposed solution can deal with the failed recommendations while keeping the user engagement. Additionally, it allows the recommender system to dynamically fine tune the preferred items and become a long-term application. Also, the adaptive filter can avoid the cost of constantly updating the recommender learning model.

Keywords: Recommender systems · Recommendation recovery · Adaptive filter · User-oriented recommendation

1 Introduction

Nowadays recommender systems (RS) have become an important tool in our everyday life: from recommending movies and songs to suggesting what to do next in your fitness routine [10,20,31]. Their development has reached the point in which RS are able to tackle difficult questions as were to travel on your next vacation [9,23]. Further, they have become so ingrained that you are able to hold a conversation with them [16].

One of the main assumptions that come into play with RS is that to obtain the highest satisfaction from the user, one has to make the best recommendation possible [13]. While this might be true, it makes the situation of the RS after not recommending the optimal item critical, more than often, ignore the reason for the failure. Thus, hurting the user base after leaving some aside: Those that do not fit under the current version of the RS. To solve some of the problems that can be linked to this, explanations have been used [26], this does not solve the failure. One of the main reasons for this idiosyncrasy lies in the current state of the art considering RS as one time operations rather than a service that is to be used in the long term [25]. With all this, for a RS it is important not only to generate the best possible recommendation but to learn from its failures.

© Springer Nature Switzerland AG 2023
M. Marchiori et al. (Eds.): WEBIST 2020/2021, LNBIP 469, pp. 107–121, 2023.
https://doi.org/10.1007/978-3-031-24197-0_7

Thus, being able to capture the preferences of the user is central to today's research in the domain. In order to do so there are some different strategies that have been implemented as, for example, analyzing the reasons that are behind the failure [4]; also expanding the experience of the RS to include a conversational aspect to it in order to be more alluring for the user. In a similar fashion [19] goes in deep on understanding the motivations and use-cases of natural language that the users might utilize when asking or finding recommendations; this approach focuses on highlighting certain aspects of the user's behaviour so it can be recognized instantly by the RS. Extending the idea of catching the user preference, it is prevalent nowadays approaches that focus on modelling the user, including her personality along her preferences [2].

With all of the above, the main aim that we are focusing on here is to propose a solution on which the recovery for failed or sub-optimal recommendations happen. This solution could be used to improve the experience of users that feel a certain level of non-satisfaction with the RS. This solution will extend the life of the RS further beyond than a one-shot operation and convert it into a long-term application that can be used frequently. Additionally, the solution will not need to expand the computational complexity beyond the limits of the current RS and would not require a cold start every time [14]. This solution is built around an *adaptive filter*, that will be in charge of discarding any items that would be deem unfit for the user after this has been given a sub-optimal item. It is also proposed an evaluation method as well as a validation in the healthcare RS domain. Let us state that the present work constitutes an extension of the techniques previously introduced in [6]. From this previous work we gather the basic notions and expand them beyond their original scope and add some crucial depth to them.

This paper is structured as follows: In Sect. 2 we review some of the most important works in relation to the state of the art of current RS. In particular we will look into works that are related to recommendation refinement and recovery. In Sect. 3 we present the technical definitions of the adaptive filter, the algorithms, as well as a process model. This process model offers a comparison to a non-adaptive filter RS. In Sect. 4 we compare our proposed solution to the critique-based RS and showcase the novelty as well as the benefits of it. In Sect. 5 we introduce a preliminary validation of the adaptive filter RS based on a real-world dataset and compare it with the performance of a regular RS. Finally, in Sect. 7 we present the conclusions to the paper as well as outline some possible future works.

2   Related Works

For framing the adaptive filter RS there are several related works that we need to take a look at. These works focus mainly on improving the user experience and finding characteristics related to the recommendation. This is the main way authors took on this improvement. The works that we are inspecting can be split in three different categories: Item Characteristics, Boost Factor and User Input. The works that we will be analyzing are grouped in Table 1.

The works of [7,8,11,32,36] are a good representations for the many valid approaches that can be found we one asks about developing a RS. These papers help to put in context the novelty of our exclusion technique that we are presenting in this very work. In particular, both [11] and [36] take the lead on showing how a RS is developed within the framework that is known as the semantic web; the first paper can be seen as a recapitulation of different techniques, while the second focuses on a more practical and applicable approach. On the other hand, the work of [32] is focused on providing a background for RS with minimal set of items so the loss of users becomes irrelevant. This is strengthened by the development of a neural-network to analyze the data. In the work of [8] a framework to fine tune the recommendation is offered, showing how the use of RS in health informatics can benefit from a having a user-in-the-loop, or in this case a medic-in-the-loop; to further reinforce their position they add a framework on which proposals like this can be evaluated. Finally, [7] further shows how the satisfaction of the user can be raised by the use of a hybrid web RS, in which the recommendation is generated from multiple techniques instead of just one.

To show how the best possible recommendations can be achieved by boosting certain factors of the RS we have to look at the works [12], and [24]. In the first one, [12], the main focus is to show how the passing of time affects the quality of the stored data and its degradation. In particular, this could lead to worse recommendations and a less satisfactory·user-experience. Therefore, the collection and usage of the data has to be as quick as possible. The other work, [24], focuses on alleviating the problem of new items and their low ranking because of the lack of data. It does so by introducing a framework on which an evaluation tool solves this ongoing problem as it is enough to position the new items amongst the popular ones.

As for the final category, the works take a look at the data that is generated by user's input, be it on her profile or be it on the usage of the RS. These works usually focus more on obtaining the best recommendations before the purchase although there are some exceptions such as [22]. In particular, it is easy to observe how these papers reinforce the need to catering the user needs and respond afterwards a purchase has been made. The work of [1] delves into context-aware RS which focus on the data that is generated by the context of the user. It drives the point that all data that the user generates, even the contextual one, has to be used to achieve the best recommendation possible. In the paper [22] the method presented focuses on introducing a group recommendation system that also has a post-rating system in which the user can express her satisfaction. They conclude their work by comparing with other more traditional approaches to collaborative filtering. [35] uses the data of the user's Twitter profile to create a RS so the items recommended are catered to her taste. It is important to note that they are able to establish a correlation between the user's tweets and the categories that the user might be more interested in. In [18] they show the effects of choosing two different characteristics to base the RS upon. They use *visual memory* and *musical sophistication* in order to provide the best recommendation possible. The paper shows that while the first characteristic could help to get better recommendations to the user thanks to a pleasing environment, a higher second one can hinder the recommendations. The work of [28] focuses on mixing data from multiple characteristics of the user so the recommendation is more tailored to her tastes. One of the main strengths is the fact that depending on which dataset is being used, the weight of the characteristic varies for a better tailoring. In the paper [3] the main topic is a unified approach based on two different versions of trust: explicit and implicit. This, added to the preference by similarity gives a rating profile for the user so the recommendation becomes more accurate. The idea of using personality tests to improve a movie RS is depicted in [27]. The paper also provides a representation of the increase in satisfaction of this method when compared to a previously available RS. In [33] a framework is proposed in such a way that the order of interaction of the user with the different elements is taken into account. It also simplifies the list of items so the election of the user is much easier and they are able to show the benefits of this approach. Finally, [29] solves the problem about "sequence recognition", in which the RS fails to recognize that the user already has a more advanced item than those that are being recommended. The solution that is developed takes a collaborative filtering RS and reinforces it with a hybrid model creating an use-case for an e-commerce.

Table 1. On how to process the recovery in recommender systems.

Driver of recovery	Items
Item characteristics	[7,8,11,32,36]
Boost factor	[12,24]
User input	[1,3,18,22,27–29,33,35]

3 Model of Adaptive Filter

Section 2 has made clear that a change in the approach and user satisfaction interpretation is in need. This is expanded even more because of the lack of resources that can help with the recovery from a failed recommendation (or a suboptimal one for that matter), and it incentives the development of this adaptive filter.

Therefore, in this section we will introduce the technical definitions on which the solution that we are presenting is based on. We begin by defining the set of items to be recommended as well as the set of users that are getting recommended an item:

Definition 1 (Items and Their Set). $\mathcal{I}$ is a non-empty and non-trivial set such that $\mathcal{I} = \{i_1, i_2, i_3, ..., i_m\}$. Each i_j represents a different item; therefore, $\mathcal{I}$ should be regarded as the set of items to be recommended. Additionally, for any item i_j, it is built as follows: $i_j = \{c_1, c_2, c_3, ..., c_l\}$. Each c_h represents a different characteristic of the item i_j.

Definition 2 (Set of Users). $\mathcal{U}$ is a non-empty and non-trivial set such that $\mathcal{U} = \{u_1, u_2, u_3, ..., u_n\}$. Each u_k represents a different user; therefore, $\mathcal{U}$ should be regarded as the set of users that are getting recommended an item.

Next we introduce the notion of a Core RS that is basic for the later definition of the adaptive filter that we are presenting.

Definition 3 (Core Recommender System). A core RS (cRS) is a function that for each user u_k in $\mathcal{U}$, orders the elements of $\mathcal{I}$ from 1 to n, where $n = |\mathcal{I}|$, according to a certain criteria. The criterion on which the items are ranked is dependant on how the

RS is set-up. For example, in a neighborhood RS, the items can be ranked according to how other users have evaluated those items. Nevertheless, given our intention to make the results as universal as possible, these criteria can be any one that the reader might like. Therefore, the set $\mathcal{I}$ is transformed into $\mathcal{I}_r$, the ranked set of items. We define $\mathcal{I}_r$ as a well-ordered set, the result of applying an ordering operation (the base algorithm of the RS), on $\mathcal{I}$. Afterwards, u_k is recommended the first element of the ordered set, $\mathcal{I}_r$. By $R(u_k, i_j)$ we mean that the user u_k is recommended the item i_j. Furthermore, by $i_j = q$ we mean that the item i_j is in the position q in the set of ranked items. All of the above can be expressed as follows:

$$\mathbf{cRS} = \forall \mathbf{u_k}, \ \mathbf{u_k} \in \mathcal{U}, \ \exists \mathbf{i_j}, \ \mathbf{i_j} \in \mathcal{I_r}, \ \mathbf{i_j} = 1, \ and \ \mathbf{R}(\mathbf{u_k}, \mathbf{i_j})$$

It is important to take into account that the proposed definition of a cRS is done with an RS that only recommends the first item in mind. Nevertheless, it could be easily modified so that the cRS actually recommends a subset of items from $\mathcal{I}_r$. In the case we are working with more than one item, the user will be recommended the items ordered from the 1st position to pth position, where p is the number of items to be recommended.

Once we have presented the cRS, it is time to define the evaluation of an item would happen in its context. Additionally we will also present the similarity between items.

Definition 4 (Evaluation of an Item). $E(u_k, i_j)$ means that the user u_k evaluates the item i_j. This has two possible outcomes: (1) $E(u_k, i_j) = Sat$ and (2) $E(u_k, i_j) = \neg Sat$. If the result of the evaluation is (1), the RS has succeeded in recommending an item; i.e., the user is satisfied and the recommended item was optimal. If the result is (2), we say that the RS has failed; i.e., the user is not satisfied and the recommended item was suboptimal.

Definition 5 (Similar Items). Any two items i_j and i_l are similar, in symbols $S(i_j, i_l)$, if and only if they share most of their characteristics.

Now, we can finally introduce the notion of adaptive filter and afterwards the similarity threshold, and also a remark on this last one item.

Definition 6 (Adaptive Filter). An adaptive filter is a cRS in which, after an evaluation such that $E(u_k, i_j) = \neg sat$, the set $\mathcal{I}_r$ is revised via filtering. For this, the set $\mathcal{I}_r$ is modified so that all the items that are similar to the suboptimal item i_j are pulled out, thus giving birth to a new ranked set of items $\mathcal{I}_{r2}$. As the set $\mathcal{I}_{r2}$ is built, so is the set $\mathcal{I}_d$, the set of discarded items. This set is built as follows:

$$\mathcal{I_d} = \{\forall \mathbf{i_n} | \mathbf{S}(\mathbf{i_j}, \mathbf{i_n}), \mathcal{I_d} \cup \{\mathbf{i_n}\}\}$$

Then, for any user u_k and a selected item i_j, the new ranked set $\mathcal{I}_{r2}$ is built from the original set $\mathcal{I}_r$ as follows:

$$\mathcal{I_{r2}} = \{\forall \mathbf{i_n} | \mathbf{S}(\mathbf{i_j}, \mathbf{i_n}), \mathcal{I_r} - \{\mathbf{i_n}\}\}$$

This can be iterated a finite number of times p at most, where $p = |\mathcal{I}_r|$. Also, $\mathcal{I}_{r2}$ can be defined from $\mathcal{I}_r$ and $\mathcal{I}_d$, we have included its definition as standalone to make everything clearer. From an implementation point of view it should be defined from both sets so it is less taxating for the system.

Definition 7 (Similarity Threshold). Definition 5 is an application of the Jaccard Index [21] and, therefore, we need to establish a Similarity Threshold (ST). This ST is equal to the ratio of the summatory of the constants of preference (k) of each characteristic, per item, multiplied by the fraction of the set of discarded items. Thus, ST is as follows:

$$\mathbf{ST} = \left(\frac{\sum \mathbf{k_{c_1}}, ..., \mathbf{k_{c_n}}}{|\mathcal{I}|} \right) \times \left(\frac{1}{|\mathcal{I_d}|} \right)$$

For qualitative characteristics, the previous applies automatically. For quantitative characteristics, they are to be considered equal if and only if, for characteristics c_f and c_g, $c_f = c_g \pm 15\%$ follows. All of the above means that when an RS fails consecutively, less and less items are pulled from the set. Therefore, even if the RS fails too many times consecutively, the set $\mathcal{I}_r$ will not be emptied.

Remark 1 (Constant of Preference). The constants of preference (k) are introduced in the previous definition to ponder the characteristics to each user. These constants of preference are to be obtained from the user in the same way the RS would deal with a cold start [14]. Some of the tools that can be used for that matter include small surveys at the beginning of the use of the RS, or emotion detection on the user's previous reviews [15] among others. The reader might choose the one that feels more adequate.

3.1 Adaptive Filtering Process

Once we have introduced the notion of the adaptive filter and how it relates to RS, we proceed to show its operation in depth with a process model. First of all we can have a comparison with a regular RS thanks to Fig. 1, the adaptive filter process model, and Fig. 2, the regular RS without the adaptive filter process model.

It begins with a set of items $\mathcal{I}$ that after being arranged by the preferences and profile of the user u, gives back a ranked set of item $\mathcal{I}_r$. The main use of this newly created ranked set $\mathcal{I}_r$ is that it allows the recommendation of an item i_1 to the user u. Once this recommendation has happened and the user makes the corresponding purchase we have two different branches: Either the user u is satisfied or it is not. In the first case, we have that $E(u, i_1) = Sat$, and $\mathcal{I}_r$, the ranked set of items, remains the same except that the recommended item is missing. In the second option, when the user u is not satisfied with the item i_1, we have $E(u, i_1) = \neg Sat$. This entails that two different sets spawn. The first one is the set of discarded items $\mathcal{I}_d$ that contains all of the items that are similar to i_1, the original recommended item to the user u. The second set is the set $\mathcal{I}_{r2}$, which is the set of items to be recommended after all the elements of $\mathcal{I}_d$ have been eliminated from the original set of ranked items, $\mathcal{I}_r$.

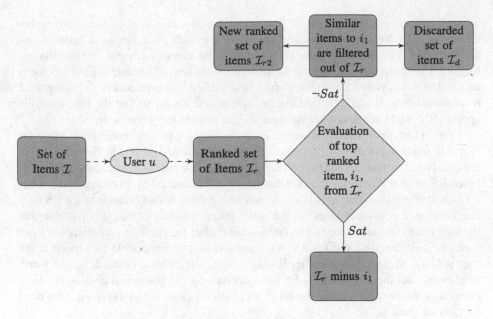

Fig. 1. Adaptive filter process model (source: [6]).

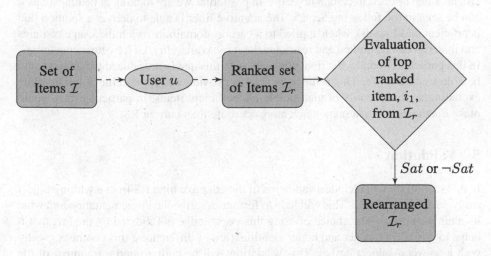

Fig. 2. Recommender system without the adaptive filter process model (source: [6]).

4 Discussion

The current state of the art when referring to addressing the suboptimal recommendations are what are known as critique-based RS [17]. It is, then, crucial to compare our solution of the adaptive filter RS with the critique-based RS. One main shared feature between the two different approaches is the fact that both are user-oriented and rely on letting the users instantly adjust the recommendation when a suboptimal recommendation is made. Nevertheless, despite this, there are multiple differences between one and the other. The main one to be pointed out is the aim of each one. While critique-based RS propose a fine-tuning of the recommendations, the adaptive filter RS focus on making impossible for the user on finding anything that is related to the suboptimal recommendation. It could be said that critique-based RS try to find the best available option [30], while adaptive filter RS does its best to hide the worst items.

From a technical point of view, the adaptive filtering process takes place **after** the user has made a purchase of a certain item and has disliked it. On the other hand, critique-based techniques can happen **before** or **after** the purchase, because for critique-based RS time in relation to the user interaction is not crucial as it is for adaptive filter RS. Another question that is vital when comparing them is that critique-based RS only flag items as low priority, does not get rid of them. Because of this it is possible that the user might encounter items that dislikes time after time, effectively decreasing her trust and enjoyment of the RS. On the contrary, that is impossible to happen if the user is faced with an adaptive filter RS, as it rules out disliked items. It is also worth mentioning that the adaptive filter RS has a decreasing computational cost, as the more items are removed, the smaller the set of recommendations is and the smaller the need for ranking them is.

As a final note, let us point that the usefulness of the proposed solution can be crucial when applied to certain domains. In particular we are looking at healthcare as it can be seen in the following Sect. 5. The adaptive filter is able to deliver a solution that is efficient and low risk when applied to a certain domain in which the usage of items and material can be limited and restricted, be it by availability, be it by time constraints. In this particular domain, the right application of this newly introduced technique could be able to save a life. This solution is able to provide a more specific solution while excluding a whole family of undesirable or inefficient items. In particular, this would make diagnosis and treatment much more accurate than current RS.

5   Validation

In this section we will include a validation of the adaptive filter RS from a within-subject study design perspective. This will help to further describe the implementation and what its main purpose is. The choice of using this perspective is validated by the fact that it helps to provide a quicker and better identification of differences; this contrasts greatly with a between-subject design. This validation will be built around a fragment of the real-world data set [34], which represents all of the medical drugs approved by the USA government. For this validation we will present two different scenarios with a common ground: A patient has arrived at the Emergency Room (ER) with an unspecific disease and gets treatment thanks to the intervention of a RS that focuses on recommending the best medical drug possible given her symptoms. In the first case, we would be looking at a regular RS without the adaptive filter, while the second one would have the proposed solution implemented into it. In both cases the RS recommends only one drug as treatments are better administered just one at a time to obtain a better diagnosis and outcome Additionally, the use of medical drugs needs to be carefully planned and healthcare teams do not work on multiple options at the same time. The fragment of interest of the set of drugs that the systems are using is the following:

$DrugsDataset = \{$Ashlyna, Daysee, Jaimiess, Malmorede, Namenda, Namzarinc, Prozac, Sarafem, Zovia$\}$

As per the definitions of Sect. 3, each one of the items, drugs, of the above set has some characteristics. In this case, these characteristics are the active ingredient, the strength and the route of the drug. Additionally, each of the RS will consider all of them when providing a recommendation. Every one of the characteristic has been selected so, as a whole, they actually are able to represent the drug itself. In particular, the active ingredient is able to point out what the drug focuses on and its usefulness; the strength can be seen as an indicator of its performance; and the route represents how easy it would be for the drug to be administered to the patient. These characteristics are just a selected part of a much bigger set of characteristics. All the characteristics of the aforementioned drugas can be seen in Table 2.

Table 2. Dataset fragment of medical drugs (source: [6]).

Drug name	Active ingredient	Strength	Route
Ashlyna	Ethinyl Estradiol; Levonorgestrel	0.03 mg; 0.01 mg	Tablet; Oral
Daysee	Ethinyl Estradiol; Levonorgestrel	0.03 mg; 0.02 mg	Tablet; Oral
Jaimiess	Ethinyl Estradiol; Levonorgestrel	0.02 mg; 0.01 mg	Tablet; Oral
Malmorede	Ethinyl Estradiol; Ethynodiol Dyacetate	0.05 mg; 1 mg	Tablet; Oral
Namenda	Memantine Hydrochloride	5 mg	Tablet; Oral
Namzaric	Donepezil Hydrochloride; Memantine Hydrochloride	10 mg; 14 mg	Capsule; Oral
Prozac	Fluoxetine Hydrochloride	10 mg	Capsule; Oral
Sarafem	Fluoxetine Hydrochloride	20 mg	Capsule; Oral
Zovia	Ethinyl Estradiol; Ethynodiol Dyacetate	0.05 mg; 1 mg	Tablet; Oral

So far, the healthcare team has proceed by administering the drugs named Malmored and Ashlyna and, thanks to them, the patient has been improving. Because of all the positive feedback so far, both RS have ranked the set of drugs as follows:

$DrugsDataset_r = \{$Daysee = 1, Jaiminess = 2, Zovia = 3, Prozac = 4, Namenda = 5, Sarafem = 6$\}$

Because of this, the healthcare team is presented with the recommendation of using Daysee, as it follows from what was said in Definition 3. It can be seen that is a natural option as it has the same active ingredient as the last recommended item, Ashlyna. In every scenario the healthcare team trusts the recommendation and applies the selected drug, despite the work of the RS, the drug has little to no effect whatsoever. Because of that, the healthcare team evaluates the recommended item as it shown in Definition 4, in both cases giving a non-satisfied evaluation. With all this, the first RS, the one without the adaptive filter proceeds to recommend the drug Jaiminess, a drug similar to the one that was just administered and that was ranked as the best next option by the RS. As this drug is quite similar to the previous ones as it can be seen in Table 2, it will not work properly and it is quite possible that the team will began to distrust the RS and its usage will decrease. In the second scenario, after the non-positive rating of the previous drug, the adaptive filter will discard any drugs that are similar to the one just administered. This discarding will happen according to the characteristics of the drugs as filtered by Definition 6. Because of this, Jaiminess that has the same active ingredient, route and the strength is within a 15% range (Cf. Definition 7), is discarded. With all this, the new ranked set of items will read as follows:

$$DrugsDataset_{r2} = \{\text{Zovia} = 3, \text{Prozac} = 4, \text{Namenda} = 5, \text{Sarafem} = 6\}$$

Additionally, a set of discarded drugs is also created:

$$DiscardedDrugs = \{\text{Jaiminess}\}$$

After all the process that builds this sets according to the algorithms of Definition 6, the RS with the adaptive filter recommends the use of Zovia. This is because of it being the top ranked item in the new set of drugs; this offers a viable alternative to the healthcare team. It can be seen that adaptive filter offers a viable alternative for a user who is facing a suboptimal recommendation. In this use-case, the healthcare team is able to recover from a critical situation, extending their trust in the RS and increasing the chance of it becoming a long term application as well as a crucial tool. All because the adaptive filter RS provides a tool to recover from any failed recommendation. Therefore, the lifespan of the RS has gone from a one-shot to a multiple-use, and may become a crucial part of the healthcare team's diagnostic cycle. The satisfaction of the user therefore also increases because there has been an effort to recover from the failure and offers an alternative that can make the team forget the bad experience. Additionally, some drugs are pulled out of the drugs dataset and they will not consider them to be recommended again for the same clinical case. This serves to improve their confidence in the agent and extend their use of the RS, since they may feel that their preferences are taken into account.

6   Evaluation of Adaptive Filter RS

The development of the Adaptive Filter RS requires also the evaluation of their implementation. As we have seen they offer an alternative to regular RS recovery, so we are in need to determine which a method for testing if the implementation of the Adaptive Filter RS offers any advantages. For that matter there are two key elements to be considered when evaluating a filtered RS:

- Cardinality of the set of discarded items $\mathcal{I}_d$
- Iterations of the RS

This means that we need to pay attention to how many times the user has actually interacted with the RS, something that goes in line with the idea that adaptive filtered RS are supposed to enhance long-term use of RS generally speaking. And the cardinality of $\mathcal{I}_d$, that is, how many items the adaptive filter RS has discarded after a failed recommendation. When the number of iterations is none, the cardinality of $\mathcal{I}_d$ is equal to zero; i.e., when $\mathcal{I}_{r0}$, then $|\mathcal{I}_d| = 0$. This is due to the fact that Filtered RS only start functioning after there has been a failed recommendation.

This however, presents us with a problem, as the cardinality of $\mathcal{I}_d$ is necessarily linked to the intrinsic similarity of the items of $\mathcal{I}_{r0}$. In the case that the items prepared for recommendation are of a closely knitted family, it is quite possible that the set $\mathcal{I}_d$ fills up pretty quickly and, within three or four iterations, its cardinality might be bigger than the original cardinality of the original set of items to be recommended. With this in mind, we need to define the familiarity of the items on based on the set $\mathcal{I}_{r0}$. This familiarity would be related to the Similarity Threshold of Definition 7. Then we define this familiarity as follows:

Definition 8 (Familiarity of Items). The familiarity of items (FI) is defined as the product of the summatory of the constants of preference (k) with the result of dividing the cardinality of the set of characteristics ($\mathcal{C}_n$) by the cardinality of the set items to be considered ($\mathcal{I}_{r0}$). Thus, the familiarity of items can be described as follows:

$$\mathbf{FI} = \sum \mathbf{k_{c_1}}, ..., \mathbf{k_{c_n}} \times \left(\frac{|\mathcal{C}_n|}{|\mathcal{I}_{r0}|} \right)$$

With this definition we have a tangible way of understanding the set of items and with that we can base the evaluation of the adaptive filter RS. This evaluation could be performed as follows:

Definition 9 (Evaluation of Adaptive Filter RS). The evaluation of adaptive filter RS (Ev) is performed by looking at percentage of items discarded, as in the cardinality of the set of discarded items ($\mathcal{I}_d$), in relation to the original set of items ($\mathcal{I}_{rn}$), weighted by the familiarity of the items (FI) and number of iterations (n). This can be expressed as follows:

$$\mathbf{Ev} = \left(\frac{|\mathcal{I}_d|}{|\mathcal{I}_{r0}| \times \mathbf{FI}} \right)$$

This would produce a fraction whose result will always be under 1. Thus, the closer the result is to zero, the better the adaptive filter RS is functioning and our evaluation would characterize it as positive. On the other hand, the closer the number gets to one, the worse the adaptive filter RS is performing.

Generally speaking, the evaluation of the adaptive filter RS would allow us to look at how quickly the set of items to be recommended depletes. In this sense, the familiarity of items that we have described before serves the purpose of making the evaluation fair for items of a closely knit family. It is to be expected for a set of items to be recommended to be depleted much quicker if the items share a really close relation. Therefore, the evaluation performed taking into account the familiarity of the items sets a much fair scenario than if we did not include it.

This evaluation allows us to compare different adaptive filter RS by just comparing the results coming out of their different evaluations. Generally speaking, the adaptive filter RS with the lowest score would be considered a better RS, while the one with a higher score would be worse. Nevertheless, this evaluation still should be able to offer some light when comparing an adaptive filter RS to a regular RS. In particular it should be able to tell us how much of an improvement the adaptive filter RS offers.

For that matter what we ought to do is to compare how many elements the adaptive filter RS has discarded through its iterations by the number of iterations that a regular RS has gone through. It means that both RS are to be implemented over the same set of items, as otherwise they would be not comparable. Then, let us propose the following:

Definition 10 (Comparison of Adaptive Filter RS). The comparison an adaptive filter RS with a regular RS (Co) is done by obtaining the relation between discarded items $(|\mathcal{I}_d|)$ per iterations (n), and the number of iterations of the regular RS (m):

$$Co = \left(\frac{\left(\frac{|\mathcal{I}_d|}{n} \right)}{m} \right)$$

This would result in a number that would measure how more effective the adaptive filter RS against the regular RS. The higher the number, the more effective our solution is. On the other hand. If the number is really small, it would come to show us that the regular RS, in that specific case would be out performing the proposed solution.

7   Conclusions

In this work we have introduced a scheme to recover the failure from RS. This solution is created by the means of an adaptive filter that can be bootstrapped to existing RS without a significant increase in computational complexity. Therefore, it is easy to incorporate into RS without modifying the algorithm. By using the context of healthcare RS we have shown the utility of the technique and performed the validation using a real-world dataset. It has shown in this proof of concept that the RS is able to fine tune the recommendations in real time and make a recovery from a non-optimal item. In particular, this solution has been able to make an impact on better patient outcome without having to deal with any risk. The evaluation result has showed that the proposed solution can efficiently avoid to recommend the items with limited impact on patients. Also, the performance evaluation has shown that the additional computational complexity is only the creation of the set of discarded items.

Some future lines of research to be followed include the implementation of the solution in pre-existing RS that are already available. This development would serve the purpose of further illustrate the functionality of this technique and compare it with the a real implementation of a traditional RS. Additionally, it would be of utmost interest to develop an implementation in the context of semantic web RS [36] by taking into consideration the inconsistency of data solution that [5] offers.

References

1. Adomavicius, G., Mobasher, B., Ricci, F., Tuzhilin, A.: Context-aware recommender systems. AI Mag. **32**(3), 67–80 (2011)
2. Alves, P., et al.: Modeling tourists' personality in recommender systems: how does personality influence preferences for tourist attractions? In: Proceedings of the 28th ACM Conference on User Modeling, Adaptation and Personalization, pp. 4–13. Association for Computing Machinery, New York (2020)

3. Ayub, M., Ghazanfar, M.A., Mehmood, Z., Alyoubi, K.H., Alfakeeh, A.S.: Unifying user similarity and social trust to generate powerful recommendations for smart cities using collaborating filtering-based recommender systems. Soft. Comput. **24**(15), 11071–11094 (2020)
4. Ben Mimoun, M.S., Poncin, I., Garnier, M.: Case study-embodied virtual agents: an analysis on reasons for failure. J. Retail. Consum. Serv. **19**(6), 605–612 (2012)
5. Blanco, J.M., Ge, M., Pitner, T.: Modelling inconsistent data for reasoners in web of things (accepted). Proc. Comput. Sci. **192**, 1265–1273 (2021)
6. Blanco., J.M., Ge., M., Pitner., T.: Recommendation recovery with adaptive filter for recommender systems. In: Proceedings of the 17th International Conference on Web Information Systems and Technologies - WEBIST, pp. 283–290. INSTICC, SciTePress (2021). https://doi.org/10.5220/0010653600003058
7. Burke, R.: Hybrid web recommender systems. In: Brusilovsky, P., Kobsa, A., Nejdl, W. (eds.) The Adaptive Web. LNCS, vol. 4321, pp. 377–408. Springer, Heidelberg (2007). https://doi.org/10.1007/978-3-540-72079-9_12
8. Calero Valdez, A., Ziefle, M., Verbert, K., Felfernig, A., Holzinger, A.: Recommender systems for health informatics: state-of-the-art and future perspectives. In: Holzinger, A. (ed.) Machine Learning for Health Informatics. LNCS (LNAI), vol. 9605, pp. 391–414. Springer, Cham (2016). https://doi.org/10.1007/978-3-319-50478-0_20
9. Carusotto, V.E., Pilato, G., Persia, F., Ge, M.: User profiling for tourist trip recommendations using social sensing. In: IEEE International Symposium on Multimedia, ISM 2021, Naple, Italy, 29 November–1 December 2021, pp. 182–185. IEEE (2021)
10. Chedrawy, Z., Abidi, S.S.R.: A web recommender system for recommending, predicting and personalizing music playlists. In: Vossen, G., Long, D.D.E., Yu, J.X. (eds.) WISE 2009. LNCS, vol. 5802, pp. 335–342. Springer, Heidelberg (2009). https://doi.org/10.1007/978-3-642-04409-0_34
11. Codina, V., Ceccaroni, L.: A recommendation system for the semantic web. In: Distributed Computing and Artificial Intelligence. In: de Leon F. de Carvalho, A.P., Rodríguez-González, S., De Paz Santana, J.F., Rodríguez, J.M.C. (eds.) Distributed Computing and Artificial Intelligence. Advances in Intelligent and Soft Computing, vol. 79, pp. 45-52. Springer, Heidelberg (2010). https://doi.org/10.1007/978-3-642-14883-5_6
12. De Pessemier, T., Dooms, S., Deryckere, T., Martens, L.: Time dependency of data quality for collaborative filtering algorithms. In: Proceedings of the Fourth ACM Conference on Recommender Systems, RecSys 2010, pp. 281–284. Association for Computing Machinery, New York (2010)
13. Fang, H., Zhang, D., Shu, Y., Guo, G.: Deep learning for sequential recommendation: algorithms, influential factors, and evaluations (2020). arXiv: 1905.01997
14. Han, D., Li, J., Li, W., Liu, R., Chen, H.: An app usage recommender system: improving prediction accuracy for both warm and cold start users. Multimed. Syst. **25**(6), 603–616 (2019)
15. Ishwarya, M.V., Swetha, G., Saptha Maaleekaa, S., Anu Grahaa, R.: Efficient recommender system by implicit emotion prediction. In: Peter, J.D., Alavi, A.H., Javadi, B. (eds.) Advances in Big Data and Cloud Computing. AISC, vol. 750, pp. 173–178. Springer, Singapore (2019). https://doi.org/10.1007/978-981-13-1882-5_15
16. Jannach, D., Manzoor, A., Cai, W., Chen, L.: A survey on conversational recommender systems. arXiv:2004.00646 [cs] (2020)
17. Jannach, D., Zanker, M.: Interactive and context-aware systems in tourism. In: Xiang, Z., et al. (eds.) Handbook of e-Tourism, pp. 1–22. Springer, Cham (2020). https://doi.org/10.1007/978-3-030-05324-6_125-1
18. Jin, Y., Tintarev, N., Htun, N.N., Verbert, K.: Effects of personal characteristics in control-oriented user interfaces for music recommender systems. User Model. User-Adap. Inter. **30**(2), 199–249 (2020)

19. Kang, J., Condiff, K., Chang, S., Konstan, J.A., Terveen, L., Harper, F.M.: Understanding how people use natural language to ask for recommendations. In: Proceedings of the Eleventh ACM Conference on Recommender Systems, pp. 229–237. ACM, New York (2017)

20. Lavanya, R., Khokle, T., Maity, A.: Review on hybrid recommender system for mobile devices. In: Hemanth, D.J., Vadivu, G., Sangeetha, M., Balas, V.E. (eds.) Artificial Intelligence Techniques for Advanced Computing Applications. LNNS, vol. 130, pp. 477–486. Springer, Singapore (2021). https://doi.org/10.1007/978-981-15-5329-5_44

21. Lee, S.: Improving jaccard index for measuring similarity in collaborative filtering. In: Kim, K., Joukov, N. (eds.) ICISA 2017. LNEE, vol. 424, pp. 799–806. Springer, Singapore (2017). https://doi.org/10.1007/978-981-10-4154-9_93

22. Li, B.H., et al.: GRIP: a group recommender based on interactive preference model. J. Comput. Sci. Technol. **33**(5), 1039–1055 (2018)

23. Mahmood, T., Ricci, F., Venturini, A., Höpken, W.: Adaptive recommender systems for travel planning. In: Information and Communication Technologies in Tourism, Vienna, Austria, pp. 1–11 (2008)

24. Mendoza, M., Torres, N.: Evaluating content novelty in recommender systems. J. Intell. Inf. Syst. **54**(2), 297–316 (2020)

25. Mimoun, M.S.B., Poncin, I., Garnier, M.: Virtual sales agents: the reasons of failure. In: Campbell, C.L. (ed.) The Customer is NOT Always Right? Marketing Orientationsin a Dynamic Business World. DMSPAMS, pp. 697–704. Springer, Cham (2017). https://doi.org/10.1007/978-3-319-50008-9_189

26. Naiseh, M., Jiang, N., Ma, J., Ali, R.: Explainable recommendations in intelligent systems: delivery methods, modalities and risks. In: Dalpiaz, F., Zdravkovic, J., Loucopoulos, P. (eds.) RCIS 2020. LNBIP, vol. 385, pp. 212–228. Springer, Cham (2020). https://doi.org/10.1007/978-3-030-50316-1_13

27. Nalmpantis, O., Tjortjis, C.: The 50/50 recommender: a method incorporating personality into movie recommender systems. In: Boracchi, G., Iliadis, L., Jayne, C., Likas, A. (eds.) EANN 2017. CCIS, vol. 744, pp. 498–507. Springer, Cham (2017). https://doi.org/10.1007/978-3-319-65172-9_42

28. Narang, K., Song, Y., Schwing, A., Sundaram, H.: FuseRec: fusing user and item homophily modeling with temporal recommender systems. Data Min. Knowl. Disc. **35**(3), 837–862 (2021)

29. Prasad, B.: HYREC: a hybrid recommendation system for E-commerce. In: Muñoz-Ávila, H., Ricci, F. (eds.) ICCBR 2005. LNCS (LNAI), vol. 3620, pp. 408–420. Springer, Heidelberg (2005). https://doi.org/10.1007/11536406_32

30. Ramnani, R.R., Sengupta, S., Ravilla, T.R., Patil, S.G.: Smart entertainment - a critiquing based dialog system for eliciting user preferences and making recommendations. In: Silberztein, M., Atigui, F., Kornyshova, E., Métais, E., Meziane, F. (eds.) NLDB 2018. LNCS, vol. 10859, pp. 456–463. Springer, Cham (2018). https://doi.org/10.1007/978-3-319-91947-8_47

31. Sanchez, O.R., Torre, I., He, Y., Knijnenburg, B.P.: A recommendation approach for user privacy preferences in the fitness domain. User Model. User-Adap. Inter. **30**(3), 513–565 (2020)

32. Sidana, S., Trofimov, M., Horodnytskyi, O., Laclau, C., Maximov, Y., Amini, M.R.: User preference and embedding learning with implicit feedback for recommender systems. Data Min. Knowl. Disc. **35**(2), 568–592 (2021)

33. Tian, X., Hao, Y., Zhao, P., Wang, D., Liu, Y., Sheng, V.S.: Considering interaction sequence of historical items for conversational recommender system. In: Jensen, C.S., et al. (eds.) DASFAA 2021. LNCS, vol. 12683, pp. 115–131. Springer, Cham (2021). https://doi.org/10.1007/978-3-030-73200-4_8

34. U. S. Food & Drug Administration: Drugs@FDA: FDA-Approved Drugs (2021). https://www.accessdata.fda.gov/scripts/cder/daf/index.cfm
35. Vajjhala, N.R., Rakshit, S., Oshogbunu, M., Salisu, S.: Novel user preference recommender system based on twitter profile analysis. In: Borah, S., Pradhan, R., Dey, N., Gupta, P. (eds.) Soft Computing Techniques and Applications. AISC, vol. 1248, pp. 85–93. Springer, Singapore (2021). https://doi.org/10.1007/978-981-15-7394-1_7
36. Ziegler, C.-N.: Semantic web recommender systems. In: Lindner, W., Mesiti, M., Türker, C., Tzitzikas, Y., Vakali, A.I. (eds.) EDBT 2004. LNCS, vol. 3268, pp. 78–89. Springer, Heidelberg (2004). https://doi.org/10.1007/978-3-540-30192-9_8

Graph-Based Recommendation Engine for Stock Investment Decisions

Artur Bugaj and Weronika T. Adrian[✉][iD]

AGH University of Science and Technology, al. A. Mickiewicza 30, 30-059 Krakow, Poland
arbugaj@student.agh.edu.pl, wta@agh.edu.pl

Abstract. Real-time recommender systems face the challenge of fast-changing data and the necessity of providing the answers in almost no time. In this paper, we discuss the case of a recommendation system for the stock market that uses knowledge about investors similar to the target user and combines it with a technical analysis of the stocks.

Keywords: Recommendation · Stock market · Graphs · Decision support

1 Introduction

With the constantly increasing amount of data on the Web, people have more and more difficulties with the choice of the information, that is interesting or useful. Browsing among all the items in a shop, all the films on a video platform, or all news on a webpage to find the ones, which appear interesting to us, we could waste a lot of valuable time. To prevent such a situation, data providers can offer a recommendation system that can select the things, that we could enjoy, omitting others, that we are not interested in. For instance, Google, Netflix, Amazon, and other companies use recommendation systems to provide things that are most appropriate for a user's needs and interests. A good recommendation can lead to an increase in the revenue of e-commerce shops, and the popularity of a specific webpage and video platform. About 80% of the streaming time on Netflix comes from recommended movies, and good recommendations have a contribution to revenue, which is estimated to 1B$ (in 2016).

However, video content, product attributes, and news' topic does not change in real time. Is it possible to make a recommendation system, which would work in an environment, where some of the items' attributes change over time? How could a recommendation system work, when recommending taking an action on stock? This work is about such a system, which could be a great tool for an investor to look for stocks, and take actions, which can produce potentially the best income. In particular, the objective of this paper is to propose a stock recommendation system, which will indicate to a user, which action is the best one to take, based on historical data as well as user-specific parameters. The data, which will be taken into account to make recommendations, will be stored in a graph database, which is faster than a relational one [15] and therefore enables making recommendations in real-time. Moreover, the work aims to check how good this type of recommendation actually can be, and if it is possible to earn money without stock-specific knowledge, relying only on recommendations.

M. Marchiori et al. (Eds.): WEBIST 2020/2021, LNBIP 469, pp. 122–148, 2023.
https://doi.org/10.1007/978-3-031-24197-0_8

The paper is structured as follows: In Sect. 2, we describe how the stock market and recommendation systems work. Section 3 overviews the related work and state-of-the-art. Section 4 describes our concept of how to design a recommendation system for the stock market, and which data to choose to receive possibly best results. In Sect. 5, we describe the process of creation of a dataset, which includes collecting, filtering out, and adjusting data. In Sect. 6 we outline the implementation, and how we do it to be efficient, optimized, and accurate. Section 7 contains the results we have achieved after testing a recommendation on real historic data. The paper is an extended version of the work presented at WebIST 2021 conference [3]. Additional material includes: (i) a description of the problem of stock investment decisions, (ii) related work in the area of graph-based recommendations and stock investment recommenders, (iii) a more detailed description of the system.

2 Preliminaries

The concept of playing in the stock market is simple - investors buy stocks as cheaply as possible and then sell them as expensive as they can. To do this, an investor makes an order to a broker. This order can be a sell/buy offer, at any price. When another investor makes an opposite order with the proper price, the transaction can be performed, e.g. if investor A wants to buy stock X for 100\$, and the lowest sell order is 101\$, their order will be active until investor B will make a sell order for at most 100\$. A plot with price value over time denotes a price which the investor could pay to buy a stock Prices on a stock depend on people's actions. Example plots and orders are shown in Fig. 1a and 1b.

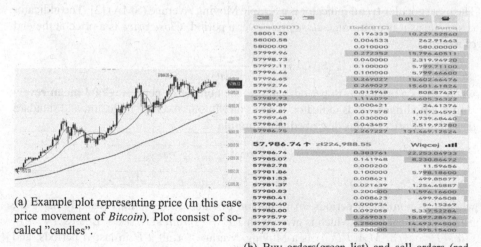

(a) Example plot representing price (in this case price movement of *Bitcoin*). Plot consist of so-called "candles".

(b) Buy orders(green list) and sell orders (red list). We can notice, that the lowest value of sell order is higher than the highest value of buy order.

Fig. 1. Plot and order list. Source: https://www.binance.com/.

There are many factors, that influence investors' decisions. It could be an information from the world (e.g. occurrence of COVID-19 in Poland made a great burst on local markets because people sold their stocks, and they decreased the price to a very low level as they could assume, that companies will bankrupt soon, so their stocks will be unworthy). But in stable periods it could also be advanced statistical analysis. How a plot shapes (chart patterns), how many people buy/sell a stock, and how fast the price grows/decrcases. Moreover, there are many formulas, that allow having a better view of price stability, and the tendency to grow, or to decrease.

2.1   Technical Analysis of the Stock Market

To predict the movement of the stock price in short term, investors use indicators, which can help them make a proper decision. Those indicators are what we can call technical analysis. They use historical prices to predict future ones. There are plenty of them, also, some of them can (and should) be used with other indicators altogether. Some indicators are concentrated on predicting direction, and where the market will move, they are called *leading*. Some other indicators give some insights into historical prices, and they are called *lagging*. Generally, indicators can be subdivided into 5 categories:

Trend. Movement of the market, if price will grow or fall (lagging)
Mean Reversion. How far the trend could go, which price could be unacceptable (lagging)
Relative Strength. Buying/selling pressure (leading)
Volume. How many transactions is made per time unit (leading)
Momentum. Speed of price change over time (leading/lagging)

The most popular **trend** indicator is a Simple Moving Average (SMA) [2]. The indicator is simple, as it is an average *close price* over a period. *Close price* is a price at the end of a period.

$$SMA = \frac{A_1 + A_2 + \cdots + A_n}{n}$$

where A_n is a price at n-th period, and n is the number of periods. Good **mean reversion** is a Boilinger Bands indicator. It bases on Moving Average indicator, and standard deviation of price, and is described with formula

$$BB_{up} = MA(TP, n) + m \cdot \sigma[TP, n]$$
$$BB_{down} = MA(TP, n) - m \cdot \sigma[TP, n]$$

where n is number of periods, m is amount of standard deviations (usually $m = 2$), TP is a "typical price" which is given with $TP = (HighestPrice + LowestPrice + ClosePrice)/3$, $MA(TP, n)$ is a Moving Average for all TP in last n periods, and $\sigma[TP, n]$ is a standard deviation for all TP in last n periods.

A popular **relative strength** indicator (and one of the most popular indicators overall) is a Relative Strength Index (RSI) [18]. It is common assumption, that a value $RSI > 70$ means, that a stock is overbought, and is likely to drop, and when a value is $RSI < 30$, then a stock is oversold, and probably a price will rise in next periods.

$$RSI = 100 - \frac{100}{1+RS}$$

$$RS = \frac{AverageGain}{AverageLoss}$$

$AverageLoss$ is a positive value, so the expression $\frac{100}{1+RS}$ is always positive. RSI should be used with other indicators, as used alone may produce many false-positive signals.

One of the momentum indicators is a Moving Average Convergence Divergence. Again, it bases on Moving Average (Exponential Moving Average). It is expressed with a formula

$$MACD = EMA_{12} - EMA_{26}$$

where EMA_{12} is Exponential Moving Average from the previous 12 days, and EMA_{26} from 26 days, respectively. Exponential Moving Average is Moving Average version, which puts a greater impact on recent periods, and can be obtained with

$$EMA_{Today} = (Value_{Today} \cdot (\frac{Smoothing}{1+n})) + EMA_{Yesterday} \cdot (1 - (\frac{Smoothing}{1+n}))$$

where usually $Smoothing = 2$, $Value_{Today}$ is today's close price, n is an amount of periods. $EMA_{Yesterday}$ is yesterday's result, but when we calculate EMA from the first period, and we don't have the previous one, we use the SMA from the selected previous period instead.

One of the most popular indicators using **volume** is an On-Balance Volume [6]. It is calculated with a formula

$$OBV = OBV_{previous} + \begin{cases} volume & close > close_{prev} \\ 0 & close = close_{prev} \\ -volume & close < close_{prev} \end{cases}$$

It can make a distinction between big buyers and small (usually less experienced) ones, e.g. when big buyers start buying, and small investors sell simultaneously, then OBV reaches a high value, although price movement is not big at the moment (but will be about to rise). However, some investors do not look at the cumulative value of OBV (formula), but for change dynamics (that is - volume from "sub-period").

Usually, it is good to use several most popular indicators. There is no need to know as many indicators, as it is possible, but it is better to master 4–5 of them. However, technical indicators are not everything, which allows for predicting if equity is worth buying or not. Also, in case of a strong fall, or strong growth, indicators may not be useful. They are preferred rather in stable times, and for a short period.

2.2 Recommendation Engine

Recommendation system uses user's data, related to items he or she interacted with, and other available data to "compare" them and return to user information on items, which the user might be interested. Recommendations can be done based on **Content-Based Filtering**, or **Collaborative Filtering**.

Content-Based Filtering compares items, how similar they are to each other. It takes many item-related factors to find proper recommendation. However, it is impossible to recommend something, which potential user can be interested in, but is not similar to item, with which they already have interacted, e.g. when user A browses only smartphones, Content-Based Filtering system will not recommend him any headphones (which could be useful). This problem is easily solved by **Collaborative Filtering**. This approach is concerned on similarity of users, and recommends things, which similar users interacted with. However, such systems could have a cold start problem, that is not enough information to make any recommendations. For example, the user A browses smartphones, but it is their first visit in this on-line shop, and Collaborative Filtering system cannot calculate, to which users user A is most similar, so results can be totally inappropriate. Generally, each recommendation system evaluates recommendations in 3 stages [1]

- **Candidate Generation** - reducing subset of potential items to those, which are most similar to what user has interacted with in past. Usually, it is achieved with e.g. "embedding" - mapping items to low-dimensional space (where we can calculate distance between nodes). Then, the closest nodes are selected, basing on similarity metric - different metrics have different properties, so for single embedding case, using different similarity metric will cause selecting different subsets
- **Scoring** - after **candidate generation** stage, we can use objective function to score items in set collected by candidate generators. Such an objective function can take into account more attributes, as it operates on smaller amount of items.
- **Re-ranking** - to ensure quality of recommendations, like imposing diversity of recommendations, boosting under-represented categories (because they can be less likely to achieve higher score), or filtering items, that user already interacted with.

Recommendation Systems based on Knowledge Graphs can return more valuable recommendations, due to potentially more information, which can be provided with high-order relationships. The simplest ones can be even created with single query (e.g. Cypher query in Neo4j database) - but it will cover only **Candidate Generation** stage. Overall, Graph-based recommendation systems can be divided into 3 categories [12]

- **Direct-relation based** - only single-order relationship. Simple, fast, but not using whole potential information graph can contain.
- **Semantic-path based** - high-order relations can be retrieved, for paths matching to defined meta-path.
- **Propagation-based** - potentially unlimited high-order relationships. They can be slower, but simultaneously they can obtain the most valuable information from graph.

All graph-based recommendation systems before creating embedding have to select subgraph. Usually, data are selected as triples (head entity, relation, tail entity). Then, for selected data, there are embeddings created (usually with *TransR* [8]). If relation is high-ordered, all this information could be aggregated into single vector. This is done by aggregation process, which is after creation of each triple embedding. Other stages are not significally different from "traditional" recommendation systems.

3   Related Work

3.1   Graph Recommendation Engines

There exist recommendation engines using knowledge graph as a source of data. Many of them base on *graph neural networks (GNN)* [11], which allow to detect "latent factors" of knowledge graph, and therefore make better recommendations. As GNN evolved over a years, being enriched with some additional mechanism, that made them more efficient in some applications [20], so authors of recommendation engines chose some of them. In the following sections, we describe some of best concepts of graph recommendation engines.

KGCN. Knowledge Graph Convolutional Network [16] is a recommendation engine, which bases on graph structure, and is capable of detecting multi-order relationships, including importance of specific relation type to speific user. In order to provide recommendation, engine must be learned prediction function $\hat{y}_{u,v} = \mathcal{F}(u, v | \Theta, \mathbf{Y}, \mathcal{G})$, where u, v are user and item, repectively, Θ is a set of parameters, which will be learned, $\mathbf{Y}$ is a user-item interaction matrix, and $\mathcal{G}$ is a knowledge graph. Process of learning includes collecting k neighbors of target node, creating their embedding representation, and aggregation of all nodes into single vector, which represents target node, and its proximity. To include a high-order relationships into such a vector, engine propagates calculations to neighbor nodes (to select another k neighbor of i-th neighbor).

KGAT. KGAT, which is a shortcut of Knowledge Graph Attention Network [17], is an engine, which, similarly to KGCN is a propagation-based one. However, instead of user-item matrix $\mathbf{Y}$ and knowledge graph $\mathcal{G}$ uses a structure called Collaborative Knowledge Graph (CKG). CKG is a Knowlege Graph with user-item matrix included in it as a set of triples $(u, interacts, v)$, for each user-item matrix entry, where $\mathbf{S} = \{(u, interacts, v) | \forall \mathbf{Y}_{u,v} = 1$. Architecture of the KGAT recommendation engine consists of 3 modules: embedding layer, which maps each node to low-dimensional vector space. Another module is an Attentive Embedding Propagation Layers, which propagate information about node towards high-order connnectivities, including weighting of nodes to which propagation goes. The last one is a prediction layer, which aggregates representation of target node and its neighbors.

AKGN. Attentive Knowledge Graph Embedding [12] is a recommendation engine, which unlike to previous two engines instead of calculating full knowledge graph, takes a subgraph of potentialy most similar nodes to target node. To achieve that, engine engages path sampling, that is, mapping nodes into low-dimensional space, and choosing those nodes, whose distance (vector norm) is close to target node. Such a subgraph is an input to Attentive Graph Neural Network, where all nodes are again mapped to low-dimensional vectors, which are propagated to neighbor nodes, and aggregated into single representation. Authors note, that embedding include not only target node data, but also relation type, and neighbor node data. After aggregation, vectors are calculated with multi-layer perceptron prediction layer.

3.2 Solutions for Stock Market Recommendations

There exist some proposals on recommendation systems for stock market. Recommendations base on news content, market trends, or investors' sentiment. In [13] authors created a recommendation system, which recommends assets and action basing on online sentiment, that is, emotions, that can be generated with specified information (e.g. authors of the publication note, that when Donald Trump won the elections, gold value increased by 5% rapidly because investors got into the panic and started buying gold). Information from *Guba*, Chineese informational service, were analyzed by finding bullish and bearish words, which can potentially make positive or negative sentiment, which influence decision.

Authors of [19] created actual stock recommendation system. The main assumption behind that system was, that big order transactions influence a stock price most. For standards of Shanghai and Shenzhen Composite Index there were transactions as big as one million yuan order, or an order for above 50,000 stocks. The recommendation system consisted of two main modules: *User clustering* and *Stock recommend*. To *User clustering* they used fuzzy clustering. Users were described with 12 variables, all of them came from survey on risk tolerance (the risk they can afford to when buying or selling on stock). All those variables were normalized in next step. Basing on there values, system creates a similarity matrix, and, using appropriate *lambda* value, or transitive closure, clusters similar users. Let us denote number of investors as n, and 12 variables describing risk tolerance for i-th investor as $x_i = \{x_{i1}, x_{i2}, .., x_{i11}, x_{i12}\}$. Then, data are standarized with formula

$$y_{ij} = \frac{x_{ij} - \min_{1 \le i \le n}\{x_{ij}\}}{\max_{1 \le i \le n}\{x_{ij}\} - \min_{1 \le i \le n}\{x_{ij}\}}, 1 \le j \le 12$$

After standarization, fuzzy matrix is created. As fuzzy matrix should contain values between 0 and 1, values are additionaly mapped with formula

$$r_{ij} = 1 - c \times d(y_i, y_j)$$

where d is Euclidean distance, and $c \in (0, 1]$ is hyperparameter, which influences on "broadening" or "narrowing" range of values

$$d(y_i, y_j) = \sqrt{\sum_{k=1}^{12}(x_{ik} - x_{jk})^2}$$

Fuzzy matrix can be mapped to a boolean one with use of $\lambda \in [0, 1]$ parameter

$$r_{ij}^{(\lambda)} = \begin{cases} 1, r_{ij} \ge \lambda \\ 0, r_{ij} < \lambda \end{cases}$$

Authors calculated transitive closure using square self-synthesis method, $t(R) = R \longrightarrow R^2 \longrightarrow R^4 \longrightarrow \ldots \longrightarrow R^{2^k}$, where $k \le \lceil \log_2^n \rceil$. Then, they choose λ value for $t(R)$, and they get $t(R)_\lambda$ matrix. To make a *Stock recommendation* for target user, it chooses the most similar users with nearest neighbour algorithm (authors do not specify, which similarity algorithm they used, but they proposed adjusted Cosine similarity or Paerson correlation-based similarity). Also, authors construct stock cluster, basing on 6 parameters, which describe their dynamics characteristics. These parameters are:

1. Daily average gains
2. Daily average amplitude
3. Days of price rise
4. Net profit in last year
5. Daily net amount of big order
6. Days with net amount of big buying order

For target user, recommended stocks are those with highest score and most occurent in neighbors stocks. If any stock, which is in stocks list of target investor, is absent in stocks lists of neighbours, then the score is calclulated with formula

$$f(u,j) = \frac{\sqrt{\sum_{k=1}^{K} sim(i,k)^2 (S_k - \overline{S_k})}}{\sqrt{\sum_{k=1}^{K} sim(i,k)^2}}$$

where $\overline{S_u}$ is a target investor's average scores for all stocks, S_k denotes kth neighbor investor scores, and $\overline{S_k}$ is an average of scores of all investors, and

$$sim(i,k) = \frac{\sum_{v=1}^{m}(R_{v_i} - \overline{R_i})(R_{v_k} - \overline{R_K})}{\sqrt{\sum_{v=1}^{m}(R_{v_i} - \overline{R_i})}\sqrt{\sum_{v=1}^{m}(R_{v_k} - \overline{R_k})}}$$

$\overline{R_i}$ is an ith stock average score for all investors, R_{v_k}, R_{v_i} denotes kth and ith neighbor score for stock v. Moreover, to simulate money inflow, they use M/G/1 Queue System. System can be in 2 states: *working* and *not working*. If system is in *working* state, then it behaves like basic M/G/1 queue. Queue System can be in state *not working* in 2 cases: when there is no work left to do, or, there is a work, but system is on a vacation. Denoting work at time t as $w(t)$, T_i as the beginning of work period i, and S_i as the end of work period i, and equations: $L(k) = min\{m : \sum_{i=1}^{m}(S_i - T_i) \geq k\}$ which is sum of all busy periods to step k, and $E(k) = \sum_{i=1}^{L(k)-1}(T_{i+1} - S_i)$ which denotes all free periods until step k, they calculate k-th workload step denoted as $l(k)$ with

$$l(k) = w(k + E(k)), k < \sum_{i+1}^{L(k)}(S_i - T_i)$$

$$l(k^+) = w(k + E(k) + T_{L(k)+1} < S_{L(k)}, l(k^-) = w(k + E(k)), k = \sum_{i+1}^{L(k)}(S_i - T_i)$$

The $l(k)$ behaves like the work in simple M/G/1 queue, if $k = \sum_{i+1}^{L(k)}(S_i - T_i)$. In M/G/1 queue probability P of the service time is dependent on random distribution $P(t_i \geq t) = B(t), i = 1, 2, 3, \ldots, B(t)$ is a general distribution function. Denoting

$A(t)$ as a number of arrival customers in $[0, t]$ time, $N(t)$ as number of customers in queue in time t and X_n as number of customers after nth customer departure. Then, $X_{n+1} = X_n + A(d_{n+1}) - A(d_n) - 1$, where d_n is a departure time of nth customer. Transition probability matrix P of Markov Chain X_n is

$$\begin{pmatrix} p_0 & p_1 & p_2 & \cdots \\ p_0 & p_1 & p_2 & \cdots \\ 0 & p_0 & p_1 & \cdots \\ \vdots & \vdots & \vdots & \ddots \\ 0 & 0 & 0 & \cdots \end{pmatrix}$$

where p_k is given by $p_k = \int_0^{\inf} \frac{e^{-\lambda t}(\lambda t)^k}{k!} dB(t), k = 0, 1, 2, \ldots$ The system processes requests from users in queue, which concers buying or selling a stock, and therefore influencing a price. Mean return rate of recommended stocks (from 20 randomly selected) in 18 trading weeks was about 30%.

Another stock recommendation system [10] was created basing on Social Network approach. Authors noticed, that information posted by influential investors on social media, like *Twitter*, can be potentially fake, but still can influence people. Thus, they propose recommendation system, which bases on trust in relationships in Social Network. To achieve this, they make use of Mutual Fund Investment Portfolio. Data used by this recommendation system consists of matrix, which describes a graph of which mutual funds uses which stock. During recommendation process, system takes into account social media, user interest, mutual funds information and equity information. Based on that information, it creates 2 graphs. First graph consists of stocks as nodes, and nodes are connected, if a single mutual fund has invested in both stocks. Second graph consists of mutual funds and equities, where funds are connected to equities (2-mode network). Stock information is: sector, industry of a stock, and parameters such as performance, expertise, and dynamism of mutual funds (credibility). Final result of recommendation depends also on a centrality measure used. Authors experimented with two: degree centrality, and eigen vector centrality. For both of them, mean return rate, based on 17 stocks was about 20%

In [5] authors made recommendations of stocks not with recommendation system, but decision support system. This expert system uses fuzzy logic, which, opposite to boolean logic, does not take discretized values, like $[true, false]$, but allows a statements be truth, or false to some extent. Authors provides example of fuzzy set, and non-fuzzy set. In non-fuzzy set, an element is present, or is not present. In case of fuzzy set, the element can be to some extent in one set, and to some extent in another set. Fuzzy inference process consist of 6 steps:

1. Identification of critical factors
2. Fuzzy rules construction
3. Fuzzification
4. Fuzzy inference module generation
5. Defuzzification
6. Comparison of the overall rating for all stocks

Critical factors had been identified with Fuzzy Delphi method, which included 3 rounds of sending questionaries to 35 experts. As the result, authors detected seven most important factors:

1. The future projects of the company
2. Stockholders
3. Earned Per Share
4. Market of stocks
5. The sale's rules
6. Size of the float stock of the company
7. Legal audit report

Those 7 factors became an input of each rule. To avoid too big number of rules (authors expressed all 7 factors with three linguistics values: *Low, Medium, Hard*, which gives $3^7 = 932$ rules). Therefore, they created fuzzy rules. Again, they used Fuzzy Delphi method, with 80 experts of *Teheran Stock Exchange*. It resulted with reduction of 932 rules to 119 most important (whose "importance degree" was higher than threshold 7.5 out from 10). Then, all factors variables had been fuzzificated, that is, discrete values were mapped to fuzzy trapezoidal number (quadruplet $A = (a_1, a_2, a_3, a_4)$), e.g. for factor *market of stock* = Low, fuzzy trapezoidal number was $(0, 0, 0.5, 7.25)$. A trapezoidal fuzzy number has a member function, which takes values, that make it look like trapezoid

$$\mu_A = \begin{cases} 0 & x < a_1 \\ (x - a_1)/(a_2 - a_1) & a_1 \leq x \leq a_2 \\ 1 & a_2 \leq x \leq a_3 \\ (x - a_4)/(a_3 - a_4) & a_3 \leq x \leq a_4 \\ 0 & x > a_4 \end{cases}$$

A fuzzy inference engine uses standard max-min algorithm. Max-min algorithm applies new association c to two associations $a(h, l)$ and $b(l, b)$, which is defined as follows

$$c = \bigcup_{H \times W} \vee_l [\mu_a(h, l) \wedge \mu_b(l, w)]/(h, w), h \in H, l \in L, w \in W$$

and

$$\mu_c(h, w) = \vee_l [\mu_a(h, l) \wedge \mu_b(l, w)], h \in H, l \in L, w \in W$$

To evaluate the degree of membership, authors use Mamdani inference [4]

$$\mu_B = \max_{i=1}^{M}[\sup \min(\mu_A(x), \mu_A(x_1)_{x \subset U}, \ldots, \mu_A(x_n), \mu_B(y))]$$

To defuzzification process, authors used *center-of-gravity method*, $x' = \frac{\int \mu(x)x dx}{\int \mu(x) dx}$. Aim of *center-of-gravity* method is to find point, where vertical line can split a plot into 2 "equal" parts. All outputs are merged into a final shape aggregated from calculated points, and a centroid of that aggregate shape is computed. According to 13 from 16 users, proposed expert system could be used instead of a "real" expert. It predicts risk ratio of specific equity, and recommends it according to risk capability of target user. After specifying critical factors of stocks (in this paper they were e.g. market of stocks, sale's rules, Earned Per Share) it creates fuzzy rules basing on instances of input.

3.3   Critical Analysis of Existing Solutions

There are many different proposals for stock recommendation systems. They differ in approach, and stock-related factors are taken into account. It shows, that there are many ways to build a relatively efficient recommendation system, but in the case of stock every decision is risky, and we cannot be 100% sure if our investment's value will grow. The system described in [19] uses user's risk tolerance to group them, and M/G/1 queue to simulate stock flow. The one from [10] uses information from mutual funds with social media as a trusted source of information, making recommendations relevant to the user's interests (category of company, whose assets can be bought). Authors of [5] designed and implemented a decision support system using fuzzy logic, and experts' knowledge about which factors are most important if it comes to estimating the chances of stock to grow. All systems have been developed for the specific stock market which means, that different stock markets can potentially have different behavior. However, this could be a matter of data rather than a model overall.

4   Proposal of a New System

Our purpose is to implement fast and reliable real-time recommendation system, which takes into account similarity to other investors' interests, their investments, as well as current stock price predictions.

4.1   Problem Statement

Prices of stocks require constant updates of recommendations. Also, investor can potentially sell or buy stock, or even change field of interest. However, as the aim of playing on stock market is to earn money, proper predictions of stock prices are the most valuable information. Proper prediction of stock prices demands not only knowledge of fundamental analysis, but also information about company, whose stocks we are going to buy. This is a huge topic for separated work. In our system we will provide stock predictions basing on only technical analysis (what can be valuable rather in short term). Our system need to be fast and available, as data will change frequently, what may cause in frequent changes of recommendations, in minutes.

4.2   System Design

Our application consists of 2 services. First, and the most important one is a recommendation engine itself. The engine has to have an access to current stock prices as well as investors database. Therefore we splitted whole application into

- Recommendation Engine - calculates recommendations
- Data Provider - provides data from database, and current database. Not to overcomplicate things, this service is also responsible for database operations.

4.3   Recommendation Engine

Recommendation Engine bases on [7], but is adapted to stock recommendation, and more important value of stock prices movements. Idea standing behind business logic is simple: we embed subgraphs of target investor, and neighbor investors to calculate distance between them. The closer both embeddings are, the more similar investors are. This similarity is a factor of stock recommendation. We check, what stocks they possess, and then we sum all stock with weight described with similarity degree. After that, we check, what their movements are, and depending on opportunities to growth, they are scored respectively. Final recommendation is a sum of stock score calculated with investors similarity, and score of current movement.

Investors data are retrieved with a query to database, which returns the following information: (i) Investor ID (ii) List of common companies (iii) List of disjoint companies investor made an investment (iv) List of common interests.

Then, basing on that information, engine creates 2 similarity matrices (to put data in square symmetric ones - Table 1).

Table 1. Metrics used to generate similarity matrix.

Data	Used	Similarity measure
Attributes	Stocks amount, Range of money per investment	Cosine
Stocks	All stocks	Jaccobi
Interests	All interests	Jaccobi

Algorithm 1. Recommendation Engine.

Result: Collection of recommended stocks

while *true* **do**

$\quad L_a, L_s, L_i \leftarrow getInvestorsData(investorsAmount);$

$\quad M_a, M_s, M_i \leftarrow similarityMatrix(L_a, L_s, L_i);$

$\quad$ **if** *first iteration* **then**

$\quad\quad | \quad E_a, E_s, E_i \leftarrow eigenDecomposition(M_a, M_s, M_i);$

$\quad$ **else**

$\quad\quad | \quad E_a, E_s, E_i \leftarrow updateEigenValuesAndVectors(M_a, M_s, M_i);$

$\quad$ **end**

$$C \leftarrow \begin{bmatrix} E_a E_a' & E_a E_s' & E_a E_i' \\ E_s E_a' & E_s E_s' & E_s E_i' \\ E_i E_a' & E_i E_s' & E_i E_i' \end{bmatrix};$$

$\quad P \leftarrow eigenDecomposition(C);$

$\quad P_{top} \leftarrow P[:][0 : investorsAmount];$

$\quad R \leftarrow [E_a, E_s, E_i] \times P_{top};$

$\quad result \leftarrow calculateDistance(R);$

end

Then, we use eigen decomposition in order to get rid of noise for each of matrices. As it is rather costly operation, we does it only first time. In next iterations, we update eigenvalues, and eigenvectors accordingly, using the following formulas:

$$\Delta\lambda_i = a_i'\Delta L_A a_i - \lambda_i a_i'\Delta D_A a_i$$

where a_i is an eigenvector (of previous iteration) associated to eigenvalue λ_i, $L_A = D_A - A$ is a Laplacian matrix, used to solve eigen-decomposition problem, D_A is a diagonal matrix with sum of row as value, $D_A(i,i) = \sum_{j=1}^n A(i,j)$. To update a eigenvector we use

$$\Delta a_i = -0.5 a_i'\Delta D_A a_i a_i + \sum_{j=2,j!=i}^{k+1}\left(\frac{a_j'\Delta L_A a_i - \lambda_i a_j'\Delta D_A a_i}{\lambda_i - \lambda_j}\right)a_j$$

Explanation of those formulas, as well as their proof is shown in [7]. However, we cannot avoid solving of eigen-problem for supermatrix, which we create to find consensus embedding - embedding, which "connects" all three matrices with finding maximal correlation between them.

Algorithm 2. Eigen decomposition.

Function *eigenDecomposition(A: Matrix) : Matrix* **is**

$$D_A \leftarrow \begin{bmatrix} \sum_{i=1}^n A(1,i) & 0 & \cdots & 0 \\ 0 & \sum_{i=1}^n A(2,i) & \cdots & 0 \\ \vdots & & \ddots & \vdots \\ 0 & \cdots & \cdots & \sum_{i=1}^n A(n,i)' \end{bmatrix};$$

$L_A \leftarrow D_A - A;$

`;       // To apply eigen decomposition, we normalize`
`diagonal matrix to I`

$$L_{A_{norm}} \leftarrow \begin{bmatrix} \frac{\sum_{i=1}^n A(1,i)-A(1,1)}{\sum_{i=1}^n A(1,i)} & \frac{A(1,2)}{\sum_{i=1}^n A(1,i)} & \cdots & \frac{A(1,n)}{\sum_{i=1}^n A(1,i)} \\ \frac{A(2,1)}{\sum_{i=1}^n A(2,i)} & \frac{\sum_{i=1}^n A(2,i)-A(2,2)}{\sum_{i=1}^n A(2,i)} & \cdots & \frac{A(2,n)}{\sum_{i=1}^n A(2,i)} \\ \vdots & & \ddots & \vdots \\ \frac{A(n,1)}{\sum_{i=1}^n A(n,i)} & \cdots & \cdots & \frac{\sum_{i=1}^n A(n,i)-A(n,n)}{\sum_{i=1}^n A(n,i)} \end{bmatrix};$$

`;       // Then we calculate standard eigen decomposition`
`problem, in our case: ` $L_{A_{norm}}v = \lambda v$
eigenValues, eigenVectors $\leftarrow$ *eigenDecomposition(* $L_{A_{norm}}$ *)*;
return eigenVectors

Algorithm 3. Update eigen values and eigen vectors.

Function *updateEigenValuesAndVectors(A: Matrix) : Matrix* **is**

for $i = 0 .. n$ **do**

$\lambda_i = \lambda_i + a_i'\Delta L_A a_i - \lambda_i a_i'\Delta D_A a_i;$

$a_i = a_i + -0.5 a_i'\Delta D_A a_i a_i + \sum_{j=2,j\neq i}^{k+1}\left(\frac{a_j'\Delta L_A a_i - \lambda_i a_j'\Delta D_A a_i}{\lambda_i - \lambda_j}\right)a_j;$

4.4 Data Provider

The aim of the data provider is to provide stocks' score basing on technical analysis. That score is later combined with stocks' score calculated with recommendation engine (we calculated most similar users, then we checked, in how many how similar investors such a stock is present, and basing on that we calculated a score). We use 3 indicators, whose combination gives us final result (for details of the following indicators see Sect. 2.1). To work, it assumes receiving a "batch" of stocks' data for initialization, and then a single record for update indicators.

- RSI - Relative Strength Index
- OBV - On-Balance Volume
- Support/Resistance

The formula for combination is

$$recommendation = 0.4\sigma(ratio_{RSI_{14}}) + 0.4\sigma(ratio_{OBV_{14}}) + 0.2\sigma(ratio_{sup/res})$$

where $recommendation \in (0,1)$, $ratio_{RSI_{14}}$, $ratio_{OBV_{14}}$ are uptrend predictions of Relative Strength Index and On-Balance Volume from last 14 periods, respectively (see Sect. 2.1). A $ratio_{sup/res}$ indicates, if it is worth to buy a stock at last recent price, that is - is the price close to support or resistance, including "strength" of that boundaries (by "strength" we mean, how many times price movement was rejected by price boundary of support or resistance).

To calculate ratios we take into account the following factors (see Table 2)

Table 2. Factors affecting a ratio value.

Ratio	Factors
RSI	Divergence RSI peaks combination
OBV	Divergence
Support Resistance	Amount of support/resistance points difference of price from support/resistance

We use 4 different algorithms, which we will describe below:

One of relatively accurate signals to predict trends can be detected with divergences. Divergence is a situation, when monotonicity of indicator is different than monotonicity of price. Not all differences can be called divergences - to describe cases it concerns we will use mathematical notations. Let's denote $Ind = i_1, i_2, \ldots i_n$ and $ClosePrice = c_1, c_2, \ldots c_n$ as values of indicator, and price in periods $p = 1 \ldots n$. Let's assume, that during period p indicator as well as price chart hit price boundary twice (by price boundary we mean support or resistance), and denote that as $Ind_{peaks} = i_{p_1}, i_{p_2}$ and $ClosePrice_{peaks} = c_{p_1}, c_{p_2}$ Then, let's normalize Ind_{peaks} and $ClosePrice_{peaks}$, that the bigger absolute value is equal to 1. Then, we find linear equation that connects i_{p_1} with i_{p_2} and c_{p_1} with c_{p_2}: $r_{ind} = a_{ind}x + b_{ind}$ and $r_{price} = a_{price}x + b_{price}$. Divergences are described in Table 3

Table 3. Divergences of price and indicators, and probable price movement direction. *Bullish* means growth of price, whereas *Bearish* - price fall.

Divergence	Trend prediction
$a_{ind} < 0, a_{price} > 0$	Bullish
$a_{ind} = 0, a_{price} > 0$	Bullish
$a_{ind} < 0, a_{price} = 0$	Bullish
$a_{ind} > 0, a_{price} < 0$	Bullish
$a_{ind} = 0, a_{price} < 0$	Bullish
$a_{ind} > 0, a_{price} = 0$	Bullish
$a_{ind} < 0, a_{price} > 0$	Bearish
$a_{ind} = 0, a_{price} > 0$	Bearish
$a_{ind} < 0, a_{price} = 0$	Bearish
$a_{ind} > 0, a_{price} < 0$	Bearish
$a_{ind} = 0, a_{price} < 0$	Bearish
$a_{ind} > 0, a_{price} = 0$	Bearish

Algorithm 4. Finding Divergences.

Function *findDivergences(peaks$_{ind}$: ((v$_{i_1}$: Double, t$_{k_1}$: Int), (v$_{i_2}$: Double, t$_{k_1}$: Int)) peaks$_{price}$: ((v$_{p_1}$: Double, t$_{k_1}$: Int), (v$_{p_2}$: Double, t$_{k_1}$: Int))) : Double* **is**

$$p_{ind_{normalized}} \leftarrow \{v_{i_1}/\max\{|v_{i_1}|, |v_{i_2}|\}, v_{i_1}/\max\{|v_{i_1}|, |v_{i_2}|\}\} = \{n_{ind_1}, n_{ind_2}\};$$

$$p_{price_{normalized}} \leftarrow \{v_{p_1}/\max\{|v_{p_1}|, |v_{p_2}|\}, v_{p_1}/\max\{|v_{p_1}|, |v_{p_2}|\}\} = \{n_{price_1}, n_{price_2}\};$$

$$a_{ind} \leftarrow \frac{n_{ind_2} - n_{ind_1}}{t_{k_2} - t_{k_1}};$$

$$a_{price} \leftarrow \frac{n_{price_2} - n_{price_1}}{t_{k_2} - t_{k_1}};$$

return $\sigma(a_{ind} - a_{price})$;

end

We find peaks, that is, extrema of indicators and price with another algorithm, which we will describe next. Peaks are rapid changes in value, which returns close to previous average value in short period. Their shape can tell us something about "price properties", like support/resistance level, or, when combined with some of technical indicators, prediction of price movement with good probability (still we have to have in mind, that every prediction on stocks is in terms of probability, and even the best quality signals are not always right). We detect peaks due to latter cause, combination with indicators. When value difference between 2 peaks from price and respective ones from indicator will not be the same (after normalization), it is potential signal for price growth or price loss. Therefore, we detect peaks to look for divergences. The algorithm we propose looks for peaks in scope of buffer. It checks, how much the price has changed, and to which level it return. To find many actual peaks, we expect, that a peak is when a price will come back to 1/3 of total difference made in that scope, e.g. if at first period a stock A has price \$10, we set minimal required change to 30% of base price (\$10) and it will grow to \$13, we find peak, when price will come back to \$12. Full algorithm is shown on Algorithm 5

Algorithm 5. Finding Peaks.

Function $findPeaks(\{c_1, \ldots, c_n\}: Double[\,], thresholds: (thr_{min}: Double, thr_{max}: Double)) : Double$ **is**

$averageChange \leftarrow \{\frac{c_2-c_1}{c_2}, \frac{c_3-c_2}{c_3}, \ldots \frac{c_n-c_{n-1}}{c_n}\} = \{a_1, a_2, \ldots, a_{n-1}\};$

$cumulativeChange \leftarrow \{a_1, \sum_{i=1}^{2} a_i, \cdots \sum_{i=1}^{n-1} a_i\} = \{s_1, s_2, \ldots s_{n-1}\};$

$i_{min} \leftarrow i \in N, \min cumulativeChange = s_{i_1};$

$i_{max} \leftarrow i \in N, \max cumulativeChange = s_{i_2};$

$maxValueAfterMin \leftarrow \max\{s_i \in cumulativeChange, i \in N : i > i_{min}\};$

$minValueAfterMax \leftarrow \min\{s_i \in cumulativeChange, i \in N : i > i_{max}\};$

$recoverValueAfterMin \leftarrow$
$\max\{s_{i_{min}} + 1, \ldots, s_{n-1}\} - \max\{s_1, \ldots, s_{i_{min}}\};$

$recoverValueAfterMax \leftarrow$
$\max\{s_1, \ldots, s_{i_{min}}\} - \max\{s_{i_{max}} + 1, \ldots, s_{n-1}\};$

$minValid \leftarrow min <= thr_{min} \wedge recoverValueAfterMin >$
$-1/3|thr_{min}| \vee maxValueAfterMin - min > 1/3|thr_{min}|;$

$maxValid \leftarrow max >= thr_{max} \wedge recoverValueAfterMax >$
$-1/3|thr_{max}| \vee max - minValueAfterMax > 1/3|thr_{max}|;$

end

Peaks reached by RSI indicator contain valuable information. One of them is probable breakout (tendency change) of stock price. It happens, when RSI goes

- from < 30 to > 70, and does not comeback to < 30 in next minimal peak
- from > 70 to < 30, and does not comeback to > 70 in next maximal peak
- from < 30 to < 70, and does comeback to < 30 in next minimal peak
- from > 70 to > 30, and does comeback to > 70 in next maximal peak

First case is signal for growth, whilst the second one predicts loss. Therefore, we calculate 3 recent peaks to catch such a "peak pattern" which allow us to find out, if the price will be more probable to grow or loss. We present values of those 3 peaks as a number, which takes negative values, when a stock price is about to loss, and positive values, when it is about to grow. Pseudocode of algorithm can be found on Algorithm 6.

Algorithm 6. Analyze RSI trend.

Function $rsiTrend(peaks = \{p_1, \ldots, p_n\}: Double[]) : Double$ **is**

    if $peaks.length \geq 3$ **then**

        $w \leftarrow \{w_1, w_2, w_3\}$;

        return $\sum_{i=1}^{3} \leftarrow boost(p_i) * w_i$

    else

        return 0;

    end

end

Function $boost(value: Double) : Double$ **is**

    return $\frac{(\frac{value-50}{5})^3}{2} + (\frac{value-50}{20})^3$;   `// RSI`$\in [0, 100]$`, so`
    `subtracting constant value 50 and dividing by 20`
    `let us discover, if peak exceeded 30 or 70 - if so,`
    `boost value`

end

Sometimes a price does not grow above, or drop below some specified value for a period of time. That value is a support/resistance. Of course, support/resistance most probably will be broken in a future, but before it will happen, it can reject at support/resistance level a few times. Sometimes a peaks can inform about such a price boundary, but also often there is a price, which slowly moves toward a price boundary, but it cannot break it. To detect such a situation, we designed an price boundary algorithm. It takes buffer as a input, rounds a price accordingly (smaller values are discretized by $0.5, bigger by $5), and basing on rounded prices it detects differences in prices, with different weights (more recent prices have stronger weight). As a result, we obtain current support/resistance value, with a weight ratio, which tells us, how strong, and how accurate the boundary is. Usually strong boundary has >0.8, while weaker one is <0.7. Whole algoritm is shown on Algorithm 7

Algorithm 7. Finding price boundary.

Function $priceBoundary(buffer = \{c_1, \ldots, c_n\}: Double[]) : (Double, Double)$ **is**

    $roundedPrice \leftarrow \{round(c_1), round(c_2), \ldots, round(c_n)\} = \{r_1, r_2, \ldots, r_n\}$;

    $roundedDifferences \leftarrow \{|c_2 - c_1|, |c_3 - c_2|, \ldots |c_n - c_{n-1}|\} = \{d_1, d_2, \ldots, d_{n-1}\}$;

    $weights \leftarrow \{w_1, w_2, \ldots, w_n\}$;

    $boundary \leftarrow \sum_{i=1}^{n-1} r_i w_i$;

    $validationDegree \leftarrow (\frac{1}{1+(average(roundedDifferences)}))^2$;

    return boundary, validationDegree ;

end

4.5   Summary of the Proposal

In order to create recommendation system we have designed 2 modules, such as Recommendation Engine and Data Provider. Both modules have a contribution to final result, where the Recommendation Engine is responsible for Scoring, and the Data Provider is responsible for Re-ranking. Candidate Generation stage is done with graph database, as we select proper sub-query, which allows us to find only those nodes, which are in relationship with target node. Recommendation Engine calculates recommendation according to relationships in sub-graph. To achieve this we use algorithm described in [7]. Data Provider consumes a stock exchange listings, and calculates a stock score according to technical analysis, and algorithms described in Sect. 4.4.

5   Dataset Preparation

In this section, we describe how we prepared a processed dataset, which is ready to be loaded into graph database. The dataset used in this work includes 1368 investors taken from website https://investorhunt.co/. Data contains business categories of investors' interests. Also, each investor invests specified amount of investments as well as average amount of money invested per single investment. Apart from investors, dataset contains data of 39 markets, and 545 companies with their stock exchange listing. All companies are taken from NASDAQ[1] market. Due to RODO, names of investors are removed from dataset.

We have scrapped investors data from https://investorhunt.co/, and we have taken information about stock exchange listing from https://www.nasdaq.com/. Both of them allows web scrapping (https://investorhunt.co/robots.txt and https://www.nasdaq.com/robots.txt)

To get investors data, we extract the following information: (i) Markets, (ii) Investment count, and (iii) Investment amount. Example view of webpage is shown on Fig. 2a Not every investor had information about investment count or investment amount, so we filtered out them, leaving only those investors, which had all demanded information. We omitted Locations, since from perspective of our recommendation system this data is not useful, and can potentially produce noise. From nearly 5700 investors, filtering operation reduced that amount to 1398. To make it possible to upload it do Neo4j[2] database, we have written all investors with all data to file *investors.csv*, with the structure shown on Listings 1.1. Also, as markets are considered as something autonomic from investors, they had been put to another file, *markets.csv*, which structure is shown on Listing 1.2. To define relationship between investors and markets, we created additional file, *investors_markets.csv* (Listing 1.3)

Listing 1.1. 'Structure of investors file.'

```
id,min_investment_amount,max_investment_amount,investment_count
0, 5000,                 100000,                13
1, 1000,                 50000,                 39
2, 1000,                 100000,                35
3, 5000,                 25000,                 17
```

---

[1] NASDAQ is a first online stock market based in New York. See https://www.nasdaq.com/.
[2] See: https://neo4j.com/.

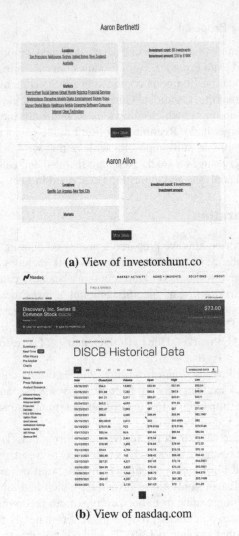

(a) View of investorshunt.co

(b) View of nasdaq.com

Fig. 2. View of nasdaq.com.

Listing 1.2. 'Structure of markets file.'

```
id,market
0, Software
1, Internet of Things
2, Digital Media
3, Marketing and Advertising
```

On https://investorhunt.co/ there were 39 most popular categories, where investors invested, whereas on NASDAQ companies were grouped on different categories and industries. It demanded manual "mapping" categories from *investorshunt.co* to industries present in NASDAQ. Due to totally different distribution, 39 categories were

Listing 1.3. 'Structure of file with investors and markets relationships.'

```
id_investor,id_market,relation
0,          0,         INTEREST
0,          5,         INTEREST
0,          3,         INTEREST
```

reduced to 14, as some of categories didn't have an equivalent, or many categories could be matched to single one. Then, for each category we selected random 35 companies (or less, if there were less companies in all industries belonging to specified category). We download historical data for all of them (we will use them for technical analysis, which will be a basis of recommendation.

After category mapping operation we had to synchronize it with already generated files containing investors, and relationships investor-market. It included changing id_market property, but also we had to take into account corner case, when an investor has no longer any relationship with any market, so they should be removed from our file. Flow of filtering algorithm was: map categories -> change market_id -> update investor-market relationships with new ids -> if there is an investor which is present but doesn't have any markets, remove them. Each category has 1 or more industries. After mapping categories, we could download stocks data related to industries. From NASDAQ (Fig. 2b) we downloaded 575 stocks historical data. We downloaded data with bot created with usage of Selenium library (nasdaq.com allows data scrapping). To distribute stocks per category equally we downloaded amounts of stock per industry.

6   Implementation of the System

In this section, we describe implementation details, like technology stack, and overall architecture of the application. We also show, how we parametrized algorithms predicting stock movement. Source code of recommendation system is available on GitHub repository.[3]

We use Neo4j as graph database. Recommendation engine and Data provider are implemented in Scala 2.12. Preprocessing code is written in plain Scala, and database operations are performed with Apache Spark library We chose Scala, since it is hybrid-paradigma language, that means, we can combine functional paradigma to process data, and object oriented paradigma to operations, that require some "memory". Usually, we have to remember previous' step result to update that in following iteration.

To create our recommendation system, a simple server-client architecture was enough, as the only thing, which requires a connection is a sending stocks' score calculated by Data Provider. *Recommendation Engine* module retrieves data from graph, so it is connected to Neo4J as well. This architecture is only "back-end" as component *Engine* has no interfaces exposed (in future work we can expose an interface to some front-end module, which could make a visualization, but it is not a part of the work). To avoid any problems related with *Database* component, we allowed only one component to communicate with it, as it ensures that data are accessed in controlled way. We didn't create separate module, e.g. *Database proxy* which could gather requests from

---

[3] Link: https://github.com/R-tooR/recommendation-system/tree/master.

several modules to avoid unnecessary architectural complications (e.g. where *Engine* could do only calculation of recommendations, while updating of graph could be done by different module). Therefore, all interfaces defined are:

updateDatabase. simulates changes investors make by selling/buying stocks, and changes graph structure accordingly

retrievedInvestorsData. retrieves data about investors, basing on which engine calculates stocks recommendation

getStocksPrediction. gets stocks prediction ratio, which result is added to recommendations calculated basing on *retrievedInvestorsData*

getCurrentListings. reads from files containing historical data listing of a "next day", used for further calculations.

Recommenation system was implemented according to concept described in [7], and developed in Sect. 4.3. We splitted implementation into 4 classes with business logic: *Engine, InvestorsDataProcessor, DataExtractor* and *Recommender*. Implementation of [7] goes in *Engine* class, whereas *DataExtractor* and *InvestorsDataProcessor* are responsible for retrieval and preparation of data in form of similarity matrices, which are input into *Engine* methods. Output of calculation goes to *Recommender* which process the result and performs re-ranking of recommendations according to data obtained from *Data Provider*.

Although there are available API's to download real-time stock data, we decided to download historical ones, due to avoiding of unnecessary costs. Main part of Data Provider is a *TechnicalCalculator* class, which is responsible for making calculations for specific stock. It uses all *Indicator* subclasses, and all algorithms described in Sect. 4.4. As an input it takes processed record of stock listing (retrieving and processing are done in *FileReader* and *DataProcessor* classes).

As we handle 356 different stocks, we need to parallelize operations of intializing and updating stocks' score, we used a simple *ConcurrentHashMap* for it, which turned out to be efficient enough for our needs. For price prediction algorithms (see sect. 4.4) we chose the following parameters (Table 4):

Table 4. Parameters of methods.

Algorithm	Parameters used
Finding divergences	2 recent peaks
Peaks detection	$buffer.length = 7$, $thresholds = -0.03, 0.03$
RSI trend analysis	$peaks.length = 3$ $w_1, w_2, w_3 = 25, 5, 1$
Price boundary	$buffer.length = 7$

Whole data provider consists of simple Java server, which stores scores for stock from current iteration. For indicators, we need some kind of memory, which allows us to update results with new portion of incoming data. Also, we store a buffer, using which we can find peaks and divergences (sect. 4.4).

We used a graph representation of data. There are 4 types of nodes (i) Investor, (ii) Industry, (iii) Category, (iv) Stock, and 4 types of relationships

- :POSSESS - *Investor* possess a *Stock* shares
- :INTERESTED - *Investor* interested in *Categories*
- :INCLUDES - *Category* contains *Industries*
- :COMPANY - *Industry* contains *Companies*.

Example subgraph is shown on Fig. 3. However, to retrieve data for further processing, we chose tabular form, as it contains information in format easier to process. We retrieve top-N investors using query to match such a graph, and then we sort investors by common companies with target investor. It ensures, that only most similar investors, and therefore, companies possibly in region of target users' interest will be considered.

Updating of graph structure is as follows: we change stocks, in which investors invest in specified iteration of simulation. To achieve that, we need to replace "old" *:POSSESS* connections with new ones. We use 3 queries which (i) Remove old connections (ii) Create new ones (iii) Update "number of companies" attribute It is a simplified version of simulation, where the optimal strategy could be "partial" replacement with taking into account current stock price forecasts as well as some "random noise" element (as some investors plays randomly as well). The aim of update is to check, how recommendation system will behave, when graph will change.

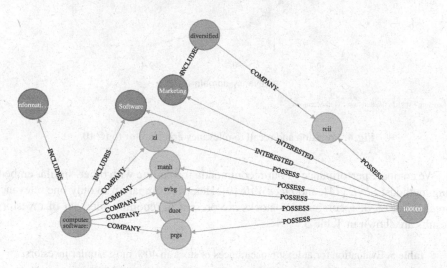

Fig. 3. Simple subgraph depicting structure of database.

7 Results and Evaluation

In this section, we discuss the results obtained by our recommendation system, and compare them to other embedding methods, as our implementation strongly bases on embedding mechanism.

For initialization we took into account 6 unrelated investors, and checked, how many of relevant stocks will occur in topN recommendations. Relevancy criterion was based on specific amount of stocks, that occurred in specific amount of most similar investors. It is expressed as percentage value of recommended investors that possess specific recommended stock. We evaluated precision and recall, where relevancy criterion varied from 12% to 46% of investors, that possess recommended stocks. It is shown on the plots Figs. 4, 5, 6.

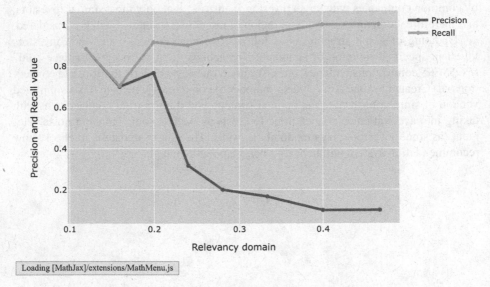

Fig. 4. Precision and recall to relevancy criterion for top@10.

We compare performance of our recommendation engine with other, similar embedding methods: *LINE* [14], and *DeepWalk* [9]. Here we compare it to only one relevancy threshold: 20% of recommended stocks are present in recommended set of investors. Results are shown in Table 5:

Table 5. Evaluation for at least 6 occurences of stock in 40% most similar investors.

		$Top@10$	$Top@25$	$Top@50$
DANE	*Precision*	63,33%	52,67%	31,67%
	Recall	63,33%	85,47%	97,9%
DeepWalk	*Precision*	25%	24%	21%
	Recall	25%	27,67%	49,17%
LINE	*Precision*	30%	32%	19%
	Recall	30%	58,88%	71,67%

Precision and Recall to Relevancy for Top@25

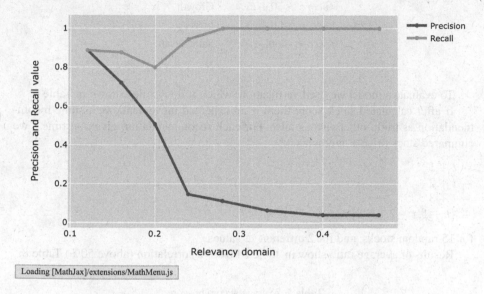

Loading [MathJax]/extensions/MathMenu.js

Fig. 5. Precision and recall to relevancy criterion for top@25.

Precision and Recall to Relevancy for Top@50

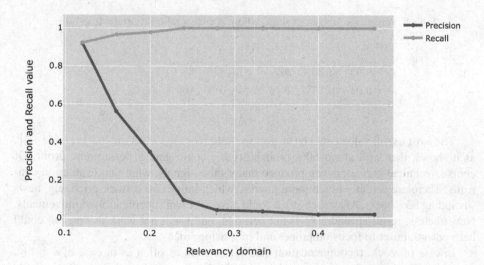

Fig. 6. Precision and recall to relevancy criterion for top@50.

Table 6. Evaluation criterion.

Stock score	Movement
$score > 50 + \Delta$	Growth
$score < 50 - \Delta$	Loss
$\|score - 50\| < \frac{score}{10}$	Same level

To evaluate a model we used verification, which follows rules shown in Table 6:

If after calculated stock score there is an expected movement, we assume recommendation as truth, otherwise as false. For each recommendation given on time t we compared stock price at moments of

- $t + 1$
- $t + 2$
- $t + 3$
- $\{t + 1, t + 2, t + 3\}$

for 15 random stocks, and for 2 different Δ values.

Results of average ratio show in Table 7 Positive correlation (above 50%) Table 8:

Table 7. Average accuracy score.

	$t + 1$	$t + 2$	$t + 3$	$\{t + 1, t + 2, t + 3\}$
$\Delta = 0.03$	45, 85%	42, 74%	41, 09%	59, 64%
$\Delta = 0.01$	51, 7%	48, 33%	47, 03%	67, 88%

Table 8. Percentage amount of stock, whose accuracy ratio was grater than 50%.

	$t + 1$	$t + 2$	$t + 3$	$\{t + 1, t + 2, t + 3\}$
$\Delta = 0.03$	33, 33%	20%	13, 33%	86, 67%
$\Delta = 0.01$	46, 67%	26, 67%	46, 67%	100%

The most useful value could be an average value for $\Delta = 0.03$ for $\{t+1, t+2, t+3\}$, as it shows, that with about 60% probability we could gain at least some profit. Of course, technical indicators can produce many false signals, what that evaluation confirms. There are actually much more factors, which influences a stock price, e.g. news (including fake ones). Also, each stock could have different specification of movements. Nevertheless, result around 60% is not bad one, but it will not work as bot, but could help potential user to focus on proper and promising stocks.

In case of stock, recommendation can not be right as often as in case of e.g. film or product recommendation, due to risk related with change of stock price. To increase accuracy there should be some additional factors, that influence final recommendation, which could "predict" people reaction, e.g. stock news analysis.

8 Summary

In this work, we designed and implemented a real-time recommendation system for the stock market. Due to being a real-time one, it gained effectiveness but lost accuracy, however, with a relatively not big amount of data it produces a satisfactory result. In Sect. 2, we described the theoretical background of this work, that is, mechanisms of how the stock market works, how a recommendation system works, and existing solutions, which combined the stock market with recommendations. In Sect. 4, we proposed our solution to the problem, with our algorithms, which calculated similarity and stock scores and used them for the recommendation. We designed a system, which contained 2 modules, and a graph database. One module was an engine, which calculated recommendations, and the second one was a data provider, which fed the recommendation engine with stock scores, which influenced the final recommendations. In Sect. 5, we described how we created a dataset, which met our needs, and how our dataset looks. In Sect. 6, we proposed the implementation of modules described in Sect. 4. We included a technology stack as well as more architectural information on system design. In Sect. 7, we evaluated the effectiveness of our recommendation system. We compared it with other methods. Results obtained are worse than in more "professional" recommendation systems, but it can be the result of some noise and false correlation in the dataset as well as lacking data, which needed to be taken into account to gain more information. To potentially improve results, the recommendation engine could be also "learned" which weights, and which formulas should be used in order to maximize recommendation accuracy.

References

1. Recommendation systems. https://developers.google.com/machine-learning/recommendation
2. Appel, G.: The Moving Average Convergence-divergence Trading Method: Advanced Version. Scientific Investment Systems (1985). https://books.google.pl/books?id=DbHzΛAAAMAAJ
3. Bugaj, A., Adrian, W.T.: Real-time recommendation system for stock investment decisions. In: Mayo, F.J.D., Marchiori, M., Filipe, J. (eds.) Proceedings of the 17th International Conference on Web Information Systems and Technologies, WEBIST 2021, 26–28 October 2021, pp. 490–493. SCITEPRESS (2021). https://doi.org/10.5220/0010714900003058
4. Chai, Y., Jia, L., Zhang, Z.: Mamdani model based adaptive neural fuzzy inference system and its application. Int. J. Comput. Intell. **5**(1), 22–29 (2009)
5. Fasanghari, M., Montazer, G.A.: Design and implementation of fuzzy expert system for Tehran stock exchange portfolio recommendation. Expert Syst. Appl. **37**(9), 6138–6147 (2010). https://doi.org/10.1016/j.eswa.2010.02.114, https://www.sciencedirect.com/science/article/pii/S0957417410001533
6. Granville, J.: New Key to Stock Market Profits. Prentice-Hall (1963). https://books.google.pl/books?id=0XVOAQAAMAAJ
7. Li, J., Dani, H., Hu, X., Tang, J., Chang, Y., Liu, H.: Attributed network embedding for learning in a dynamic environment. In: Proceedings of the 2017 ACM on Conference on Information and Knowledge Management, pp. 387–396 (2017)

8. Lin, Y., Liu, Z., Sun, M., Liu, Y., Zhu, X.: Learning entity and relation embeddings for knowledge graph completion. In: Proceedings of the AAAI Conference on Artificial Intelligence, vol. 29 (2015)
9. Perozzi, B., Al-Rfou, R., Skiena, S.: DeepWalk: online learning of social representations. In: Proceedings of the 20th ACM SIGKDD International Conference on Knowledge Discovery and Data Mining, pp. 701–710 (2014)
10. Sankar, C.P., Vidyaraj, R., Kumar, K.S.: Trust based stock recommendation system-a social network analysis approach. Proc. Comput. Sci. 46, 299–305 (2015)
11. Scarselli, F., Gori, M., Tsoi, A.C., Hagenbuchner, M., Monfardini, G.: The graph neural network model. IEEE Trans. Neural Netw. 20(1), 61–80 (2008)
12. Sha, X., Sun, Z., Zhang, J.: Attentive knowledge graph embedding for personalized recommendation. arXiv preprint arXiv:1910.08288 (2019)
13. Sun, Y., Fang, M., Wang, X.: A novel stock recommendation system using Guba sentiment analysis. Pers. Ubiquit. Comput. 22(3), 575–587 (2018)
14. Tang, J., Qu, M., Wang, M., Zhang, M., Yan, J., Mei, Q.: LINE: large-scale information network embedding. In: Proceedings of the 24th International Conference on World Wide Web, pp. 1067–1077 (2015)
15. Vicknair, C., Macias, M., Zhao, Z., Nan, X., Chen, Y., Wilkins, D.: A comparison of a graph database and a relational database: a data provenance perspective, vol. 10, p. 42 (2010). https://doi.org/10.1145/1900008.1900067
16. Wang, H., Zhao, M., Xie, X., Li, W., Guo, M.: Knowledge graph convolutional networks for recommender systems. In: The World Wide Web Conference, pp. 3307–3313 (2019)
17. Wang, X., He, X., Cao, Y., Liu, M., Chua, T.S.: KGAT: knowledge graph attention network for recommendation. In: Proceedings of the 25th ACM SIGKDD International Conference on Knowledge Discovery & Data Mining, pp. 950–958 (2019)
18. Wilder, J.: New Concepts in Technical Trading Systems. Trend Research (1978). https://books.google.pl/books?id=WesJAQAAMAAJ
19. Yujun, Y., Jianping, L., Yimei, Y.: An efficient stock recommendation model based on big order net inflow. Math. Probl. Eng. 2016 (2016). https://doi.org/10.1155/2016/5725143
20. Zhou, J., et al.: Graph neural networks: a review of methods and applications. AI Open 1, 57–81 (2020). https://doi.org/10.1016/j.aiopen.2021.01.001, https://www.sciencedirect.com/science/article/pii/S2666651021000012

LDViz: A Tool to Assist the Multidimensional Exploration of SPARQL Endpoints

Aline Menin[1]([✉])(iD), Pierre Maillot[1](iD), Catherine Faron[1](iD), Olivier Corby[1](iD),
Carla Dal Sasso Freitas[2](iD), Fabien Gandon[1](iD), and Marco Winckler[1](iD)

[1] University Côte d'Azur, CNRS, Inria, I3S (UMR 7271), Nice, France
{aline.menin,pierre.maillot,catherine.faron,olivier.corby,
fabien.gandon,marco.winckler}@inria.fr
[2] Institute of Informatics, Federal University of Rio Grande do Sul, Porto Alegre, Brazil
carla@inf.ufrgs.br

Abstract. Over recent years, we witnessed an astonishing growth in production and consumption of Linked Data (LD), which contains valuable information to support decision-making processes in various application domains. In this context, data visualization plays a decisive role in making sense of the large volumes of data created every day and in effectively communicating structures, processes, and trends in data in an accessible way. In this paper, we present LDViz, a visualization tool designed to support the exploration of knowledge graphs via multiple perspectives: (i) RDF graph/vocabulary inspection, (ii) RDF summarization, and (iii) exploratory search. We demonstrate the usage and feasibility of our approach through a set of use case scenarios showing how users can perform searches through SPARQL queries and explore multiple perspectives of the resulting data through multiple complementary visualization techniques. We also demonstrate the reach and generic aspects of our tool through an evaluation that tests the support of 419 different SPARQL endpoints.

Keywords: Linked data · Linked data visualization · RDF visualization · Visual exploratory search · SPARQL

1 Introduction

An increasing amount of data is published as RDF (Resource Description Framework) datasets and is made available as Linked Open Data (LOD) in different domains, providing valuable information to support decision-making processes in various application domains [15]. However, the value of these data depends on the ability of decision makers to grasp the relevant information to describe the phenomena embedded in the data. Information visualization, through the use of visual representations of abstract data, reinforces human cognition to support the discovery of unstructured insights only limited by human imagination and creativity, making it a suitable approach to communicate the knowledge described by RDF datasets. In particular, we observe an increasing interest in using visual and interactive techniques to explore LOD resources via multiple criteria and levels of abstraction by the Semantic Web community to accomplish three main goals: (i) to explore the relevant concepts of an application domain via ontology

© Springer Nature Switzerland AG 2023
M. Marchiori et al. (Eds.): WEBIST 2020/2021, LNBIP 469, pp. 149–173, 2023.
https://doi.org/10.1007/978-3-031-24197-0_9

representation; (ii) to inspect RDF graphs (e.g., "for debugging triples") [1]; and (iii) to analyze the instances based on their types/classes.

Among the many evolution trends of the Web, knowledge graphs (KGs) are now widely used to describe in standard ways the semantics of entities in the real world and their relations [16], and to link descriptions with additional information in semantic LOD repositories. Typically, KGs are generated through the integration of many different data sources, which results on highly heterogeneous information. This heterogeneity represents both a leverage and a challenge in their effective utilization. Further to the often unknown structure and nature of the data, visualizing linked data requires a preceding KG processing to retrieve suitable data, which requires knowledge of the underlying RDF vocabulary used to build the KG, less and less familiar even to data producers and analysts, as different vocabularies can be used to describe the same phenomenon, and nearly inaccessible to application domain users. Furthermore, retrieving suitable data often requires combining data from different KGs (available from the same or different SPARQL endpoints), which results in several data quality issues (e.g., missing data, inconsistency, etc.). Thus, visual methods are a necessary and suitable approach to support an effective exploration of knowledge graphs.

The design process of every visualization tool follows a well-known pipeline (i.e., import $\rightarrow$ transform $\rightarrow$ map $\rightarrow$ render $\rightarrow$ interact) [4,31]. In particular, a visualization pipeline for LOD data should also take into account the linked nature of these datasets by leveraging/supporting/exploiting these links while being capable of processing and visualizing the data appropriately. In a previous work [25], we presented and discussed a visualization pipeline for LOD exploration that supports a high level of flexibility in every step. This versatility is found in the drafting of SPARQL queries in a way that appropriately addresses the links in the linked data, in the possibility of tuning the parameters of the graphic display and the associated interaction, and in the availability of multiple visualization techniques that can help users see data according to diverse and complementary viewpoints. To demonstrate the feasibility of our visualization pipeline, we had implemented a proof of concept in the form of a web-based visualization tool called LDViz. In this paper, we further explore the genericity and flexibility of LDViz by defining a scope of SPARQL queries to support the exploration of RDF graphs via different methods and by evaluating the extent to which LDViz can support LOD visualization. In particular, our contributions are summarized as follows:

- A generic web-based visualization tool for LOD exploration, LDViz, that supports data visualization through multiple perspectives from any SPARQL endpoint that is W3C compliant.
- A classification of the scope of SPARQL queries with respect to KGs exploration methods. This classification cover RDF graph/vocabulary inspection, RDF summarization, and exploratory search.
- An analysis of LDViz using 419 SPARQL endpoints, which results shows an average coverage of 41.77% of SPARQL endpoints by our approach.

The remaining of this document is organized as follows. Section 2 presents the proposed visualization tool. Section 3 presents the scope of SPARQL queries in terms of KG exploration methods and illustrate their use in LDViz. Section 4 presents a coverage analysis of the genericity and reach of our approach. Section 5 summarizes previous contributions for LOD visualization and compares them with our approach. Section 6 discusses our results and concludes the paper.

2   Visual Exploration of LOD

In this section, we present the Linked Data Visualizer (LDViz), a web-based visualization tool for LOD exploration. Our visualization techniques are implemented using *D3.js* (Data-Driven Documents) library, while the *nodejs* library is used to manage the linked data access server that handles data retrieval through SPARQL queries. We also use *Stencil JS* to implement visualization techniques as reusable Web components. LDViz implements each step of the visualization pipeline (i.e., import → transform → map → render → interact) as described in [25] and summarized hereafter:

Import. Data import is handled via SPARQL queries. The generality of LDViz relies on the fact that users can query any SPARQL endpoint as long as it can return result sets in a JSON format. We provide an interactive interface where the user can test and debug SPARQL queries or import predefined queries, which they may modify at will. The data import process can be launched at different times throughout the exploration process by using follow up queries, which allows to import external data (a different subset of data from the same SPARQL endpoint or data from a different SPARQL endpoint) into the exploration process to enrich the analysis (bring supplementary information to the analysis or compare datasets).

Transform. Data transformation occurs in three moments during the exploration process. First, at the definition of the SPARQL query, the RDF graph is filtered to retrieve the appropriate data to solve a particular domain question and reshaped into the required data model (see Subsect. 2.1) to be visualized. Second, in the transformation engine, the SPARQL result sets are cleaned and re-shaped into a suitable data model for visualization, handled by MGExplorer [23], a visualization interface to explore multidimensional network data. Finally, as the user filters the input data set through a selection operation in a particular view to explore it in another, the data are filtered and reshaped to fit the selected visualization technique.

Visual Mapping. Visual mapping occurs during the transformation of the SPARQL results set into the LDViz data model, followed by the mapping of data variables into the visual variables of each technique, and the tuning of certain variables through the use of a Graph Style Sheet (e.g., by defining colors to represent them) (see Subsect. 2.2).

Rendering. This is handled by MGExplorer [23], the visualization interface to explore multidimensional network data mentioned before.

Interaction. Via the MGExplorer interface, we provide selection operations that allow the user to subset the input data to be explored using different visualization techniques, which present complementary views of the data.

2.1   Importing Data from SPARQL Endpoints

SPARQL Result Sets. The W3C Recommendation [29] describes a specific data format to represent SPARQL SELECT query results using JSON. The results of a SPARQL query are serialized in a single top-level JSON object with two keys: head and results. The results key is an object with a single key, bindings, which is an array with zero or more elements, one element per query solution. The Listing 1.1 illustrates this data format through an extract of the results of the SELECT query presented in Listing 1.5. Each SPARQL query solution is a JSON object whose keys are the variable names of the query solution. A solution describes an RDF term that has a type and a value key, and other keys depending on the specific kind of RDF term (e.g., language, datatype). In LDViz, we use this data format, which means that our approach supports data from any SPARQL endpoint, as long as it can return SPARQL result sets in a JSON format that is W3C compliant.

```
{head: { link: [], vars: [ "s", "p", "o", "label", "type", "date" ] },
 results: { distinct: false, ordered: true, bindings: [
    {s: { type: "literal", xml:lang: "en", value: "Maximilian Schell" },
    p: { type: "uri",
        value: \url{http://dbpedia.org/resource/A_Bridge_Too_Far_(film)},}
    o: { type: "literal", xml:lang: "en", value: "Dirk Bogarde"},
    label: { type: "literal", xml:lang: "en",
        value: "A Bridge Too Far (film)"},
    type: { type: "literal", xml:lang: "en", value: "non-fiction" },
    date: { type: "typed-literal",
        datatype: \url{http://www.w3.org/2001/XMLSchema#date,}
        value: "1977-06-15" }}
] } }
```

Listing 1.1. Example of a SPARQL SELECT result set serialized in a JSON object as specified by the W3C Recommendation.

LDViz Data Model. The data model corresponds to a custom graph model defined through a SPARQL SELECT query, which uses arbitrary query patterns on RDF graphs to generate the edges ?s ?p ?o of the graph that one wants to visualize, where ?s and ?o represent the nodes of the graph while ?p corresponds to labeled edges between them. Listing 1.5 illustrates an example SPARQL query supported by LDViz. In this example, ?s and ?o are bound to the actors and ?p to the films. The result of this SPARQL query will be used to build a visualization of the social network of actors co-starring in films. In addition to these three variables, the data model allows three other reserved variables to be used to describe the edges (?p) of the output graph in visualization: ?type, ?label, and ?date. Variable ?type can be used to type the edges of the output graph (e.g., in a graph where films connect actors, films can be "typed" or classified by their genre). Due to human perceptual and cognitive limits towards visualizations, only a certain number of graphic elements can be perceived on the screen. For that, we allow the variable ?type to be bound to only four different values that describe the edges. If the variable ?type is bound to more than four distinct values in the SPARQL query result, the system automatically determines the three more relevant ones based on the number of bindings and considers the remaining values as the"Other" category. The variable ?label is intended to provide a description of the edges in natural language (e.g., the value of properties rdfs:label that describe resources). Finally, the ?date variable is used to provide a visual representation of the distribution of edges over time (e.g., if edges are films, it could correspond to the release year).

2.2   SPARQL Query Editor

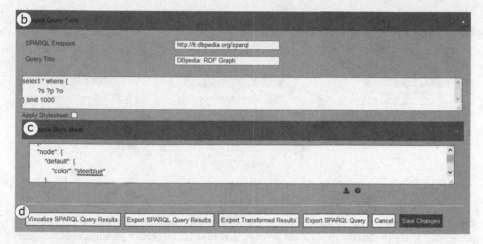

Fig. 1. SPARQL Query Management Interface. (a) Listing of predefined queries. (b) The querying area. (c) The GSS editing area. (d) Control buttons to visualize and export the results. Image reused from [25].

The query editor (Fig. 1) allows users to create, test, and debug SPARQL queries. Users can also clone predefined queries and adapt them according to specific needs[1]. The interface expects a SPARQL endpoint, a name for the SPARQL query and the query code itself. Users can retrieve data from more than one endpoint by leveraging the full strength of the SPARQL language, including the SERVICE clause by using the Corese proxy [9], for example. The action buttons at the bottom (Fig. 1d) allow to visualize the SPARQL query results using MGExplorer or export them as a JSON file.

```
(a) {"node": { "fst": {"color": "green"},
    "snd": {"color": "orange"} },
    "services": { "Corese Browser": { "url":
    "http://corese.inria.fr/srv/service/covid?uri="}}}

(b) select * where { ?s ?p ?o
    bind("fst" as ?style1) bind("snd" as ?style2)}
```

Listing 1.2. Example of (a) GSS and (b) its usage in a SPARQL query.

---

[1] For security reasons, authentication is required to use the editor. Interested readers might contact the authors to acquire access.

Each query is associated with a **Graph Style Sheet (GSS)** that can be used to transform the default node-link diagram through a declarative specification of visibility, layout, and styling rules [28]. So that, it is possible to define styling rules as classes in a style sheet of reference (JSON format) (e.g., Listing 1.2a) and bind them to dedicated variables in the SPARQL query (i.e. ?style1 to style ?s, ?style2 to style ?o, and ?style for both). This information is then processed in the transformation engine, which associates the style classes to the visual variables used in the visualization. Moreover, the GSS supports a behavior feature that enables exploring data (the graph nodes) via an external service (e.g., the Corese browser [9], which allows browsing the original repository of open data) as long as an URL is provided (see Listing 1.2a).

2.3 Using Predefined Queries

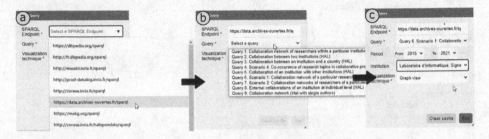

Fig. 2. Using a query panel, users can (a) choose a SPARQL endpoint they want to explore, (b) a predefined query to start the exploration process, and (c) custom certain parameters of the query such as time period, location, etc.

We assume that many users might be expert on the application domain of an endpoint and interested in exploring such as data sets. However, an expertise in the application domain does not imply that the user knows SPARQL. For that kind of user, the visualization tool includes a querying process that allows the use of predefined queries (defined by expert users in the SPARQL query editor) to retrieve data from endpoints without having to understand SPARQL or the complexity of the underlying knowledge graph. From a query panel (see Fig. 2) users can select a SPARQL endpoint (Fig. 2a) and have a simple access to the queries (Fig. 2b) that have been specifically created for that endpoint. That panel also displays a set of custom parameters that allow users to filter the data (e.g. in a bibliometric network, these could be the publication period and research institution of scholarly articles) (Fig. 2c). The button "Run" at the bottom of the panel, will trigger the query against the chosen endpoint, prompt the system to transform the resulting data, and then launch the visualization technique to display the resulting data. For the purpose of optimizing the process, we use a cache that stores the results of queries for a certain amount of time (i.e. 15 days), thus reducing the requests to the data server. To acquire fresh data, the user can deliberately clear the results stored in the cache by using the button "Clear cache" at the bottom, which will force the system to apply the query to the SPARQL endpoint at the next execution.

Table 1. Visualization techniques available in MGExplorer according to the given perspective to the data.

Graph View	Cluster View	Egocentric View	Pairwise Relationship View	Distribution View	Listing View
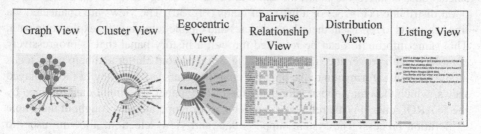					

2.4 Data Visualization Using MGExplorer

In our approach, data visualization is provided through MGExplorer [23], a tool that assists in the exploration of multidimensional and multivariate graphs. The tool provides a set of complementary visualization techniques (see Table 1) that can be instantiated at will during the exploration process to further explore the data through different perspectives. The **graph view** shows the nodes as items and the edges between them as relationships. This visualization provides an overview of the network defined by the SPARQL query. The **cluster view** [6] shows clusters according to some relationship among the data items. The technique features a multi-ring layout, where the innermost ring is formed by the data items (represented by circles), and the remaining rings display the data attributes (represented by rectangles). The items belonging to the same cluster are connected via curved lines. The **egocentric view** isolates a data item of interest (in the center) and shows all other data items with which it has a specific relationship in a circular view [7]. The data attributes of the pairwise relationships are encoded by the height and color of a bar placed between the item of interest and each related item. The user can place any item in the field of view center by clicking on it, switching the focus of the IRIS. The **pairwise relationship view** [5] features a matrix in which rows and columns represent data items, and cells contain glyphs that encode attributes that describe the relationship between these items. The default glyph is a star-plot-shaped object with a variable number of axes that are used to encode the values of the selected data attributes. By pointing a glyph to the matrix, it is possible to enlarge the glyph to see the details of the data attributes. The **distribution view** shows the data attributes of an item or a set of items distributed over a particular variable. For example, in one of our use-case scenarios, the x-axis encodes temporal information (in years), while the y-axis encodes the counting of publications co-authored by an author or a set of authors. The data is displayed as a single bar per time period or multiple colored bars to represent categorical information of attributes. The **listing view** displays the elements that form the relationship between two or more nodes in the graph. Each item of the list is linked to a descriptive web page in the dataset where the user can obtain more information about it.

Figure 3 shows an overview of the exploration process using MGExplorer. It starts with a query panel, where the user can choose a SPARQL endpoint and a predefined query (Fig. 3a), or directly with a graph view of the data (Fig. 3b), when the visualization is launched from the SPARQL query editor. From the graph view, the user can select nodes of interest to subset the data and explore it using other views, such as a temporal distribution (Fig. 3c) or a listing of items (Fig. 3d). The views are connected via line segments to represent their dependencies and enable retracing the exploration path. This same information can be retrieved through a history panel that is progressively completed with provenance information (Fig. 3e). To avoid clutter and help users focus on the relevant information to the ongoing analysis, users can hide any of the displayed views, which they may revisit later using the history panel. The input data (defined by the SPARQL query) is the reference data for selection operations throughout the whole exploration process. The system supports data and view selection, allowing users to specify subsets of interest from the whole input graph and suitable views to explore them. Upon selection of elements, the system filters the input dataset accordingly, and the resulting subset undergoes a transformation and mapping process that properly filter and reshape the data to be visualized with the selected visualization technique. The history records information about the selection operation, the data subset, the chosen view, and the transformed data.

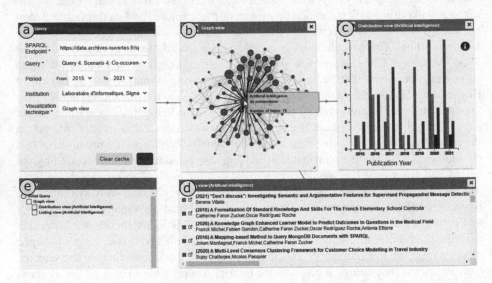

Fig. 3. Overview of MGExplorer exploration process. In the query panel (a), the user chooses a SPARQL endpoint and a predefined query, which results are displayed in the graph view (b). By right-clicking on a node of interest, the user can subset the data and explore it through different views such as a distribution (c) or listing view (d) of items. The lines between views represent their dependency, which is also displayed in the history view (e).

2.5 Visualizing Multiple SPARQL Endpoints During Exploration

The tool proposes a feature, called *Follow-up Queries*, that allows users to simultaneously explore multiple SPARQL result sets on the visualization dashboard [24]. This feature supports exploratory tasks such as (i) the comparison of a particular phenomenon described by different KGs and (ii) the inclusion of complementary data (from

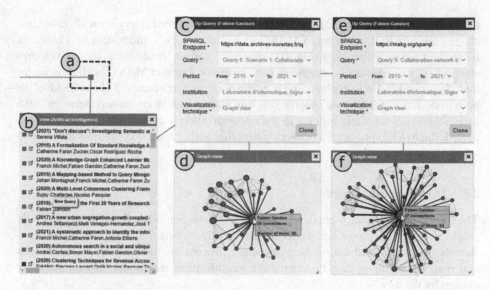

Fig. 4. Usage of follow up queries. We hide the views that are no longer necessary (a) and launch a new query by right-clicking on an item displayed on the listing view (b). In the new query panel (c), we choose an endpoint and query, which results are displayed in a new graph view (d). We can clone the query to reuse information, which creates a new query panel (e) where we can modify the information if necessary and relaunch the query. The results are then displayed in a new graph view (f).

the same or a different SPARQL endpoint) to enrich the ongoing analysis. Figure 4 illustrates the usage of follow-up queries subsequent to the exploration process depicted in Fig. 3. To avoid clutter, we first hide the views that are no longer necessary, which replaces the view by an icon (Fig. 4a) that serve to retrace the exploration process and is interactive to allow users to display the view again by clicking on it. In the listing view (Fig. 4b), suppose we are interested in the paper entitled "A Survey of the First 20 Years of Research on Semantic Web and Linked Data" and we want to know more about the author, "Fabien Gandon" and, particularly, about his scientific collaborations. For that purpose, we will query the HAL SPARQL endpoint to retrieve the coauthorship network of "Fabien Gandon". We right-click on the name of the author and select the option "New Query" (Fig. 4b), which instantiates a query panel giving the author's name as input data to be used as a parameter in the new query. As for the initial query, we select the endpoint of interest and the query (Fig. 4c), which results are displayed on a new graph view (Fig. 4d). This process allowed us to bring complementary data to the exploration process.

Up to this point, we have explored the scientific collaboration network of "Fabien Gandon" from the perspective of the HAL knowledge graph. Now, let us compare these data with the coauthorship network of this researcher retrieved from another KG (i.e., the Microsoft Academic Knowledge Graph[2]. The tool allows us to clone the query view

---

[2] Available at https://makg.org/sparql.

to reuse information and speed up the process. In the cloned query view (Fig. 4e), we change the SPARQL endpoint to MAKG and select query 9, the results of which can be seen in a new graph view (Fig. 4f). We can compare these visualizations side-by-side, where we can quickly observe that the network found in MAKG is slightly larger than that found in HAL. By hovering over the node that represents "Fabien Gandon" in both node-link diagrams, we observe that this author had 36 co-authors between 2015 and 2021 in 28 scholarly articles in the network retrieved from HAL. For the same period, the MAKG provided a network where this author had 64 co-authors through 64 scholarly articles.

2.6   Transformation Engine

The LDViz transformation engine consists of a converter module from SPARQL JSON results to the MGExplorer data model and a set of algorithms (i.e., mappers) that process subsets of data defined during the exploratory process via visual querying operations and map the resulting data to a particular visualization technique, also interactively chosen by the user.

From SPARQL Results to MGExplorer Data Model. The system receives the SPARQL JSON results set, which undergoes a transformation process to extract an attributed graph, encoded in the JSON format, that will serve as input data to MGExplorer. In addition to identifying mandatory and optional variables from the dataset, the process also derives indicators to describe the relationship between each pair of nodes, such as the total count of items and the count of items per type, when this information is provided.

MGExplorer Mappers. Every selection operation triggers a transformation process that filters and transforms the data and maps it to the selected visualization technique via: the *cluster view mapper*, which extracts clusters of nodes grouped according to the existing links among them, e.g., in a co-authorship network, the algorithm detects groups of authors co-authoring the same publication(s); the *egocentric view mapper*, which extracts pairwise relationships between the selected node and the other nodes in the subset; the *pairwise relationship view mapper*, which extracts pairwise relationships by analyzing every possible combination of pairs of nodes within the subset; the *distribution view mapper*, which extracts the distribution of items in the subset according to a particular attribute (e.g., date); and the *listing view mapper*, which extracts the list of links in the graph and their descriptive information (if provided). Regardless of the resulting relationship type, every mapper keeps information on the count and type of items per relationship.

3   KG Exploration Methods and SPARQL Queries

LDViz covers three domains of data exploration: (i) RDF graph/vocabulary inspection, (ii) RDF graph summarization, and (iii) exploratory search. In this section, we present the spectrum of SPARQL queries capable of extracting the necessary data from RDF graphs to support such as data. We then demonstrate the generic use of LDViz by applying those queries on two distinct SPARQL endpoints giving access to the DBpedia FR dataset[3] (over 400 million triples describing the content generated in the Wikipedia project) and the *HAL* dataset[4] (an open archive for scientific publications in all domains).

3.1 RDF Graph/Vocabulary Inspection

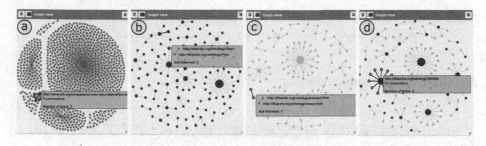

Fig. 5. Graph view of an extract of DBpedia's (a) RDF graph, (b) hierarchy of classes, (c) hierarchy of properties, and (d) signatures of properties linking classes (orange) and properties (light green). (Color figure online)

When working with the Semantic Web, a recurring task is to inspect the RDF graph and its ontology to learn its content. In particular, we consider exploration tasks where the user wants to (1) display the RDF graph with no particular goal in mind and (2) get an idea of the ontology used in the RDF graph. The RDF graph can be extracted through a simple SPARQL SELECT query retrieving every triple ?s, ?p, ?o in the graph, without specific matching (Listing 1.3a). To support the exploration of the RDF vocabularies, we define three SPARQL query templates based on the RDF Schema data-modeling vocabulary to retrieve the (a) *hierarchy of classes*, defined by the rdfs:subClassOf property (Listing 1.3b), (b) the *hierarchy of properties*, defined by the rdfs:subPropertyOf property Listing 1.3c), and (b) the *signature of properties*, defined by the properties rdfs:domain and rdfs:range, which give the class to which the subject of an RDF statement using a given property belongs, and the class of its object (value), respectively (see Listing 1.3d). These SPARQL query templates are generic enough to retrieve information from any SPARQL endpoint, as long as it includes the RDF Schema description.

To demonstrate the feasibility of these SPARQL queries, we apply them to the DBPedia endpoint and visualize the results using LDViz. Figure 5a shows an interactive graph view of the 1000 first statements in the DBpedia graph. The graph views in Figs. 5b–d show the above mentioned methods of RDF vocabulary inspection: hierarchy of classes and properties, and the signatures of properties. Users can hover over nodes to inspect and navigate within hierarchies and explore property signatures by hovering over nodes that represent properties to inspect their signature or classes to identify

---

[3] SPARQL endpoint: http://fr.dbpedia.org/sparql.
[4] SPARQL endpoint: http://sparql.archives-ouvertes.fr/sparql.

all the properties to whose signatures the selected class belongs (e.g., `dbo:Athlete` is related to eleven properties). In this example, we leverage the GSS feature to assign meaningful visual elements to certain variables as shown in Fig 5d, where color encodes property (light green) and class nodes (orange), assisting visual search and understanding of relationships between nodes of different types.

```
(a) select * where { ?s ?p ?o }          (b) select * where { ?s ?p ?o
                                              filter(?p = rdfs.subClassOf) }
(c) select * where { ?s ?p ?o            (d) select * where { ?s ?p ?o
        filter(?p = rdfs:subPropertyOf) }     filter(?p = rdfs:domain ||
                                                  ?p = rdfs:range)}
```

Listing 1.3. SPARQL query templates for RDF graph/vocabulary inspection via the (a) RDF graph, (b) hierarchy of classes, (c) hierarchy of properties, and (d) signature of properties.

3.2 RDF Graph Summarizations

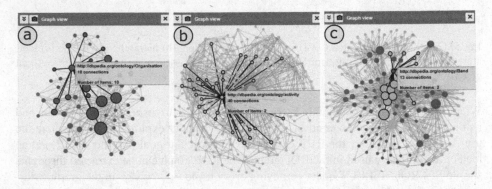

Fig. 6. Graph views of DBpedia RDF summarizations representing (a) class paths, (b) property paths, and (c) paths of type class → property → class.

A benefit of visualization for exploring RDF graphs relies on its capacity to reveal tendencies and patterns within the data. However, visualization knows its limitations as one tries to display millions of triples on the screen, resulting in a huge and cluttered graph that hinders the discovery of meaningful information. Structural RDF graph summarization addresses this issue by providing indices or summaries of RDF graphs to aggregate the triples in meaningful ways. We consider three methods of RDF graph summarization, which we support through three SPARQL query templates (Listing 1.4) capable of extracting (i) the existing paths between classes of resources in an RDF graph, (ii) the existing property paths between the resources of the graph, or (iii) the paths between classes and properties (i.e. Class → Property → Class path). To demonstrate the feasibility of these queries, we applied them on the DBPedia SPARQL endpoint. The graph view in Fig. 6a summarizes the DBPedia RDF graph by showing how classes are connected through properties, while the graph view in Fig. 6b shows how properties are connected through resources. Finally, Fig. 6c shows how properties and classes are connected together through resources.

```
prefix ldv: <http://ldv.fr/path/>
(a) select distinct ?s ?p ?o
    where { ?a ?p ?b . ?a a ?s . ?b a ?o }

(b) select distinct ?s (ldv: as ?p) ?o where {
    ?x ?s ?y . ?y ?o ?z . filter (?s != ?o)}

(c) select distinct ?s (ldv: as ?p) ?o where {
    {?a ?b ?c. ?a a ?s . bind (?b as ?o)} UNION
    {?a ?b ?c. ?c a ?s . bind (?b as ?o)}}
```

Listing 1.4. SPARQL query templates for exploring RDF summarizations through (a) class paths, (b) property paths, and (c) paths of type class → property → class.

3.3 Exploratory Search of Knowledge Graphs

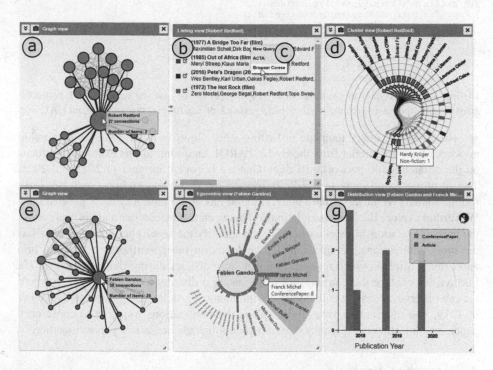

Fig. 7. Exploratory path of Robert Redford's co-starring network (a–d) and Fabien Gandon's co-authorship network (e–g).

The set of KG exploration methods presented above are useful to support data producers while inspecting or discovering the RDF graph. As for any dataset, KGs provide data that describes a particular phenomenon, which analysis could support decision-making processes on a particular application domain. Therefore, we support exploratory search in KG starting from a question or hypothesis, which is then formulated as SPARQL query to retrieve an initial dataset used in the exploration. Hereafter, we define SPARQL query templates to support exploratory search in KGs with focus on relationship networks.

The SPARQL query template presented in Listing 1.5a is able to retrieve the co-starring network of a given artist described by the DBPedia KG. In this example, we focus on Robert Redford, which resulting graph view shown in Fig. 7a consists of 28 nodes (actors) and 137 links (movies). We see that Redford has 27 co-stars across four movies where details are available at the Listing view (Fig. 7b). The resources can be explored using the Corese browser (Fig. 7c) or any other service enabled in the GSS. Furthermore,the cluster view (Fig. 7d) shows Redford's co-stars grouped by movie.

```
(a) prefix dbo: <http://dbpedia.org/ontology/>
    prefix dbp: <http://dbpedia.org/property/>
    select * where { ?x rdfs:label {artist name} .
        ?p dbo:starring ?x, ?a1, ?a2; rdfs:label ?label;
            dbp:released ?date ; dbp:genre ?type .
        ?a1 rdfs:label ?s . ?a2 rdfs:label ?o . }

(b) prefix dc:<http://purl.org/dc/terms/>
    prefix foaf:<http://xmlns.com/foaf/0.1/>
    prefix hsc:<http://data.archives-ouvertes.fr/schema/>
    select * where { ?p dc:creator ?x, ?x1, ?x2 ;
        dc:type ?type ; dc:title ?label ; dc:issued ?date.
        ?x hsc:person ?a . ?a foaf:name {researcher name}.
        ?x1 hsc:person ?a1 . ?a1 foaf:name ?s .
        ?x2 hsc:person ?a2 . ?a2 foaf:name ?o . }
```

Listing 1.5. SPARQL query template for retrieving (a) the co-starring network of a particular artist from DBpedia and (b) the co-authorship network of a particular researcher from HAL

The SPARQL query template in Listing 1.5b allows to retrieve the co-authorship network of any researcher from the HAL SPARQL endpoint. In this example, we focus on the co-authorship network of Fabien Gandon between the year of 2015 and 2021. The resulting graph view in Fig. 7e is formed by 35 nodes (authors) and 109 links (publications). We observe that Fabien Gandon has 36 co-authors via 28 publications. We further explore the pairwise relationship between this researcher and his peers using the pairwise relationship view, where we can identify the researcher with whom he has the most publications. As an example, we focus on the co-authorship between him and Franck Michel, which resulted in 8 scholarly articles during that period (Fig. 7f). Further, we explore these articles over time using a distribution view (Fig. 7e), where we can observe a constant collaboration with the most articles being published together in 2019. The distribution view also displays the publications' types (i.e., conference paper, article), showing that they have mostly published conference papers together.

4   Coverage Analysis

To demonstrate the extent to which LDViz can support the exploration of LD datasets, we implemented a script that tested 419 different SPARQL endpoints to identify whether the SPARQL result set could be visualized by our tool.

4.1   Data

The 419 SPARQL endpoints used in this analysis were obtained from IndeGx [21], a framework designed to index public KGs that are available online through a SPARQL endpoint. The indexing process uses SPARQL queries to either extract the available metadata from a KG or to generate as much metadata as the endpoint allows it. The generated metadata not only describes KGs and their endpoints but also conveys an esti- mation of certain quality criteria. The queries used by IndeGx to index KGs and their endpoints are available in a public repository at https://github.com/Wimmics/dekalog, and the results of its indexations are publicly available through a SPARQL endpoint at http://prod-dekalog.inria.fr/sparql, from which we retrieved the list of endpoints using the query presented in Listing 1.6. These SPARQL endpoints are present in the dataset generated by IndeGx because they appeared in different publicly available catalogs of datasets. In particular, they were retrieved from the LOD Cloud website[5], Yummy Data [34], Wikidata[6], Linked Wiki[7], SPARQLES [33] and the OpenLink company end- point[8].

```
prefix index: <http://ns.inria.fr/kg/index\#>
prefix desc: <http://www.w3.org/ns/sparql-service-description\#>
SELECT DISTINCT ?endpointUrl where {
    GRAPH ?g {  ?metadata index:curated ?dataset .
        ?dataset desc:endpoint ?endpointUrl . } }
```

Listing 1.6. SPARQL query used to retrieve the list of available endpoints from the IndeGx RDF graph.

4.2   Procedure

The queries in the exploratory search category require a knowledge of the RDF graph and vocabulary to retrieve suitable data to start the exploration. Thus, we ran the evalua- tion using only queries that serve to inspect the RDF graph or vocabulary, and those that provide RDF summarizations as they are rather generic to any endpoint. The only spe- cific vocabulary used by these queries is the RDF Schema, which provides a data mod- eling vocabulary for RDF data and would be therefore expected to appear in most RDF graphs. We implemented a *nodejs* script that applies each query against every one of the 419 SPARQL endpoints retrieved from the IndeGx endpoint using the fetch API provided by the node-fetch module. We limited each query to 10 solutions to speed up the process, as our goal was to inspect the resulting data format to check whether we could visualize it using LDViz; the actual data was not important for this analysis. A request would have mainly two possible outcomes. In case of a successful request, we inspect the resulting data format to verify whether it matches the SPARQL JSON result set defined by W3C Recommendation. If the data does not match the expected format, we inspect it further to identify its format, which may sometimes be HTML or CSV, for instance. In case of a failed request, we inspect the error thrown to understand why we were unable to retrieve data from that particular endpoint.

4.3   Results

Figure 8 presents a TreeMap graph showing the distribution of different responses obtained while querying 419 SPARQL endpoints obtained from IndeGx [21]. The top

---

[5] https://lod-cloud.net.

[6] https://www.wikidata.org/.

[7] https://linkedwiki.com/.

[8] http://lod.openlinksw.com/sparql/.

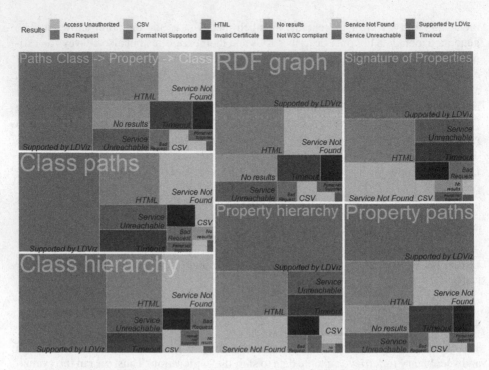

Fig. 8. Summary of results per type of query. In the case where results cannot be visualized with LDViz, we display the issues encountered while querying the SPARQL endpoints.

level of the TreeMap graph contains seven rectangles each of which covers a specific query type (i.e. Paths→Properties→Class, Class paths, Class hierarchy, RDF graph, property hierarchy, signature of properties, and properties path). These rectangles are further divided in smaller colored rectangles that summarize the results obtained per query type including SPARQL endpoints supported by LDViz and issues encountered while accessing the endpoints (e.g., Access Unauthorized, Service not found, etc.). The size of the rectangle encodes the number of results obtained for each query.

On average, 41.77% of the SPARQL endpoints returned a valid result set that could be explored using LDViz. We noticed that the queries seeking for class and property hierarchy, and signature of properties were slightly less successful than the remaining, where only about 38.19% of SPARQL endpoints returned a valid result set. Regarding the issues found while querying the SPARQL endpoints, we could identify 11 different reasons for why it cannot be explored using LDViz. Table 4 summarizes the percentage of issues per query type. Hereafter we present the issues in decreasing order of occurrence:

- **HTML:** About 16.06% of the requests returned an HTML object, which may contain valid results from the SPARQL endpoint, but cannot be processed by the LDViz transformation engine.

- **Service Not Found:** The SPARQL endpoint could not be found (request status 404 and 410). We encountered this issue in about 14.18% of requests.
- **Service Unreachable:** This issue is identified when the connection is refused by the server (throwing the ECONNREFUSED error), or the protocol encountered an unrecoverable error for that endpoint (throwing the EPROTO error). On average, 7.06% of requests encountered this issue. We noticed that this issue appeared slightly more often for the SPARQL query recovering the RDF summarization through class paths then for the remaining, where we observed the issue in 8.59% of requests.
- **Timeout:** About 6.27% of the requests encountered a timeout issue. This is due to the request response not being received within the default timeout of the fetch request, which is of about 300 s (request statuses 408 and 504) or the Virtuoso server estimating the query processing time to be longer than its established timeout of 400 s.
- **No Results:** This issue means that the request returned a valid JSON object, but the bindings array was empty. In average, 4.30% of SPARQL endpoints did not provide results to our queries. However, once again, we observe that this number is higher for SPARQL queries seeking for the signature of properties, class, and property hierarchies, where we observe that about 8.35% of endpoints did not provide results against an average of only 1.25% of endpoints not providing results for the remaining queries.
- **Invalid Certificate:** The request could not be completed due to an invalid certificate on the SPARQL endpoint side. This issue was observed in about 3.10% of requests, which correspond to 13 SPARQL endpoints.
- **CSV:** On average, 2.18% of the requests returned a string object which content follows a CSV format. The result set may contain valid data but cannot be processed by the LDViz transformation engine.
- **Bad Request:** The request could not be fulfilled due to bad syntax (request status 400). This error was thrown by 2.18% of requests, which correspond to 9 to 11 SPARQL endpoints. We could observe that the SPARQL queries seeking for the RDF graph and an RDF graph summarization through class paths were slightly less affected than the remaining.
- **Format Not Supported:** Requests for 6 different SPARQL endpoints have responded with this error (1.43% of requests), which means that the server can only generate a response that is not accepted by the client (status 406).
- **Access Unauthorized:** This issue encompasses the following request responses: the server refuses to respond (status 401 and 403), and authentication is required (status 407 and 511). We observed that three endpoints (0.95% of requests – 4 SPARQL endpoints) required authentication, which we could not provide.
- **Not W3C Compliant:** The request responded with a JSON object that does not follow the JSON format specified by the W3C Recommendation. This issue was observed in 2 SPARQL endpoints (0.48%).

To better understand the issues, we further inspected some of the SPARQL endpoints using the KartoGraphi application[9] [21], which provides an overview of the state

---

[9] Accessible at http://prod-dekalog.inria.fr/.

of the 419 endpoints used in this analysis through the metadata generated by IndeGx. It shows, for instance, that not every SPARQL endpoint is transparent regarding the used vocabularies (only 110 endpoints provide the list of vocabularies used). Furthermore, only 95 endpoints contain a RDF Schema vocabulary, revealing that not every SPARQL endpoint contains the description of RDF Schema, which may explain the higher rate of empty results for the queries retrieving the hierarchies and signature of properties using RDF Schema properties such as subClassOf, subPropertyOf, domain, and range. Moreover, we noticed that some of the SPARQL endpoints do not support the majority of the SPARQL features, which could explain why they did not recognize the syntax of the queries, throwing a bad request error.

5   Related Work

A complete survey of tools designed for LOD exploration is beyond the scope of this paper. For that, we suggest the reading of the comprehensible survey of 70 such tools [12], previous surveys of linked-data based exploration systems [22], and the definitions and models of exploratory search [26]. In this section, we focus on LOD visualization tools that support the exploration of (i) OWL or RDF Schema, (ii) the RDF graph, and (iii) custom datasets represented according to data types, while examining their support to perform tasks of (i) RDF graph/vocabulary inspection, (ii) RDF summarization, and (iii) exploratory search. Table 2 summarizes the reviewed tools according to supported data format, access methods, represented aspects of data, visualization, and interaction tools.

OWL/RDF Schema Visualization. Kremen et al. [20] represent the structure of RDF datasets and the relationship with other datasets by using class/properties statistics, spatial and temporal information, and a dataset summary. Similarly, the tool proposed by Anutariya and Dangol [2] uses a node-link diagram to visualize schema information inferred via SPARQL queries using ontological characteristics of the triples in the LOD data sources.

RDF Graph Visualization. Aiming at simplifying the exploration of large RDF graphs, various visualization tools have been proposed in the literature to support the progressive visual exploration of LOD, which would simply require a particular resource or a RDF dataset as starting point [10,11,19]. In such tools, the RDF graph is represented via a node-link diagram and the user can incrementally reveal or hide neighboring resources via selection operations to explore and visualize relevant data from very large RDF graphs [11], while discovering linked RDF graphs in the Web [19], and inspecting information and internal relations of data subsets [10]. To assist the user in interpreting all nodes and links of an RDF graph as knowledge structures by keeping only interesting triples, Chawuthai and Takeda [8] use graph simplification methods to visualize an RDF graph, which remove redundant triples to present a sparse graph to the user, while ranking triples according to topics of interest.

Frasincar et al. [14] propose an RDF data format plugin for a general-purpose visual environment that supports browsing and editing graph data. Users can define new operations for data processing, visualization, and interaction while being able to modify

Table 2. Summary of related work: publication reference, year, name (if provided), input data type, represented information, data access, visualization type (**CO**: comparison, **CL**: clustering, **D**: distribution, **G**: geographical, **H**: hierarchical, **P**: proportional, **PT**: patterns, **R**: relationship, **T**: temporal, **TT**: text and table), and interaction operations (**CC**: chart customization, **E**: chart export, **F**: data filtering, **M**: visual mapping, **V**: view operations, **DD**: details on demand). **N/A** stands for non-available.

Ref.	Year	Tool	Input Data	Rep.	Data Access	Visualization	Interaction
[13]	2020	S-Paths	RDF Dataset	Per Datatype	RDF Dump	CO, G, H, P, PT	CC, F
[14]	2018	N/A	RDF Dataset	RDF Graph	RDF Dump	H, PT, R	CC, F, M
[2]	2018	VizLOD	RDF Dataset	OWL/RDF Schema	SPARQL / RDF Dump	R	F, V
[20]	2018	Dataset Dashboard	RDF Dataset	OWL/RDF Schema	RDF Dump	R, TT	F, V
[19]	2018	LOD Explorer	RDF Dataset	RDF Graph	JSONP	R	DD, F
[18]	2018	JLO/GIG	SPARQL Result Sets	RDF Graph	SPARQL	CL, R	CC, F, M, V
[8]	2016	N/A	RDF Dataset	RDF Graph	SPARQL construct	R	CC, F
[27]	2016	N/A	SPARQL Result Sets	Per Datatype	SPARQL / RDF Dump	CO, G, P, R	N/A
[32]	2015	LinkDaViz	RDF Dataset	Per Datatype	RDF Dump	CO, D, G, P, T	CC, E, M, V
[10]	2014	LOD/ VizSuite	RDF Dataset	RDF Graph	SPARQL	R	CC, F
[17]	2013	VisualBox	SPARQL Result Sets	Per Datatype	SPARQL	G, R, T	E, F
[3]	2012	LDVM	Non/RDF Dataset	Per Datatype	RDF Dump	G, H, P	F, M, V
[30]	2012	Sgvizler	SPARQL Result Sets	Per Datatype	SPARQL select	CO, D, G, H, R, P, T	N/A
[35]	2011	ViziQuer	SPARQL Result Sets	OWL/RDF Schema	SPARQL	R	F, V
[11]	2007	PGV	RDF Dataset	RDF Graph	SPARQL	R	CC, F, V

visual mapping by changing the shape, size, and color of nodes and edges. Graziosi et al. [18] provide a user-friendly SPARQL query builder to support non-programmers users in extracting data from the Web and exploring it through a node-link diagram.

Likewise, users can modify visual attributes of nodes (shape, color, border, etc.) via a customizable template for the visualization of entities and properties.

Visualization per Datatype. In an attempt to improve the visualization of LOD by considering the characteristics of the data, a few tools have been proposed to analyze the RDF vocabulary of the input data to visualize it accordingly (e.g., data containing properties such as `xsd:date` and `ical:dtstart` would be visualized through timeline or calendar visualizations) [3,27,32]. Similarly, the S-Paths visualization tool [13] supports the visualization of resources sets based on semantic paths by identifying and ranking a set of visualization techniques suitable to explore the data. Via interaction tools, the user can explore different resource sets and/or use different visualization techniques to get a different perspective to the dataset delivered via different semantic paths.

The Visualbox tool [17] generates graph, temporal, and geographical visualizations to explore SPARQL result datasets; it also exports the visualization in a format suitable for incorporation into hypertextual documents. Similarly, the JavaScript wrapper proposed by Skjaeveland [30] generates visualizations of SPARQL result sets via HTML elements, such as web components, embedded with SPARQL SELECT queries, which are rendered to contain the specified visualization type on page load or function call.

Table 3. Summary of related work regarding task support: RDF profiling, RDF summarization, or exploratory search.

Tool & Ref.	RDF graph / vocabulary inspection	RDF Summarization	Exploratory Search
S-Paths [13]			✓
[14]	✓		
VizLOD [2]	✓		
Dataset Dashboard [20]	✓	✓	
LOD Explorer [19]	✓		
JLO/GIG [18]	✓		✓
[8]	✓	✓	
[27]	✓		✓
LinkDaViz [32]	✓		
LOD/ VizSuite [10]			✓
VisualBox [17]			✓
LDVM [3]			✓
Sgvizler [30]			✓
ViziQuer [35]	✓		
PGV [11]	✓		
LDViz	✓	✓	✓

Table 3 presents these related works according to the type of KG exploration they support, i.e. RDF graph/vocabulary inspection, summarization, and exploratory search. To our knowledge, there is no LOD visualization tool that supports all three types of analysis, which can be achieved with LDViz. In particular, the advantage of our approach compared to existing solutions relies on a flexibility that allows users to define meaningful datasets via SPARQL SELECT queries applied to any SPARQL endpoint, so that they can explore multiple aspects of RDF datasets, as well as to progressively explore the LOD Cloud through the usage of follow-up queries launched on the fly to include external data into the exploration process. It also allows users to perform exploratory searches using various complementary visualization techniques, instantiated on demand, focusing on meaningful subsets of data according to the task at hand, instead of a single visualization technique that represents the whole data set, restricting the analysis to a single view of the data.

6 Discussion, Conclusion and Future Work

In this paper, we present a web-based interactive visualization tool for LOD exploration called LDViz. It provides access to any SPARQL endpoint by allowing users to perform searches with SPARQL queries and visualize the results via multiple perspectives delivered through complementary visualization techniques.

KG Exploration Methods. Our approach supports the exploration of KG through a set of methods which we support via a set of SPARQL query templates that allow (i) RDF graph/vocabulary inspection, (ii) RDF summarizations exploration, and (iii) exploratory search. We defined the scope of SPARQL queries through templates that can be reused over any SPARQL endpoint, either directly or after slight modifications to accommodate the RDF vocabulary. We demonstrated their usage and feasibility through a set of use case scenarios and a coverage analysis that apply those queries over 400 SPARQL endpoints.

Visual Design and Interactions. We support exploration search via MGExplorer, a visualization tool for progressively exploring multidimensional network data via multiple complementary views. Users can select subsets of data through visual queries and display the results in a separate view that shows a different perspective to the data. The multiple views can be hidden, revisited, and arranged in the display area in meaningful ways to support efficient data exploration while reducing cognitive overhead and clutter-related issues. The tool provides yet a *follow up query* feature that allow the user to bring external data into the exploration process via predefined queries processed on-the-fly. The different datasets can be simultaneously explored in the same dashboard, enriching the ongoing analysis, while allowing the progressive exploration of the Web.

User Support. When exploring KGs, a great deal of time and effort is spent in testing and debugging SPARQL queries to ensure that the resulting data is sufficient to accomplish the task at hand. Thus, we support data producers and analysts via a SPARQL query editor, where users can test and debug their queries, or import predefined queries, which they may use as templates to create new queries, simplifying the process. Furthermore, to support domain users on their decision-making processes without having to deal with the complexity of the SPARQL language, LDViz includes an interface where users can perform exploratory search through predefined queries. The tool is available at http://dataviz.i3s.unice.fr/ldviz.

Generalization. Through the scope of SPARQL queries defined in this paper, our results showed that LDViz can support the exploration of KGs from about 42% of the 419 analyzed SPARQL endpoints. We noticed that certain queries, such as the ones describing the signature of properties, class and property hierarchies of KGs were less successful encountering issues such as bad request and no results more often than the remaining queries, which may be explained by the SPARQL endpoint missing RDF Schema vocabulary description. In general, we observe that most issues encountered were rather caused by accessibility limitations at the SPARQL endpoint side. We follow the W3C standards, as we believe this ensures the accessibility and homogeneity of data throughout the Web. However, this could be considered a limitation of our approach, as it prevents the visualization of SPARQL endpoints that are not W3C compliant (about 18% of endpoints in our analysis).

Usability and Suitability. Although our use case scenarios and our coverage analysis are enough to support the feasibility and genericity of our approach, user-based evaluations are essential and should be performed to determine the usability and suitability of LDViz. Thus, future work includes developing user-based evaluations to investigate the usability of LDViz to assist the resolution of these and other use cases by expert users in Semantic Web, as well as to assist decision-making processes via exploratory search of RDF graphs, involving expert users in diverse application domains.

Acknowledgements. We are grateful to Ricardo A. Cava, who provided us with the first version of MGExplorer, which was developed as part of his Ph.D. thesis at the Federal University of Rio Grande do Sul. C.D.S. Freitas is funded by the Brazilian funding agencies CNPq and CAPES (Finance Code 001). This work is also partially funded by University of Côte d'Azur through its IDEX[JEDI] program (CC: C870A06232 EOTP: LINKED_OPEN_DATA DF: D103).

Appendix

A - Results of the Coverage Analysis

Table 4. Percentage of SPARQL endpoints per response and per SPARQl query.

Result	RDF graph/vocabulary inspection				RDF Summarization		
	RDF graph	Class hierar-chy	Property hierarchy	Signature of Properties	Class paths	Property paths	Paths Class → Property → Class
Supported	45.35	38.42	37.71	38.42	41.77	45.11	45.58
HTML	16.71	16.71	16.71	15.75	15.99	15.51	15.27
Service Not Found	14.08	14.08	14.08	14.08	14.32	14.32	14.32
Service Unreachable	6.68	6.68	6.68	6.92	8.59	6.92	6.92
Timeout	6.21	5.97	5.97	5.97	7.88	5.97	5.97
No results	0.72	7.88	8.59	8.59	1.43	1.67	1.19
Invalid Certificate	3.10	3.10	3.10	3.10	3.10	3.10	3.10
Bad Request	1.91	2.15	2.15	2.15	1.91	2.39	2.63
CSV	2.39	2.15	2.15	2.15	2.15	2.15	2.15
Format Not Supported	1.43	1.43	1.43	1.43	1.43	1.43	1.43
Access Unauthorized	0.95	0.95	0.95	0.95	0.95	0.95	0.95
Not W3C compliant	0.48	0.48	0.48	0.48	0.48	0.48	0.48

References

1. Antoniazzi, F., Viola, F.: RDF graph visualization tools: a survey. In: 2018 23rd Conference of Open Innovations Association (FRUCT), pp. 25–36. IEEE (2018). https://doi.org/10.23919/FRUCT.2018.8588069
2. Anutariya, C., Dangol, R.: VizLOD: schema extraction and visualization of linked open data. In: 2018 15th International Joint Conference on Computer Science and Software Engineering (JCSSE), pp. 1–6. IEEE (2018). https://doi.org/10.1109/JCSSE.2018.8457325
3. Brunetti, J.M., Auer, S., García, R., Klímek, J., Nečaský, M.: Formal linked data visualization model. In: Proceedings of International Conference on Information Integration and Web-based Applications & Services, pp. 309–318 (2013). https://doi.org/10.1145/2539150.2539162
4. Card, S.K., Mackinlay, J.D., Shneiderman, B. (eds.): Readings in Information Visualization: Using Vision to Think. Morgan Kaufmann Publishers Inc., San Francisco, CA, USA (1999)
5. Cava, R., Freitas, C.D.S.: Glyphs in matrix representation of graphs for displaying soccer games results. In: The 1st Workshop on Sports Data Visualization, vol. 13, p. 15. IEEE (2013)

6. Cava, R., Freitas, C.M.D.S., Winckler, M.: ClusterVis: visualizing nodes attributes in multivariate graphs. In: Proceedings of the Symposium on Applied Computing, pp. 174–179 (2017). https://doi.org/10.1145/3019612.3019684

7. Cava, R., Freitas, C.M., Barboni, E., Palanque, P., Winckler, M.: Inside-in search: an alternative for performing ancillary search tasks on the web. In: 2014 9th Latin American Web Congress, pp. 91–99. IEEE (2014). https://doi.org/10.1109/LAWeb.2014.21

8. Chawuthai, R., Takeda, H.: RDF graph visualization by interpreting linked data as knowledge. In: Qi, G., Kozaki, K., Pan, J.Z., Yu, S. (eds.) JIST 2015. LNCS, vol. 9544, pp. 23–39. Springer, Cham (2016). https://doi.org/10.1007/978-3-319-31676-5_2

9. Corby, O., Gaignard, A., Faron-Zucker, C., Montagnat, J.: KGRAM versatile data graphs querying and inference engine. In: Proceedings of the IEEE/WIC/ACM International Conference on Web Intelligence. Macau (2012)

10. De Vocht, L., et al.: A visual exploration workflow as enabler for the exploitation of linked open data. In: IESD 2014 Proceedings of the 3rd International Conference on Intelligent Exploration of Semantic Data, vol. 1279, pp. 30–41. CER-WS. org (2015)

11. Deligiannidis, L., Kochut, K.J., Sheth, A.P.: RDF data exploration and visualization. In: Proceedings of the ACM First Workshop on CyberInfrastructure: Information Management in eScience, pp. 39–46 (2007). https://doi.org/10.1145/1317353.1317362

12. Desimoni, F., Po, L.: Empirical evaluation of linked data visualization tools. Futur. Gener. Comput. Syst. **112**, 258–282 (2020). https://doi.org/10.1016/j.future.2020.05.038

13. Destandau, M., Appert, C., Pietriga, E.: S-Paths: set-based visual exploration of linked data driven by semantic paths. Semant. Web **12**(1), 99–116 (2021). https://doi.org/10.3233/SW-200383

14. Frasincar, F., Telea, A., Houben, G.J.: Adapting graph visualization techniques for the visualization of RDF data. In: Geroimenko, V., Chen, C. (eds.) Visualizing the Semantic Web, pp. 154–171. Springer, London (2006). https://doi.org/10.1007/1-84628-290-X_9

15. Gandon, F.: A survey of the first 20 years of research on semantic web and linked data. Rev. Sci. Technol. Inf. (2018). https://doi.org/10.3166/ISI.23.3-4.11-56

16. Gandon, F., Hall, W.: A never-ending project for humanity called "the Web". In: WWW 2022 - ACM Web Conference. Lyon (virtual), France (2022). https://doi.org/10.1145/3485447.3514195

17. Graves, A.: Creation of visualizations based on linked data. In: Proceedings of the 3rd International Conference on Web Intelligence, Mining and Semantics, pp. 1–12 (2013). https://doi.org/10.1145/2479787.2479828

18. Graziosi, A., Di Iorio, A., Poggi, F., Peroni, S., Bonini, L.: Customising LOD views: a declarative approach. In: Proceedings of the 33rd Annual ACM Symposium on Applied Computing, pp. 2185–2192 (2018). https://doi.org/10.1145/3167132.3167367

19. Jacksi, K., Zeebaree, S.R., Dimililer, N.: LOD explorer: presenting the web of data. Int. J. Adv. Comput. Sci. Appl. IJACSA **9**(1), 1–7 (2018)

20. Kremen, P., Saeeda, L., Blasko, M.: Dataset dashboard-a SPARQL endpoint explorer. In: VOILA@ ISWC, pp. 70–77 (2018)

21. Maillot, P., Corby, O., Faron, C., Gandon, F., Michel, F.: KartoGraphI: drawing a map of linked data. In: ESWC 2022. LNCS, vol. 13384, pp. 112–117. Springer, Berlin (2022). https://doi.org/10.1007/978-3-031-11609-4_21

22. Marie, N., Gandon, F.: Survey of linked data based exploration systems. In: IESD 2014 - Intelligent Exploitation of Semantic Data. Riva Del Garda, Italy (2014). https://hal.inria.fr/hal-01057035

23. Menin, A., Cava, R., Freitas, C.M.D.S., Corby, O., Winckler, M.: Towards a visual approach for representing analytical provenance in exploration processes. In: 2021 25th International Conference Information Visualisation (IV), pp. 21–28 (2021). https://doi.org/10.1109/IV53921.2021.00014

24. Menin, A., et al.: Using chained views and follow-up queries to assist the visual exploration of the web of big linked data. Int. J. Human-Comput. Int., 1–7 (2022). https://hal.archives-ouvertes.fr/hal-03518845

25. Menin, A., Faron Zucker, C., Corby, O., Dal Sasso Freitas, C.M., Gandon, F., Winckler, M.: From linked data querying to visual search: towards a visualization pipeline for LOD exploration. In: WEBIST 2021 17th International Conference on Web Information Systems and Technologies. France (2021). https://doi.org/10.5220/0010654600003058

26. Palagi, E., Gandon, F., Troncy, R., Giboin, A.: A survey of definitions and models of exploratory search. In: ESIDA 2017 - ACM Workshop on Exploratory Search and Interactive Data Analytics, pp. 3–8. Limassol, Cyprus (2017). https://doi.org/10.1145/3038462.3038465

27. Peña, O., Aguilera, U., López-de Ipiña, D.: Exploring LOD through metadata extraction and data-driven visualizations. Program (2016)

28. Pietriga, E.: Semantic web data visualization with graph style sheets. In: Proceedings of the 2006 ACM Symposium on Software Visualization, pp. 177–178 (2006)

29. Recommentation, W.: SPARQL 1.1 query results JSON format. https://www.w3.org/TR/2013/REC-sparql11-results-json-20130321/. Accessed 11 Apr 2022

30. Skjæveland, M.G.: Sgvizler: a javascript wrapper for easy visualization of SPARQL result sets. In: Simperl, E., et al. (eds.) ESWC 2012. LNCS, vol. 7540, pp. 361–365. Springer, Heidelberg (2015). https://doi.org/10.1007/978-3-662-46641-4_27

31. Telea, A.C.: Data Visualization: Principles and Practice. CRC Press, Boca Raton (2014)

32. Thellmann, K., Galkin, M., Orlandi, F., Auer, S.: LinkDaViz – automatic binding of linked data to visualizations. In: ISWC 2015. LNCS, vol. 9366, pp. 147–162. Springer, Cham (2015). https://doi.org/10.1007/978-3-319-25007-6_9

33. Vandenbussche, P.Y., Umbrich, J., Matteis, L., Hogan, A., Buil-Aranda, C.: SPARQLES: monitoring public SPARQL endpoints. Semant. Web 8(6), 1049–1065 (2017). https://doi.org/10.3233/SW-170254

34. Yamamoto, Y., Yamaguchi, A., Splendiani, A.: YummyData: providing high-quality open life science data. Database 2018, 1–12 (2018). https://doi.org/10.1093/database/bay022

35. Zviedris, M., Barzdins, G.: ViziQuer: a tool to explore and query SPARQL endpoints. In: Antoniou, G., et al. (eds.) ESWC 2011. LNCS, vol. 6644, pp. 441–445. Springer, Heidelberg (2011). https://doi.org/10.1007/978-3-642-21064-8_31

Flexible Detection of Similar DOM Elements

Julián Grigera[1,2,3]([✉]), Juan Cruz Gardey[1,2], Gustavo Rossi[1,2], and Alejandra Garrido[1,2]

[1] LIFIA, Fac. de Informática, Univ. Nac. La Plata, 1900 La Plata, CP, Argentina
`{juliang,jcgardey,gustavo,garrido}@lifia.info.unlp.edu.ar`
[2] CONICET, Buenos Aires, Argentina
[3] CICPBA, La Plata, Argentina

Abstract. Different research fields related to the web require detecting similarity between DOM elements. In the field of information extraction, many approaches emerged to extract structured data from web documents, most of which require comparing sample documents to extract their underlying structure. Other fields of applicability like web augmentation or transcoding also require analyzing structural similarity, but on UI components with smaller structures than full documents, making them unsuitable for the algorithms generally used in information extraction. Instead, these approaches tend to rely on the DOM elements' location, but this does not resist structural changes in the document, and cannot locate similar elements placed in different positions. In this paper we present two flexible algorithms to measure similarity between DOM elements by using a mixed approach that considers both elements' location and inner structure, together with a wrapper induction technique. We evaluated our algorithms with respect to other known approaches in the literature by comparing how they cluster a dataset of 1200+ DOM elements, using a manual clustering as ground truth. Results show that both proposed algorithms outperform all baseline ones. The proposed algorithms run in linear time, so they are faster than most approaches that analyze structural similarity.

Keywords: DOM · Information extraction · Web adaptation

1 Introduction

Detecting similar elements in web interfaces is an important task in different fields of research. In Information Extraction's, the goal is to retrieve information from structured documents, which in turn requires analyzing similar documents for understanding their common underlying structure. In the Web Augmentation field, is usually necessary to detect similar elements in the web interfaces, so they can all be reached and modified in the same way. Both fields have naturally devised different algorithms to determine whether 2 elements in the DOM (Document Object Model) are similar, which usually means that they share a common template.

Since information extraction generally focuses in retrieving data from full documents, these algorithms tend to analyze the structure of their DOM (Document Object Model) for comparison. Conversely, in web augmentation, there is more interest in detecting smaller DOM elements, so it is usual to use their location within the document to compare them. and rely less on their inner structure. For instance, a product

M. Marchiori et al. (Eds.): WEBIST 2020/2021, LNBIP 469, pp. 174–195, 2023.
https://doi.org/10.1007/978-3-031-24197-0_10

page in an e-commerce application could typically be structured by a layout template (which defines a header, menu and footer) and a list of ratings, each defined by the same smaller-scaled template, as shown in Fig. 1.

Using locators to establish similarity is quite effective for detecting elements that appear repeatedly in a same or different pages, but could present problems if these elements appear in different places, or when the outer structure suffer changes (hence, changing the elements' location).

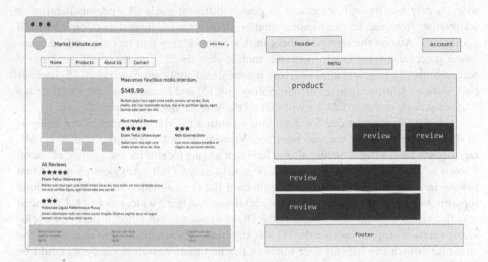

Fig. 1. A sample page with different templates. The review widget is highlighted.

1.1 DOM Structure Detection in Information Extraction

The field of Information Extraction aims at retrieving structured information from web applications, which requires to understand the semantics of the data. In the example shown in Fig. 1, it is important to tell apart the rating text from the author and the date of submission. This is usually achieved by analyzing the underlying structure of web documents. Given that information extraction is generally performed on repeating structures (e.g. all product pages in an e-commerce website), this field usually resorts to find the underlying HTML template, since most data intensive websites generate their content dynamically. In consequence, several approaches were devised to discover such templates by studying the structure of many similar pages [25].

A common way of doing this consists in clustering functionally equivalent components and then designing cluster-specific mining algorithms [17,24]. These approaches typically produce a *wrapper*, which can be though of as a reverse-engineered template. Once the similar pages are grouped in clusters, the wrapper is generated by identifying the common structure within each cluster [17]. Wrappers are then used to analyze similar pages and extract their raw contents, in a similar way than regular expressions can be used to extract information from structured text.

Several algorithms used to cluster similar pages compute **tree edit distance** between the DOM structure of entire pages [24,25]. Since these algorithms are computationally expensive, other approaches have been proposed to measure structural similarity with improved execution time, but mostly at the expense of accuracy [4]. Other approaches in the area of Web Engineering even use variants of Web Scraping to make the application development process easier [23].

1.2 DOM Structure Detection in Web Augmentation

Web augmentation is another area that requires understanding DOM structure in order to externally modify web interfaces to pursue different goals like personalization or adaptation. However, in these cases, smaller elements are detected as opposed to full documents. Among the research works in this area we may find techniques like adaptation mechanisms for touch- operated mobile devices [22], transcoding to improve accessibility [2], augmentation to create personalized applications versions [5] and our own work on refactoring to improve usability [14, 15] and accessibility [9]. For the sake of conciseness, in this article we will call all these techniques *web adaptations*.

A widely used technique for detecting repeating HTML structures is the analysis of the DOM structure of the web interface. Viewing the page as a collection of HTML tags organized in a tree structure allows having a unique locator for each single element, known as XPath. Using an XPath, it is relatively easy to tell equivalent elements that belong in a repeating structure, like items on a list (`<li>` within a `<ul>`), or simple repetition of generic `<div>` tags. This technique has been widely used [1, 12] and it usually works well for detecting similar DOM elements, but since it depends exclusively on their locations within the HTML structure, it is not resilient to changes in the structure (which can happen over time) or the fact that equivalent elements could be located at different positions in the same page (or even different pages). In the example presented in Fig. 1, the product page has a list of ratings at the bottom, but there is also a short list of the 2 most helpful ratings at the top. In this case, relying only on the XPath of the rating widgets would lead to incorrect results.

1.3 Contributions

The work presented in this paper intends to overcome the issues of both families of algorithms previously described, i.e. internal structure comparison (like tree edit distance) and path comparison (like XPath analysis). For this purpose we propose an algorithm that combine the strenghts of both approaches, with enough flexibility to prefer one over the other depending on the situation. This means that, when needing to compare large DOM elements, it should rely on inner structure comparison, but when these elements have few inner nodes, and hence the risk of grouping dissimilar elements is higher, it should switch to comparing their location within the document.

In this paper we describe a web widget comparision algorithm that's designed to adapt to differently sized DOM elements. This algorithm is based on the comparison of both XPath locators and inner structure, including relevant tag attributes. Additionally, a variant of this algorithm is shown, which considers also on-screen dimensions and position of the elements. Our algorithms can successfully compare and cluster elements as small as single nodes but has also the flexibility to compare larger elements with the same accuracy, or even better than state-of-the-art methods. These algorithms, namely **Scoring Map** and **Scoring Map Dimensional Variant** were first presented on a previous article [13], and in this work we extend it in different directions.

More specifically, the contributions of this paper are the following:

- We extend the related work section with other works that are relevant to our proposal.
- We describe the Scoring Map and its dimensional variant algorithms with greater detail, including improvements on their past implementation, and the rationale behind the algorithm's design.
- We show how we optimized the algorithm's parameters in order to get better results.
- We extend the previous experiment with new samples and analysis, and evaluate the performance of the algorithms with an additional measure.

2 Related Work

Detecting DOM element similarity has been covered in the literature in the context of different research areas, like web augmentation or web scraping. Because of the broad applicability of this simple task, many different techniques have emerged. Some of these techniques are applicable to any tree structure, and some are specific to XML or HTML structures. Many of these methods can be found in an early review by Buttler [4].

In this section we describe many of these works, and organize them in three main groups: tree edit distance algorithms, bag of paths methods, and other approaches. We also briefly describe some other algorithms that serve the same purpose but take radically different approaches.

2.1 Tree Edit Distance Algorithms

Since DOM elements can be represented as tree structures, they can be compared with similarity measures between trees, such as edit distance. This technique is a generalization of string edit distance algorithms like Levenshtein's [18], in which two strings are similar depending on the amount of edit operations required to go from one to the other. Operations typically consist in adding or removing a character and replacing one character for another.

Since the Tree Edit Distance algorithms are generally very time-consuming (up to quadratic time complexity), different approaches emerged to improve their performance. One of the first of such algorithms was proposed by Tai [26], and it uses mappings (i.e. sets of edit operations without a specific order) to calculate tree-to-tree edition cost. Following Tai's, other algorithms based on mappings were proposed, mainly focused on improving the running times. A popular one is RTDM (Restricted Top-Down Distance Metric) [25], which uses mappings such as Tai's but with restrictions on the mappings that make it faster. Building on RTDM, Omer et al. [24] developed SiSTeR, which is an adaptation that weights the repetition of elements in a special manner, in order to consider as similar two HTML structures that differ only in the number of similar children at any given level (e.g. two blog posts with different amounts of comments).

Other restricted mapping methods were developed, like the bottom-up distance [27], but RTDM and its variants are best suited for DOM elements where nodes closer to the root are generally more relevant than the leaves.

Griasev and Ramanauskaite modified the TED algorithm to compare HTML blocks [11]. They weight the cost of the edit operations depending on the tree level in which they are performed, giving a greater cost to those that occur at a higher level. Moreover, since different HTML tags can be used to achieve the same result, their version of the algorithm also accounts for tag interchangeability. Fard and Mesbah also developed a variant of the TED algorithm to calculate the diversity of two DOM trees [7], in which the amount of edit operations are normalized by the number of nodes of the biggest tree.

TED algorithms have also been proposed to compare entire web pages [28]. This work defines the similarity of two web pages as the edit distance between their block trees, which are structures that contain both structural and visual information.

2.2   Bag of Paths

Another approach to calculate similarity between trees is by gathering all paths/ sequences of nodes that result from traversing the tree from the root to each leaf node, and then comparing similarity between the bags of paths of different trees. An implementation of this algorithm for general trees was published by Joshi et al. [17], with a variant for the specific case of XPaths in HTML documents. The latter was used in different approaches for documents clustering [12].

The bag of paths method has one peculiarity: the paths of nodes for a given tree ignore the siblings' relationships, and only preserve the parent-child links. This results in a simpler algorithm that can still get very good results in the comparisons. We have similar structural restrictions in our algorithms, as we explain later on in Sect. 3. The time complexity of this method is $O(n2N)$, where n denotes the number of documents and N the number of paths.

Another proposal similar to the Bag of Paths approach in the broader context of hierarchical data structures, is by using pq-grams [3]. This work takes structurally rich subtrees and represents them as pq-grams, which can be represented as sequences. Each tree to be compared is represented as a set of pq-grams, then used in the comparison. This performs in $O(n \log n)$, where n is the number of tree nodes. Our approach is similar to the aforementioned one in how it generates linear sequences to represent and eventually compare tree structures, although relying less on topological information and more on nodes' specific information (such as HTML attributes).

2.3   Locator-Based Comparison

Most of the previous methods focus on the inner structure of documents, but few consider external factors (amongst the ones commented here, only the work of Grigalis and Çenys [12] use inbound links to determine similarity). The reason is that these approaches are generally designed to compare full documents. There are however some works focused on comparing smaller elements where external factors like location play a key role. Amagasa, Wen and Kitagawa [1] use XPath expressions to identify elements in XML documents, which is an effective approach given that XML definitions usually have more diverse and meaningful labels than, for instance, HTML.

Other works focused on HTML elements also use tag paths: Zheng, Song, Wen, and Giles generate wrappers for small elements to extract information from single entities [31]. The authors propose a mixed approach based on a "broom" structure, where tag paths are used identify potentially similar elements, and then inner structure analysis is performed to generate wrappers. Our approach is also a combined method that considers some of the inner structure of the elements, but also their location inside the document that contain them.

2.4 Other Approaches

Different approaches have been developed that have little or no relation with tree edition distance or paths comparison. Many approaches like the one proposed by Zeng et al. [30], rely on visual cues from browser renderings to identify similar visual patterns on webpages without depending on the DOM structure. Another interesting work is that of using fingerprinting to represent documents [16], enabling a fast way of comparing documents without the need of traversing them completely, but by comparing their hashes instead. Locality preserving hashes are particularly appealing in this context, since the hash codes change according to their contents, instead of avoiding collisions like regular hash functions.

String-based comparison have also been proposed to find differences and similarities between DOM trees. The work of Mesbah and Prasad uses a XML-differencing tool to detect DOM-level mismatches that have a visual impact on web pages rendered on different browsers [21]. Moreover Mesbah et al., developed a DOM tree comparison algorithm to derive the different states of a target UI to support automatic testing of AJAX applications [20]. This comparison is based on a pipeline of"comparators", in which each comparator eliminates specific parts of the DOM tree (such as irrelevant attributes). At the end, after all the desired differences are removed, a simple string comparison determines the equality of the two DOM strings.

3 Proposed Algorithm

We devised an algorithm that has the capability of comparing DOM elements of different sizes. This flexibility is achieved considering both the element's internal structure and location within the DOM tree. As the inner structure grows larger, the more relevant it becomes in the final score. Conversely, when the structure is small, the location path gains more relevance. This design makes the algorithm actually prefer the inner structure when possible, since it is a better strategy to resist DOM changes or compare differently located but equivalent elements. It will rely on the element's location when the inner structure size is insufficient to tell DOM elements apart. We also introduce a variant that considers also the elements' dimensions and position as rendered on the screen.

The algorithm generates a dictionary-like structure (i.e. a map) for each DOM element, which contains structural information through its HTML tags and attributes (keys) and relevance scores (values). These maps can be compared to obtain a similarity score between any two DOM elements. This map, and the comparison algorithm are both used for a wrapper induction technique, which is important for different applicabilities of the algorithm.

3.1 Rationale

The main idea behind the algorithm is to compare elements' structure and location, in terms of inner HTML tags and path from the document's root, respectively. In order to do this, it first captures both structure and location of each element to compare, as shown in Fig. 2.

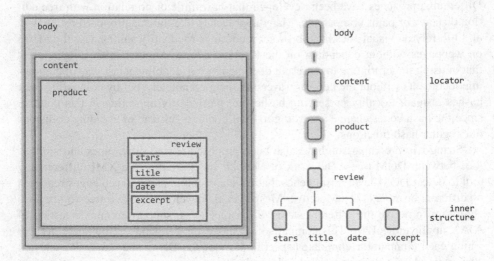

Fig. 2. A schematic of a DOM element as seen in its containing document (left), and the catured data for comparison in terms of location and structure (right).

Regarding inner structure comparison, the algorithm looks for matches in the tags that are at the same level. For instance, if the root tag of both elements being compared is the same, that counts as a coincidence. If a direct child of the root matches a direct child of the other element, it also counts as a coincidence, but to a lesser degree than the root element. This degree is defined by a score that decreases as the algorithm moves farther away from the root towards the leaves. The criterion behind this decision is that equivalend DOM elements usually present some kind of variability, e.g. two product panels may come from the same template, but only one of them shows a discount price. This variability tends to happen farther from the root of the element, so the algorithm was designed for this to have a lesser impact in the comparision, making it resistent to small variations but sensitive to more prominent ones.

Inner structure comparison doesn not only compare tag names, but it also considers tag attributes. Attributes are only captured by their name, and not their values, since their presence and number is usually enough to determine equivalent tags. There is only one exception, the `class` attribute, since it's abundantly present in many tags, and its values are usually shared between equivalent DOM elements that, in this case, makes them more useful than the simple tag presence. It is worth mentioning that the `id` attribute's value would not be helpful in this case, since this value is meant to be unique in the document, hence hindering the algorithm's ability to match equivalent elements that will naturally have different ids.

The outer comparison, which is the comparison of the elements' paths, is similar to the inner part. The main difference is that the way to the root of the document is a list and not a tree, so there is exactly one tag at each level.

3.2 Scoring Map Generation

The proposed algorithm processes the comparison in two steps: first, it generates a map of the DOM elements to be compared, where some fundamental aspects are captured, such as tag names organized by level (i.e., depth within the tree), along with relevant attributes (e.g. class), but ignoring text nodes. Then, these maps are compared to each other, generating a similarity score, which is a number between 0 and 1. The main benefit of constructing such map structure, which is created in linear time, is that it enables computing the similarity measure also in linear time (with respect to the number of nodes). The map summarizes key aspects of the elements' structure and location. Considering a single DOM element's tree structure, the map captures the following information for each node:

- Level number, which indicates depth in the DOM tree, where the target node's level is 0, its children 1, and so on. Parent nodes are also included using negative levels, i.e. the closest ancestor has level -1.
- Tag name, often used as label in general tree algorithms.
- Relevant attributes, in particular CSS class.
- Score, which is a number assigned by the algorithm representing the relevance of the previous attributes when comparison is made.

In the map, the level number, tag name and attributes together compose the key, and the score is the value, but since HTML nodes can contain many attributes, there will be one key for each, with the same level number and tag name. This way, a node will in fact generate many entries in the map, one for each attribute. For example, if a DOM element contains the following node:

```
<div id="container" class="main zen">
```

the map is populated with 3 entries: one for the div label alone, one for the div label with the id attribute, and 2 more for the class attribute, one for each value: main and zen. Only values of the class attribute are considered, other attributes are kept without their values. In this case, all three entries would get a same score (later in this section we explain how this is determined). Also, if this element were repeated, only one set of entries would be entered since a map cannot have repeated keys, which is actually a desirable property for an algorithm that applies to HTML elements. Documents generated by HTML templates typically contain iteratively generated data, e.g., comments in a post. In this case, two posts from a same template should always be considered similar, no matter the different amounts of comments on each one. Therefore, comparing only one entry for a set of equivalent DOM elements is likely to obtain better results than considering them as distinct [24].

This map organization is important in the second step of the algorithm, where the actual comparison is made based on these scores. A full example of a DOM element and its scoring map is depicted in Fig. 3.

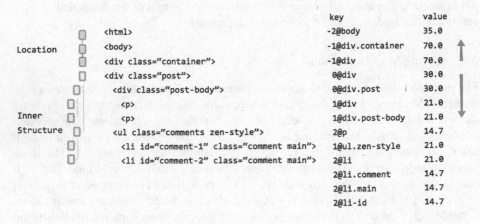

	key	value
`<html>`	-2@body	35.0
`<body>`	-1@div.container	70.0
`<div class="container">`	-1@div	70.0
`<div class="post">`	0@div	30.0
`<div class="post-body">`	0@div.post	30.0
`<p>`	1@div	21.0
`<p>`	1@div.post-body	21.0
`<ul class="comments zen-style">`	2@p	14.7
`<li id="comment-1" class="comment main">`	1@ul.zen-style	21.0
`<li id="comment-2" class="comment main">`	2@li	21.0
	2@li.comment	14.7
	2@li.main	14.7
	2@li-id	14.7

Location — Inner Structure

Fig. 3. A DOM element along with its generated scoring map. Yellow indicates outer path and green indicates inner structure. (Color figure online)

Two initial score values are set in the map: one at the root, and one at the first parent node (levels 0 and −1, respectively). These scores decrease sideways, i.e. from the root down to the leaves, and from the first parent node up to the higher ancestors.

In the original algorithm [13] the initial score for the parent node was generated inversely proportional to the height of the tree. The rationale behind this is to give the algorithm the flexibility to detect similar elements relying less on their location when the trees are large enough, so the inner structure scores get more weight on the overall comparison. In the new algorithm, we simply allow any initial relevance, both outer and inner. This still keeps the same properties, since the number of levels determine the amount of key/value tuples that will populate the map. The taller the inner tree is, the more values in the map to represent it. Conversely, when the tree is shorter, the external path entries gain more relevance. This design made the algorithm simpler, while keeping its flexibility.

Another distinctive aspect of the map structure is the elements' limited knowledge of their tree structure. Notice that the only information for each node regarding this structure is the level number (or depth), which ignores the parent-child relationships and also the order. The results obtained in the experiment described in the following section, showed that this makes the algorithm simpler and faster, and does not implicate a significant decrease in the obtained scores.

3.3   Maps Comparison

Once there is a map for the 2 elements to be compared, they are used to get a score that's based on the values at each level. The final similarity score between the two elements is made by comparing the values of their maps. The following formula describes how we obtain the similarity S between two elements once their maps m and n are generated:

$$S(m,n) = \frac{\sum_{k \in (K(m) \cap K(n))} max(m[k], n[k]) * 2}{\sum_{k \in K(m)} m[k] + \sum_{k \in K(n)} n[k]}$$

The function K(m) answers the set of keys of map m, and m[k] returns the score for the key k in the map m. In the dividend summation, we obtain the intersection of the keys for both maps. For each of these keys, we obtain the scores in both maps and get the highest value (with max(m[k],n[k])) times 2. The divisor term adds the total scores of both maps.

Intuitively, this function compares similitude between maps by their common keys with respect to the total number of combined keys. This is similar to the Jaccard index for sample sets, which calculates the ratio between intersection and union. This makes sense for comparing maps, since for comparison purposes they can be seen as sets of keys - that cannot be repeated. The way the Bag of Paths algorithm calculates similarity in the same way [17].

3.4   Scoring Map with Dimensional Awareness

We devised an alternative algorithm that also considers size and position of the elements to improve the detection of similar elements when their inner structure is scarce. This criterion relies on geometric properties to determine if two elements are part of a series of repetitive, similar widgets.

It is usual for repeating DOM elements to be aligned, either vertically or horizontally. In such cases, it is also usual for one of their dimensions to be also equal; in the case of horizontal alignment, the height (e.g. a top navigation menu), and in the case of vertical alignment, the width (e.g. products listing). By using these properties in repetitive elements, we obtain a dimensional similarity measure between 0 and 1 for either of the two cases (i.e. vertical or horizontal alignment), in the compared elements.

For each of the two potential alignments, this measure is calculated by obtaining the absolute values of the proportional differences in position and dimension. The higher of both alignment measures is then considered as an extra weighted term to the similarity formula. A visual example is shown in Fig. 4.

In current web applications, it is usual to find responsive layouts that adapt their contents to different devices. This could harm the dimensional scores when different sized elements are the same but rendered in different devices. Depending on the case, this may lead to wrong results, but also can be beneficial to detect them as different elements, e.g. in the field of applicability of web adaptation where different adaptations can be applied to the UI depending on the device.

This variant has shown improvements over the base algorithm in elements with little structure, but imposes an extra step in the capture to gather the elements' bound boxes. The base algorithm, on the other hand, can be applied to any DOM element represented with the HTML code only.

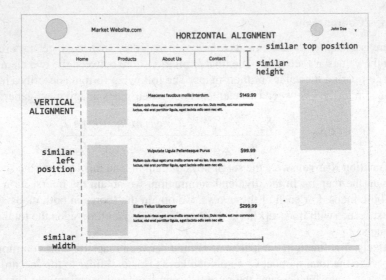

Fig. 4. Dimensional alignment example with DOM Elements.

3.5 Time Complexity

The proposed algorithm runs in O(n), i.e. linear time, with respect to the size of the compared trees (being n the total number of nodes). Since stages of the comparision, i.e. the generation of the scoring map and the maps comparison, happen in linear time, we can conclude that the algorithm runs in linear time too.

It should be noticed that calculating the intersection of keys for the second step (function $K(m)$ in the formula) is linear given that only one of the structures is traversed, while the other is accessed by key, which is generally considered constant (O(1)) for maps or dictionaries (although it can be, depending on the language, linear with respect to the size of the key).

When applying the algorithm to larger DOM structures, e.g. full documents, some improvements could be made to make this time worst case O(n) in practice, by applying a cutoff value when the relevance score drops below a certain level. This could reduce the trees traversing significantly, and consequently decrease the size of the maps, while keeping the most relevant score components.

3.6 Wrapper Induction

Being information extraction one of the potential areas of applicability of our algorithm, it is important to be able to generate a matching template for the elements being "scraped", i.e. a *wrapper*.

We developed a way of generating wrappers with the same maps that we use for comparing elements. A first element is taken as reference to generate a base map the same way we explain in Sect. 3.2. Then, as new elements are taken into consideration, we refine the base map to iteratively generate the wrapper. The way to achieve this is by generating a new map for each new element (we will refer to as candidate map) and apply the comparison algorithm, also described in Sect. 3.2. Depending on the result of this comparison, we apply either positive or negative reinforcements over the base map.

When comparing a candidate map with the base map, if the result of the comparison exceeds a given similarity threshold, we will first find all the intersecting keys of both maps. The scores for these keys on the base maps are positively reinforced, by adding a value that is calculated as a proportion of the score for the same key in the candidate map. During our experiments, we have obtained best results with a proportion of 0.35. When the result of the comparison between candidate and base maps do not reach the similarity threshold, a negative reinforcement is applied in a similar way, also to the intersecting keys, by subtracting the same reinforcement value. It is important that, no matter how much negative reinforcement a score gets, it never reaches a value below zero.

Intuitively, those keys that are shared among similar elements, will get a higher score once the wrapper induction is done. Conversely, those keys that are too common, i.e. present in many different elements in the document, will get a lower score, until eventually reaching zero. This way, only the distinctive keys (which represent tags and attributes) end up being the most relevant in the wrapper.

4 Validation

In order to test the efficacy of our algorithm, we carried out an experiment using DOM elements from several real websites. The main objective was to compare the ability of the algorithm to group together DOM elements that are equivalent, that is, show the same kind of structured data, or serve the same purpose (in the case of actionable elements such as menu items or buttons). We compare the algorithm's performance with 3 others used as baselines, using a manual clustering as reference.

A similar experiment is described in our previous work [13], but we have extended the number of samples and cases. We also show different post-hoc analyses that offer new insights of the results. All the resources for replicating the validation are available online[1].

4.1 Dataset Generation

We created a dataset with small and medium DOM elements from real websites. To do this, we first had to create a tool for capturing the elements, and then generate the reference groups. The tool allows for selecting DOM elements from any website with the help of a highlighter to accurately display the limits of each element, and grouping them together for generating a reference cluster. We implemented our tool as a Grease-Monkey[2] script, with a Pharo Smalltalk backend[3], storing the elements in a MongoDB database.

---

[1] https://github.com/juliangrigera/scoring-map.

[2] https://addons.mozilla.org/en-GB/firefox/addon/greasemonkey/.

[3] https://pharo.org.

Using our tool, we captured **1204** DOM elements grouped in **197** reference clusters from a total **54** websites. The elements ranged from medium sized widgets like forum comments or item presentations (such as products) to smaller components like menu items, buttons or even atomic components like dates within larger elements. We also aimed at capturing equivalent elements placed in different locations of the page to represent the situations where a template is reused, but it was also a good approximation for the scenario where the document DOM structure changes over time. These, however, were a small proportion with respect to the total dataset.

Clustering comparison is not a trivial task, and different metrics can favor (or fail at) particular scenarios. For this reason, we selected 2 different metrics to evaluate all the algorithms. The first one, also used in the original experiment, is f-score, which is based on a precision/recall analysis of counting pairs. The second analysis is an asymmetric index based on cluster overlapping.

4.2   Preparation

We implemented 3 algorithms from the literature to use as baseline, each one representing a family of algorithms covered in Sect. 2. For the tree edit distance algorithms, we chose RTDM [25], for being more performant than starndard tree edit distance, and having available pseudocode. In the bag of paths area, we chose the Bag of XPath algorithm [17]. Finally, for the locator-based algorithms we implemented a straightforward XPath comparison, which is the root of many of such algorithms, which usually add variations. Using this algorithm, two DOM elements are considered similar if their XPaths match, considering only the labels, i.e., ignoring the indices. For example, the following XPaths:

```
/body/div[1]/ul[2]/li[3]
/body/div[2]/ul[2]/li[2]
```

would match when using this criterion, since only the concrete indices differ.

After implementing the algorithms, we performed parameter optimization: almost all the algorithms required a similarity threshold to be set. XPath comparision was the only exception, since it does not produce a similarity score but a boolean result, the clustering procedure does not depend on the order in which the elements are fed. Additionally, the Scoring Map algorithm requires two initial scores for creating the maps of the elements to be compared: one for the root of the target element (inner relevance), and the other one for the parent node (outer relevance).

With the aim of finding the parameters values that give the highest performance (in terms of f-score described in next section), we performed a bayessian hyperparameter optimization. Bayessian methods can find better settings than random search in fewer iterations, by evaluating parameters that appear more promising from past iterations.

We used HyperOpt Python library[4] which requires four arguments to run the optimization: a search space to look for the scores, an objective function that takes in the scores and outputs the value to be maximized, and a criteria to select the next scores in each iteration. The search space for both the inner and outer relevance was an interval

---

[4] https://github.com/hyperopt/hyperopt/.

between 0 and 100 uniformly distributed, while the space for the threshold was an interval between 0 and 1. The objetive function runs the maps comparison with the selected threshold and relevance scores in the target dataset and returns the resulting f-score negated, because the optimization algorithm expects from the objetive function a value to minimize. Lastly, the criteria to select the scores is Tree of Parzen Estimators (TPE).

We ran the optimizer perfoming 100 iterations over the search space for each of the implemented algorithms. The highest reached f-score for the Scoring Map was 0.9916, with *outer relevance* = 39.65, *inner relevance* = 57 and *threshold* = 0.7. Regarding RTDM and Bag of XPath, the highest f-score was 0.338 and 0.339 with the thresholds 0.8 and 0.54 respectively.

4.3   Procedure

We ran all 5 algorithms (the 3 baseline ones, plus the 2 proposed in this paper) on the dataset, and then analyzed the clustering that each one produced. The clustering procedure consisted in adding the elements one by one; if a group was found in which at least one element was considered similar, then the new element was added to that group, otherwise, a new group with the new element was created. Since for some algorithms the clustering is prone to change depending on the order in which the elements are added, we ran these algorithms with 20 different random orders and obtained the average numbers, and also calculated Standard Deviation to find the degree of this alteration in the results. The results for the XPaths algorithm showed no alteration whatsoever with different orders of elements, given that in this case there is no similarity metric involved but equality comparisons.

We compared all the clusterings with the manual one. For the f-score analysis we used pair comparison: since clusterings are not simple classification problems with predefined classes, there is a special interpretation for calculating precision and recall. Given two elements:

- if both the automated and reference clustering place them in the same group, then we consider this case a **true positive**.
- if both the automated and reference clustering place them in different groups, then we consider this a **true negative**
- if both elements are in the same group in the reference clustering but not in the automated clustering, we consider it a **false negative**
- if the automated clustering incorrectly groups the two elements together when the reference clustering does not, we consider this case a **false positive**.

Thanks to this method, we were able to calculate precision, recall and f-score for the automated clustering methods.

Given the interpretation for false/true positives and negatives, the formula for calculating the precision and recall metrics is standard. In the case of the f-score, we specifically use a F1-Score formula, since we want to value precision and recall the same:

$$F1 = 2 * \frac{precision * recall}{precision + recall}$$

This value represents a weighted average of precision and recall measures.

188   J. Grigera et al.

In addition to the f-score measure, we calculated an overlapping baser measure proposed by Meilă and Heckerman [19], which is relevant to our work since all baseline clusterings are compared to a reference clustering taken as ground truth. The formula used is the following:

$$MH(C, C') = 1/n \sum_{i=1}^{k} \max_{C'_j \in C}(|C_i \cap C'_j|)$$

where C' is the manual reference clustering, and C is the clustering automatically generated by the algorithm. In the rest of the paper we will refer to this measure as *MH*.

4.4 Results

Results are shown in Table 1 and Fig. 5. Regarding the f-score analysis, it is important to remark that, the precision/recall and f-score values are averaged from a set of 20 executions with different elements' order (except for the XPath algorithm), so obtaining an f-score by applying the formula to the Precision and Recall values on the corresponding columns will not necessarily match the values on the f-score column.

Table 1. Evaluation results, including number of false positives and negatives for f-score analysis.

Algorithm	F. Positives	F. Negatives	Precision	Recall	F-Score	MH
Bag of XPaths	17503	380	0.2070	0.9231	0.3863	0.3382
RTDM	17060	467	0.2080	0.9056	0.3384	0.4088
XPaths	1252	420	0.7834	0.9151	0.8442	0.5780
Scoring Map	0	358	1.0	0.9276	0.9625	0.8219
Scoring Map (D)	0	436	1.0	0.9117	0.9538	0.7847

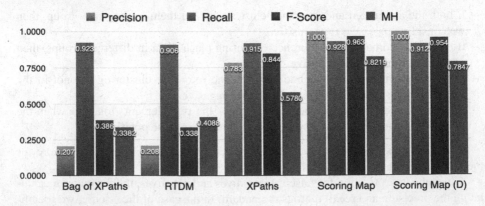

Fig. 5. Evaluation results. Precision, Recall and F1 Score, and Meilă-Heckerman measure.

There is a pronounced difference both in f-score and MH measure, between the algorithms that consider the elements' inner structure, more prepared for comparing full documents, and the algorithms that consider the location of the elements, namely XPath, Scoring Map and Scoring Map dimensional variant.

Both Scoring Map and Scoring Map dimensional variant outperformed the baseline ones in f-score and MH measure. Regarding precision and recall, our algorithms got perfect precision, while shared a similar recall value with all baseline algorithms (although Scoring Map was still the highest). In this context, high precision means lower false positives ratio, which indicates that fewer elements considered to be different (in the reference grouping) were grouped together by the algorithm. High recall, on the other hand, means that most matching couples of elements were correctly grouped together by the algorithm, even if it means that many other elements were incorrectly grouped together. The worst performing algorithms in this analysis showed high recall values, but when precision drops to low levels (below 0.3) as shown in Table 1.

While still outperforming all baseline algorithms, the dimensional variant of the Scoring Map algorithm got slightly lower results than the original algorithm. By examining the samples, we could observe that the dimensional variant worked well in some particular cases where the structure was different but the spatial properties similar (e.g. a menu item that has a submenu in a list where its siblings don't have any).

Since the results were averaged, we analyzed the Standard Deviation to assess the variations in the different orders of elements, but we found it to be very low in all cases. The standard deviation in the f-score for the resulting clusters depending on the order was 0.0006 for RTDM, 0.0003 for bag of XPaths, 0.0002 for our scoring map algorithm and 0.0004 for the dimensional variant. With MH measures, it was also very low: 0.0071 for RTDM, 0.0021 for Bag of XPaths, 0.0022 for Scoring Map and 0.0045 for the dimensional variant.

4.5 Post-hoc Analysis

The dataset allowed us to make different analyses, since there is more data in the captured DOM elements than their structure.

The first analysis, also present in our previous work, is the analysis per element size, defined by the height of the DOM tree. This is especially relevant to our proposal because it allows to validate the alleged flexibility of the Scoring Map algorithm. In line with the previous experiment, we observed that the baseline algorithms focused on inner structure perform poorly when height is 1 (single nodes), but quickly ascends as height increases. Our algorithms keep a high score at all levels, showing their flexibility. The results by level are shown in Fig. 6. The second analysis consisted in restricting the groups of DOM elements by their domain. We were interested in this analysis since working on a single application is a very common use case for all the applicabilities previously listed. Results show a major improvement across all algorithms, especially those performing poorly in the general analysis. This is most likely due to the reduced search space. Both our algorithms still outperform all baseline ones, although in this particular study the dimensional variant is the best one for a small margin. These results can be seen in Fig. 7.

4.6 Threats to Validity

When designing the experiment, we faced many potential threats that required special attention. Regarding the construction of the elements' set, we had to make sure the

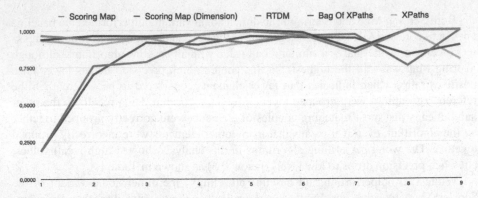

Fig. 6. F-score results by DOM element height for each algorithm.

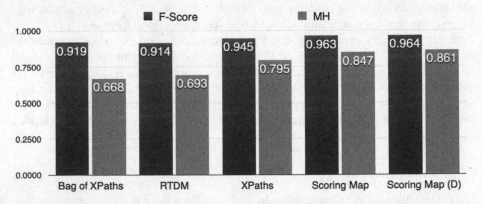

Fig. 7. Evaluation results of restricted clustering by domain. F1 Score and Meilã-Heckerman measure.

reference groups were not biased by interpretation. To reduce this threat, at least two authors acted as referees to determine elements' equivalence in the reference groups.

Another potential threat is the size of the dataset itself. Since there is manual intervention to create the groups of elements, and there were also restrictions with respect of their heights, building a large repository is very time-consuming. The set is large enough so adding new elements does not alter the results noticeably, but a larger set would prove more reliable.

There is also a potential bias due to the clustering algorithm, which is affected by the order in which elements are supplied to the algorithms. We tacked this by running the algorithms repeatedly, as explained in Sect. 4.3.

5   Use Cases

We used our algorithms to measure structural similarity in the context of three web adaptation approaches in the specific areas of UX and accesibility. These approaches are described in the next subsections.

5.1   Automatic Detection and Correction of Usability Smells

The first use case for the Scoring Map algorithm is automatic detection of usability problems on web applications. This was developed to ease usability assessment of web applications, since it is usually expensive and tedious [8]. Even when there are tools that analyze user interaction (UI) events and provide sophisticated visualizations, the repair process mostly requires a usability expert to interpret testing data, discover the underlying problems behind the visualizations, and manually craft the solutions.

The approach is based on the refactoring notion applied to external quality factors, like usability [6] or accessibility [9]. We build on the concept of "bad smell" from the refactoring jargon and characterize usability problems as "usability smells", i.e., signs of poor design in usability with known solutions in terms of usability refactorings [10].

The scoring map algorithm is then used in the tool that supports this approach, the Usability Smell Finder (USF). This tool analyses interaction events from real users on-the-fly, discovers usability smells and reports them together with a concrete solution in terms of a usability refactoring [15]. For example, USF reports the smell "Unresponsive Element" when an interface element is usually clicked by many users but does not trigger any actions. This happens when such elements give a hint because of their appearance. Typical elements where we have found this smell include products list photos, website headings, and checkbox/radio button labels. Each time USF finds an instance of this smell in a DOM element, it calculates the similarity of this element with clusters of elements previously found with the same smell. When the number of users that run into this smell reaches certain threshold, USF reports it suggesting the refactoring "Turn Attribute into Link".

The wrapper induction technique presented in this paper becomes useful at a later stage. The toolkit is able in some cases to automatically correct a reported usability smell by means of a client-side web refactoring (CSWR) [9], i.e., generic scripts that are parameterized to be applied on DOM elements in the client-side. Our proposal includes applying CSWR automatically by parameterizing them with the specific details of a detected usability smell and making use of the wrapper to find all matching elements that suffer from a same specific smell.

We obtained better results with the Scoring Map algorithm than simple XPath comparison, given that it works better on large elements, resisting HTML changes (small elements get similar results, since Scoring Map works in a similar way in these cases).

5.2   Use of Semantic Tags to Improve Web Application Accessibility

According to W3C accessibility standards, most Web applications are neither accessible nor usable for people with disabilities. One of the problems is that the content of a web page is usually fragmented and organized in visually recognizable groups, which added to our previous knowledge, allows sighted users to identify their role: a menu, an advertisement, a shopping cart, etc. On the contrary, unsighted users don't have access to this visual information. We developed a toolkit that includes a crowdsourcing platform for volunteer users to add extra semantic information to the DOM elements [29] using predefined tags, in order to transcode the visual information into a more accessible data presentation (plain text). This extra information is then automatically added on the client-side on demand, which is aimed to improve some accessibility aspects such as screen-reader functionalities.

By using an editor tool, when a user recognizes a DOM element, the tool applies the structural similarity algorithm to find similar elements that should be identically tagged within the page. For example, as soon as the user tags a Facebook post, all other posts are recognized as such and highlighted with the same color. At this stage we applied our wrapper induction method on the selected element to automatically tag the similar ones. Small structural differences are ignored, like the number comments. By adjusting the threshold, users can cluster elements with higher precision, e.g., successfully filtering out ads disguised as content. The Scoring Map algorithm was actually first developed during this work, since other comparison methods didn't have an adjustable similarity threshold, or the required speed.

A screenshot of the tool capturing YouTube videos thumbnails can be seen in Fig. 8, where the threshold is adapted to include or exclude video lists in the clustering. This way, we can easily reduce the entire web page into a limited set of semantically identifiable UI elements that can be used to create accessible and personalized views of the same web application, by applying on-the-fly transformations to each semantic element of the requested page. This happens in real time, as soon as the page loads, even on DOM changes, such as continuous content loading applications like Facebook or Twitter. On each refresh, the application applies different strategies to look for DOM elements that match the previously defined semantic elements, by applying the induction wrapper, the application is able to recognize those similar DOM elements where the new semantic information has to be injected. This process must be fast enough to avoid interfering on the user experience, which is achieved with our method.

Fig. 8. Web Accessibility Transcoder capturing similar DOM elements, using two different threshold values. Figure originally published in the previous work [13].

5.3   UX-Painter

UX-Painter is a web-extension to apply CSWRs on a web page with the aim of improving the user experince. These transformations are meant to perform small changes on the user interface (UI) without altering the application functionality. The tool is intended for UX-designers, who may not have programming skills, to be able to freely excercise design alternatives directly on the target application. CSWRs are applied without the need of coding the changes, by selecting the target elements on the UI and configuring specific parameters, and can be saved in different application versions which then can be re-created to perform UX evaluations such as user tests or inspection reviews.

On a first version of the tool, each refactoring was applied on a single UI element on a specific page. Later, by conducting interviews with professional UX designers, we discovered that it was important to allow applying a refactoring to multiple instances of a UI element that can be spreaded across different pages, since it is common to re-use certain UI elements in different parts of the target application. In this way, we improved UX-Painter with Scoring Map to generate a wrapper for each element refactored by the user in order to identify similar elements to apply the same transformation on. Finding similar elements with the wrapper induction technique is more flexible and robust than using XPath expressions because the elements location can differ in each case, and because XPath expressions tend to break as web pages evolve.

6   Conclusions and Future Work

In this paper we have presented an algorithm to compare individual DOM elements, along with a variant that uses the elements' dimensions and positioning. Both algorithms are flexible enough to successfully compare DOM elements of different sizes, overcoming limitations of previous approaches. We also presented a wrapper induction technique that's based on the comparison algorithm's implementation.

Thanks to the simple map comparison technique, the algorithm is relatively easy to implement, especially in contrast to the known tree edit distance approaches. It is also very flexible since it allows to weight the two comparison aspects. Both algorithms run in order $O(n)$, being n the total number of nodes of both trees added together.

Through a validation with 1200+ DOM element, we compared our proposal with others from the literature, spanning different strategies. We compared the clusterings generated by each algorithm against a ground truth, and used two different metrics to compare them. The results showed that our algorithms outperform all the baseline algorithms according both metrics.

We performed other analyses derived from the evaluation: one showed the flexibility of our algorithm, which was able to keep a stable performance across different levels (heights) of DOM elements, and the other demonstrated the adjusted performance of all algorithms when the clustering was restricted by application domain.

Another relevant extension to the validation could be testing the resistance of the algorithm to DOM structure changes. This is, however very complicated to set up because of the difficulty of gathering realistic samples of elements that change places over time. A controlled experiment with generated test data could be carried out, but it would have low external validity.

Acknowledgements. The authors acknowledge the support from the Argentinian National Agency for Scientific and Technical Promotion (ANPCyT), grant number PICT-2019-02485.

References

1. Amagasa, T., Wen, L., Kitagawa, H.: Proximity search of XML data using ontology and XPath edit similarity. In: Wagner, R., Revell, N., Pernul, G. (eds.) DEXA 2007. LNCS, vol. 4653, pp. 298–307. Springer, Heidelberg (2007). https://doi.org/10.1007/978-3-540-74469-6_30
2. Asakawa, C., Takagi, H.: Web accessibility: a foundation for research, chapter transcoding (2008)
3. Augsten, N., Böhlen, M., Gamper, J.: Approximate matching of hierarchical data using pq-grams. In: Proceedings of the 31st International Conference on Very Large Data Bases, pp. 301–312 (2005)
4. Buttler, D.: A short survey of document structure similarity algorithms. Technical report Lawrence Livermore National Lab. (LLNL), Livermore, CA (United States) (2004)
5. Díaz, O.: Understanding web augmentation. In: Grossniklaus, M., Wimmer, M. (eds.) ICWE 2012. LNCS, vol. 7703, pp. 79–80. Springer, Heidelberg (2012). https://doi.org/10.1007/978-3-642-35623-0_8
6. Distante, D., Garrido, A., Camelier-Carvajal, J., Giandini, R., Rossi, G.: Business processes refactoring to improve usability in e-commerce applications. Electron. Commer. Res. 14(4), 497–529 (2014). https://doi.org/10.1007/s10660-014-9149-0
7. Fard, A.M., Mesbah, A.: Feedback-directed exploration of web applications to derive test models. In: 2013 IEEE 24th International Symposium on Software Reliability Engineering (ISSRE), pp. 278–287 (2013). https://doi.org/10.1109/ISSRE.2013.6698880
8. Fernandez, A., Insfran, E., Abrahão, S.: Usability evaluation methods for the web: a systematic mapping study. Inf. Softw. Technol. 53(8), 789–817 (2011)
9. Garrido, A., Firmenich, S., Rossi, G., Grigera, J., Medina-Medina, N., Harari, I.: Personalized web accessibility using client-side refactoring. IEEE Internet Comput. 17(4), 58–66 (2012)
10. Garrido, A., Rossi, G., Distante, D.: Refactoring for usability in web applications. IEEE Softw. 28(3), 60–67 (2010)
11. Griazev, K., Ramanauskaitė, S.: HTML block similarity estimation. In: 2018 IEEE 6th Workshop on Advances in Information, Electronic and Electrical Engineering (AIEEE), pp. 1–4. IEEE (2018)
12. Grigalis, T., Čenys, A.: Using XPaths of inbound links to cluster template-generated web pages. Comput. Sci. Inf. Syst. 11(1), 111–131 (2014)
13. Grigera, J., Gardey, J.C., Garrido, A., Rossi, G.: A scoring map algorithm for automatically detecting structural similarity of DOM elements (2021)
14. Grigera, J., Garrido, A., Panach, J.I., Distante, D., Rossi, G.: Assessing refactorings for usability in e-commerce applications. Empir. Softw. Eng. 21(3), 1224–1271 (2016). https://doi.org/10.1007/s10664-015-9384-6
15. Grigera, J., Garrido, A., Rivero, J.M.: A tool for detecting bad usability smells in an automatic way. In: Casteleyn, S., Rossi, G., Winckler, M. (eds.) ICWE 2014. LNCS, vol. 8541, pp. 490–493. Springer, Cham (2014). https://doi.org/10.1007/978-3-319-08245-5_34
16. Hachenberg, C., Gottron, T.: Locality sensitive hashing for scalable structural classification and clustering of web documents. In: Proceedings of the 22nd ACM International Conference on Information & Knowledge Management, pp. 359–368 (2013)
17. Joshi, S., Agrawal, N., Krishnapuram, R., Negi, S.: A bag of paths model for measuring structural similarity in web documents. In: Proceedings of the Ninth ACM SIGKDD International Conference on Knowledge Discovery and Data Mining, pp. 577–582 (2003)
18. Levenshtein, V.I., et al.: Binary codes capable of correcting deletions, insertions, and reversals. In: Soviet Physics Doklady, vol. 10, pp. 707–710. Soviet Union (1966)

19. Meilă, M., Heckerman, D.: An experimental comparison of model-based clustering methods. Mach. Learn. **42**(1), 9–29 (2001). https://doi.org/10.1023/A:1007648401407
20. Mesbah, A., van Deursen, A., Roest, D.: Invariant-based automatic testing of modern web applications. IEEE Trans. Softw. Eng. **38**(1), 35–53 (2012)
21. Mesbah, A., Prasad, M.R.: Automated cross-browser compatibility testing. In: Proceedings of the 33rd International Conference on Software Engineering, ICSE (2011), pp. 561–570. Association for Computing Machinery, New York, NY, USA (2011)
22. Nebeling, M., Speicher, M., Norrie, M.: W3Touch: metrics-based web page adaptation for touch. In: Proceedings of the SIGCHI Conference on Human Factors in Computing Systems, pp. 2311–2320 (2013)
23. Norrie, M.C., Nebeling, M., Di Geronimo, L., Murolo, A.: X-themes: supporting design-by-example. In: Casteleyn, S., Rossi, G., Winckler, M. (eds.) ICWE 2014. LNCS, vol. 8541, pp. 480–489. Springer, Cham (2014). https://doi.org/10.1007/978-3-319-08245-5_33
24. Omer, B., Ruth, B., Shahar, G.: A new frequent similar tree algorithm motived by DOM mining using RTDM and its new variant-SiSTeR (2012)
25. Reis, D.D.C., Golgher, P.B., Silva, A.S., Laender, A.: Automatic web news extraction using tree edit distance. In: Proceedings of the 13th International Conference on World Wide Web, pp. 502–511 (2004)
26. Tai, K.C.: The tree-to-tree correction problem. J. ACM (JACM) **26**(3), 422–433 (1979)
27. Valiente, G.: An efficient bottom-up distance between trees. In: spire, pp. 212–219. Citeseer (2001)
28. Xu, Z., Miller, J.: Estimating similarity of rich internet pages using visual information. Int. J. Web Eng. Technol. **12**(2), 97–119 (2017)
29. Zanotti, M.: Accessibility and crowdsourcing: use of semantic tags to improve web application accessibility. University of La Plata, Argentina (2016)
30. Zeng, J., Flanagan, B., Hirokawa, S.: Layout-tree-based approach for identifying visually similar blocks in a web page. In: 2013 IEEE/ACIS 12th International Conference on Computer and Information Science (ICIS), pp. 65–70. IEEE (2013)
31. Zheng, S., Song, R., Wen, J.R., Giles, C.L.: Efficient record-level wrapper induction. In: Proceedings of the 18th ACM Conference on Information and Knowledge Management, pp. 47–56 (2009)

GeoSoft: A Language for Soft Querying Features Within GeoJSON Information Layers

Paolo Fosci[1] , Stefania Marrara[2] , and Giuseppe Psaila[1(✉)]

[1] University of Bergamo, DIGIP, Viale Marconi 5, 24044 Dalmine, BG, Italy
{paolo.fosci,giuseppe.psaila}@unibg.it
[2] Cefriel, Viale Sarca 226, 20126 Milan, Italy
Stefania.Marrara@cefriel.com

Abstract. *GeoJSON* has become one of the most popular format for representing spatial information. Its popularity is due to the fact that it relies on *JSON* as hosting syntactic structure. Currently, querying in an effective way a *GeoJSON* document, to extract features of interests, can be hard, for various reasons.

In this paper, we propose a domain-specific language named *GeoSoft*: it is a high-level tool that hides details of the *GeoJSON* format, which enables soft querying of features, to express imprecise queries. The paper shows that a *GeoSoft* query can be effectively and automatically translated into a *J-CO-QL* script, which is executed by the *J-CO* Framework, i.e., the execution engine we chose for *GeoSoft*.

Keywords: GeoJSON documents · Soft querying of GeoJSON documents · Fuzzy *J-CO-QL* queries

1 Introduction

In the era of Big Data and Open Data, the *JSON* format has become the *de-facto* standard for representing and sharing data and documents over the Internet. Indeed, it is possible to obtain *JSON* documents from Open Data portals, as well as from APIs (Application Programming Interfaces) of social media and, more in general, Web Services.

The GIS (Geographical Information Systems) community has defined *GeoJSON*[1]: it is an international standard whose goal is to describe "spatial information layers". In Geography, an information layer is a set of geographical (or spatial) entities, which are located on the Earth globe according to a determined set of spatial coordinates. GIS tools are able to import and export *GeoJSON* documents; furthermore, public administrations publish authoritative geographical data in form of *GeoJSON* documents on their Open Data portals.

The relevance of *GeoJSON* in the current panorama is a matter of fact: *GeoJSON* layers are used by analysts to get information about a given territory. Conceptually, a *GeoJSON* layer is a set of "features", where each feature has its set of "properties" and its "geometry". Consequently, the idea of "querying" features in a *GeoJSON*

---

[1] https://geojson.org/, accessed on 30/10/2021.

© Springer Nature Switzerland AG 2023
M. Marchiori et al. (Eds.): WEBIST 2020/2021, LNBIP 469, pp. 196–219, 2023.
https://doi.org/10.1007/978-3-031-24197-0_11

layer is straightforward. However, it is not easy to perform: GIS tools does not provide query languages as people used to work on relational databases could think; relational databases extended with support for geographical data (such as *PostgreSQL* extended with *PostGIS*) usually do not natively ingest *GeoJSON* documents (consequently, long and complex preprocessing activities are needed); finally, *NoSQL* document stores (such as *MongoDB*) deal with *GeoJSON* documents as pure *JSON* documents, forcing users to write preprocessing queries to extract features from *GeoJSON* information layers. Consequently, we guessed that if users wishing to query features in a *GeoJSON* document were provided with a DSL (Domain-Specific Language) for querying *GeoJSON* features, they would greatly increase their efficiency and effectiveness.

What characteristics should be provided by such a query language for *GeoJSON* layers? Moving from our previous research work on soft querying in relational databases [5,6], we argued that a soft approach is more favorable, because very often it is not possible to know the data set to query in a precise way, in particular as far as values of numerical properties are concerned. Indeed, the soft approach allows analysts to perform imprecise matching. A second important decision we had to make was the level of the language: usually, query languages provided by *NoSQL JSON* document stores are too low-level, because they must be generic. In contrast, we decided for a high-level query language, specifically designed for *GeoJSON* documents, which provides a simplified view of the problem of querying features within *GeoJSON* documents. The first result was the language for soft querying *GeoJSON* documents that we presented in [16].

In this paper, we present *GeoSoft*: it is the first assessment of the language for soft querying *GeoJSON* layers proposed in [16]. Specifically, we have consolidated the syntax, in order to make it practically feasible to be applied in a real context. Second, we implemented a prototype translator on top of the *J-CO* Framework [19,28] and its query language named *J-CO-QL*; the *J-CO* Framework is a research framework under development at University of Bergamo, aimed to gather, transform, integrate and query possibly-large collections of *JSON* documents, which can possibly describe spatial entities (through a geo-tagging); currently, the *J-CO-QL* language has been extended with partial support for evaluating fuzzy sets on *JSON* documents, so as to enable soft querying on them. Third, this paper presents a novel case study, based on EU NUTS (acronym from the french *Nomenclature des Unités Territoriales Statistiques* that is a hierarchical system for dividing up the economic territory of the European Union for statistical purposes)[2] to illustrate the potential application of *GeoSoft*.

The paper is organized as follows. Section 2 discusses the relevant related works. Section 3 presents the *J-CO* Framework, its main characteristics and how *J-CO-QL* (its query language) actually supports soft querying on *JSON* documents. Section 4 introduces the *GeoJSON* format; furthermore, a running example is introduced. Section 5 actually presents the *GeoSoft* language, by means of the running example introduced in Sect. 4. Section 6 presents the translation technique we implemented in the prototype translator, which converts a *GeoSoft* query into a *J-CO-QL* query. Finally, Sect. 7 draws the conclusions and sketches future work.

---

[2] https://ec.europa.eu/eurostat/web/nuts/background, accessed on 30/10/2021.

2   Related Work

Talking about a flexible language for geographical *JSON* documents, we need to evaluate three different research topics: languages to express *JSON* data, language to express flexible queries and, finally, languages specifically designed for geographical data. The first two topics have been covered in our previous work [19], here we just summarize the most important contributions.

With the rise of *JSON* as new *de-facto* standard for data exchange on the Web, many systems specifically designed to store *JSON* documents have been designed as subclass of *NoSQL* databases; the most popular is *MongoDB*[3], which is used for storing and querying large collections of small *JSON* documents. Another important example is *CouchDB*[4] [21], which has been chosen as the underlying database engine for the *HyperLedger Fabric* BlockChain platform [8]. As a consequence, many query languages for *JSON* data sets have been proposed by the database community. The most popular ones are: *Jaql* [25], *SQL++* [26], *JSONiq* [14] and the query language provided by *MongoDB* [11].

In the domain of soft query languages, there are two main approaches: the first one extends the relational data model towards a fuzzy database model (as in *FSQL* [20]). The second approach does not modify the relational data model but extends the SQL query language with the capability to fuzzy query a conventional relational database (such as *SoftSQL* [6] and *SQLf* [7]).

The topic of this paper is closely related to the area of Geographical Information Systems; in this domain, several proposals have been made, especially for data storage, indexing and query optimization [1]. GIS are supposed to store huge amounts of complex data, so as to graphically represent them. Many extensions of the SQL language have been proposed [12,13]. These extensions are necessary in order to allow Data Base Management Systems (DBMS) to store and retrieve spatial information. However, these languages are not designed for end-users, due to the complexity of the SQL language. To overcome this issue, other proposals include tabular approaches [30] defined as extensions of QBE (Query By Example) [22]), graphical languages [23], visual languages [24], and *hypermaps* [10] (integrated into hypermedia techniques [2]).

If the geographical information is stored as *GeoJSON* documents, most systems provide traditional *JSON* query languages to access them. Talking about query languages that are specifically targeted to *GeoJSON*, the number of available proposals is very low. We can cite *GeoPQLJ* [15]: it is a pictorial query language that allows users to formulate their queries by using drawing facilities, so as to help users correctly interpret the query syntax and semantics on the basis of its underlying algebra. *GeoPQL* has been conceived as a stand-alone GIS client which uses the *ESRI* Library[5].

---

[3] *MongoDB*. 2021. Available online: https://www.mongodb.com/ accessed on 30/10/2021.

[4] CouchDb. 2021. Available online: https://couchdb.apache.org/ accessed on 30/10/2021.

[5] https://www.esri.com/arcgis-blog/products/arcgis-hub/announcements/welcome-to-the-content-library/ accessed on 30/10/2021.

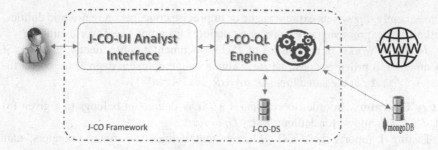

Fig. 1. Components of the *J-CO* framework.

3 Soft Querying *JSON* Documents: The *J-CO* Framework

In this section, we introduce the background on which our work relies, i.e., the *J-CO* Framework and its main features, in particular as far as soft querying of *JSON* documents is concerned.

The *J-CO* Framework is the result of a research work [3,4,27,28] conducted at University of Bergamo, towards the definition of a tool able to retrieve, integrate, transform, manage and query possibly-large collections of *JSON* documents either stored in *JSON* document store or directly provided by Web sources.

The core of the framework is *J-CO-QL*, a novel query language specifically designed to query heterogeneous *JSON* data sets, by natively supporting geo-spatial aggregations of geo-tagged documents. In [17–19,29], we proposed to extend the language in order to support fuzzy sets and soft querying.

The *J-CO* Framework is composed by several software tools, as depicted in Fig. 1. We report a brief summary of them (the interested reader can refer to [28]).

The *J-CO-QL Engine* actually processes *J-CO-QL* scripts. It is able to access Web sources and can connect to *JSON* stores like *MongoDB*.

J-CO-DS is a *JSON* document store developed within the *J-CO* Framework, which can store very-large single *JSON* documents.

Finally, *J-CO-UI* is the user interface of the framework: users can use it to interact with the *J-CO-QL Engine*.

Fuzzy Sets. Fuzzy-Set Theory was introduced by Zadeh [31]. Let us consider a non-empty universe X, either finite or infinite. A fuzzy set $A \in X$ is a mapping $A : X \rightarrow [0, 1]$. The value $A(x)$ is referred to as the *membership degree* of the element x to the fuzzy set A. In other words, given a fuzzy set $A \in X$, a membership function $A(x)$ associates each element $x \in X$ with a real number in the interval $[0, 1]$; given x, the value $A(x)$ is the degree of membership of x to A.

If $A(x) = 1$, x fully belongs to A. If $A(x) = 0$, x does not belong at all to A. An intermediate value $0 < A(x) < 1$ means that x belongs to A in a partial way (i.e., $A(x) = 0.9$ means that x does not completely belong to A). For example, if A stands for "old people" and x_1 and x_2 are two persons, the fact that $A(x_1) = 0.9$ and $A(x_2) = 0.3$ denotes that neither x_1 nor x_2 are completely old, but certainly x_1 is older than x_2.

Consequently, fuzzy sets express vague or imprecise concepts on real-world entities, as well as they express vague or imprecise relationships among real-world entities.

J-CO-QL works on collections of *JSON* documents; consequently, given a *JSON* document d, it provides constructs to evaluate its membership degrees to several fuzzy sets $A_1, \ldots, A_n$ at the same time, i.e., $A_1(d), \ldots, A_n(d)$.

Fuzzy Operators. In order to evaluate if a *JSON* document belongs to a given fuzzy set, *J-CO-QL* allows for defining *Fuzzy Operators*.

Listing 1 reports the *J-CO-QL* script that defines two fuzzy operators, named `Has_Decreasing_Population` and `Has_Increasing_GDP`. Hereafter, we briefly describe their definitions.

Listing 1. Defining Fuzzy Operators.

```
1:  CREATE FUZZY OPERATOR Has_Decreasing_Population
      PARAMETERS
        Pop1 TYPE Float,
        Pop2 TYPE Float
      PRECONDITION
            Pop1 > 0
        AND Pop2 > 0
      EVALUATE 100*(Pop2-Pop1) / Pop1
      POLYLINE
        [ (-2.0, 1.0),
          (-1.0, 0.7),
          (-0.5, 0.1),
          ( 0.0, 0.0) ];


2:  CREATE FUZZY OPERATOR Has_Increasing_GDP
      PARAMETERS
        GDP1 TYPE Float,
        GDP2 TYPE Float
      PRECONDITION
            GDP1 > 0
        AND GDP2 > 0
      EVALUATE 100*(GDP2-GDP1) / GDP1
      POLYLINE
        [ (  0, 0.0),
          (  2, 0.1),
          (  4, 0.5),
          (  7, 0.8),
          ( 10, 0.9),
          ( 15, 1.0) ];
```

Consider the first fuzzy operator, named `Has_Decreasing_Population`. Given the population in two consecutive years (referring to the same area), it expresses the fact that the population decreases.

The `PARAMETERS` clause specifies the two formal parameters, named `Pop1` and `Pop2`, whose actual values are the amounts of population to compare.

The `PRECONDITION` clause specifies a condition on actual parameters that must be met before proceedings with the evaluation of the operator. If it is not met, an error signal is raised and the evaluation is stopped.

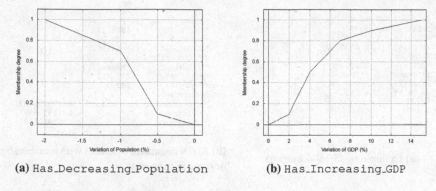

(a) `Has_Decreasing_Population`   **(b)** `Has_Increasing_GDP`

Fig. 2. Membership functions of fuzzy operators in Listing 1.

The EVALUATE clause is used to specify an expression to evaluate on the basis of actual parameters; in this case, the expression computes the percentage of variation of population, which can be either positive or negative.

The POLYLINE clause provides the coordinates of vertices of a polyline function actually used to evaluate the membership degree of the operator. The polyline defined in the Has_Decreasing_Population operator is depicted in Fig. 2a: the value obtained by evaluating the expression in the EVALUATE clause is used as x coordinate; the corresponding y value on the polyline is the output membership degree. Notice that the percentage of population variation could be less than -2%, as well as it could be greater than 0%: in these cases, the left extreme value (i.e., 1) and, respectively, the right extreme value (i.e., 0) are returned as membership values.

The second fuzzy operator is named Has_Increasing_GDP. Its goal is to evaluate positive variations of GDP (Gross Domestic Product) of a region.

Similarly to the previous operator, two formal parameters are defined, named GDP1 and GDP2; the condition in the PRECONDITION clause ensures that the operator is evaluated only for positive values of the parameters.

The EVALUATE clause defines the expression that computes the percentage of GDP variation. Then, the POLYLINE clause defines the membership function, which is depicted in Fig. 2b. The reader can see that the two polylines are mirrored: the left one must be 1 for negative variations of population, while the right one must be 1 for positive variations of GDP.

Soft Querying a Collection of Documents. Let us suppose that we have a collection of *JSON* documents, named NUTSCollection, stored within the NUTS_Info database (managed by a *MongoDB* server), where each document describes a level-3 European NUTS (corresponding to a province or a county, depending on the country). An example of document (describing a NUTS) is shown in Fig. 3a. It reports the code (NUTSCode), the name (NUTSName), the level (NUTSLevel), the country code (CountryCode), the population in 2017 (population2018) and in 2018 (population018) and the GDP in 2017 (GDP2017) and in 2018 (GDP2018).

Listing 2 reports the second part of the *J-CO-QL* script, whose goal is to select those documents that describe a NUTS for which a significant reduction of population was

```
{                                              {
    "CountryCode"  :  "RO",                        "CountryCode"  :  "RO",
    "GDP2017"      :  1523.11,                      "GDP2017"      :  1523.11,
    "GDP2018"      :  1720.9,                       "GDP2018"      :  1720.9,
    "NUTSCode"     :  "RO413",                      "NUTSCode"     :  "RO413",
    "NUTSLevel"    :  3,                            "NUTSLevel"    :  3,
    "NUTSName"     :  "Mehedinti",                  "NUTSName"     :  "Mehedinti",
    "Pop2017"      :  247.25,                       "Pop2017"      :  247.25,
    "Pop2018"      :  243.3                         "Pop2018"      :  243.3,
}                                                  "~fuzzysets"   :  {
                                                       "Decreasing_Population" : 0.879271987,
                                                       "Increasing_GDP"        : 0.959718592,
                                                       "Wanted"                : 0.879271987 }
                                               }
```

(a) Example of *JSON* document.   (b) *JSON* document extended with membership degrees to fuzzy sets.

Fig. 3. Example of *JSON* document describing a NUTS (a), later extended (b) with membership degrees to fuzzy sets.

```
{
    "CountryCode"  :  "RO",
    "NUTSCode"     :  "RO413",
    "NUTSLevel"    :  3,
    "NUTSName"     :  "Mehedinti",
    "rank"         :  0.879271987
}
```

Fig. 4. Example of document obtained by the soft query.

registered, jointly with a significant increase of GDP, from 2017 to 2018. To illustrate the script, we have to introduce both the data model and the execution model of *J-CO-QL* scripts.

– *Data Model.* J-CO-QL works on standard *JSON* documents; however, root level fields whose name begins with the "~" character play a special role. For example, the ~fuzzysets field works as a map *fsn* → *md*, where *fsn* is a fuzzy-set name and *md* is the corresponding membership degree; this way, the degrees of membership of a document to multiple fuzzy sets can be simultaneously represented. The model encompasses the ~geometry field too, for representing spatial geometries [3, 28].
– *Execution Model.* A clear and linear execution model has been defined. The query (or script) is a sequence of instructions. The *query-process state* s contains the so-called *temporary collection* $s.tc$: an instruction i_j works on the $s_{(j-1)}$ query-process state and generates a new query-process state s_j, meaning that i_j receives the $s_{(j-1)}.tc$ temporary collection as input and generates the new $s_j.tc$ temporary collection as output; in the initial state s_0, it is $s_0.tc = \emptyset$. Consequently, instructions are *piped*, so as the user can write them following the natural flow with which they are thought.

We can now present the instructions of the script in Listing 2.

Listing 2. Soft querying with *J-CO-QL*.

```
3:  USE DB NUTS_Info
      ON SERVER MongoDB 'http://127.0.0.1:27017';

4:  GET COLLECTION NUTSCollection@NUTS_Info;

5:  FILTER
      CASE
        WHERE  WITH .Pop2017, .Pop2018, .GDP2017, .GDP2018
          CHECK FOR FUZZY SET Decreasing_Population
            USING Has_Decreasing_Population (.Pop2017, .Pop2018)
          CHECK FOR FUZZY SET Increasing_GDP
            USING Has_Increasing_GDP (.GDP2017, .GDP2018)
          CHECK FOR FUZZY SET Wanted
            USING ( Decreasing_Population AND Increasing_GDP )
          ALPHA-CUT 0.8 ON Wanted
        DROP OTHERS;

6:  FILTER
      CASE
        WHERE KNOWN FUZZY SETS Wanted
          GENERATE
          { .NUTSName      : .NUTSName,
            .NUTSCode      : .NUTSCode,
            .NUTSLevel     : .NUTSLevel,
            .CountryCode   : .CountryCode,
            .rank          : MEMBERSHIP_OF (Wanted) }
          DROPPING ALL FUZZY SETS
        DROP OTHERS;

7:  SAVE AS DetectedNUTS@NUTS_Info;
```

- On line 3, the USE DB instruction connects the *J-CO-QL Engine* to a *MongoDB* database named NUTS_Info, managed by a *MongoDB* server running on the same server where the *J-CO-QL Engine* is running.
- The GET COLLECTION instruction on line 4 retrieves the collection named NUTSCollection from the NUTS_Info database, so as to make it the new temporary collection. Figure 3a reports an example document in the collection (remember that each document describes a level-3 NUTS).
- The FILTER instruction on line 5 actually performs the soft querying of *JSON* documents in the current temporary collection.
  Given a document d in the temporary collection, the CASE WHERE selection clause evaluates if it has the fields specified in the WITH predicate; if d satisfies the condition, it is considered for further processing. Notice the dot notation used to refer to fields: the initial dot (e.g. .Pop2017) means that the field is at the root level of d.
  The three CHECK FOR FUZZY SET clauses evaluate the membership degrees of d to three fuzzy sets, named Decreasing_Population, Increasing_GDP and Wanted.
  The first CHECK FOR FUZZY SET clause applies the fuzzy operator named Has_Decreasing_Population on d's fields in the USING sub-clause, which is a fuzzy condition. The resulting membership degree is associated to d by adding a new field named ~fuzzysets, as depicted in Fig. 3b: within it, the nested field named Decreasing_Population denotes the membership degree of d to the

Decreasing_Population fuzzy set.

The second CHECK FOR FUZZY SET clause behaves similarly: it evaluates the membership degree of d to the fuzzy set named Increasing_GDP, through the Has_Increasing_GDP fuzzy operator.

The last CHECK FOR FUZZY SET clause evaluates the membership of d to the Wanted fuzzy set, by means of a soft condition based on the AND operator, i.e., the minimum membership degree to the Decreasing_Population and Increasing_GDP fuzzy sets is considered as membership degree to the Wanted fuzzy set. The final structure of d is reported in Fig. 3b.

At this point, the ALPHA-CUT clause specifies a minimum threshold on the Wanted fuzzy set: if d has a membership degree that is less than the threshold of 0.8, it is not inserted into the output temporary collection.

Notice the final DROP OTHERS option, which discards all documents that do not meet the CASE WHERE condition from the output temporary collection.

- The FILTER instruction on line 6 has to *de-fuzzify* the selected documents and add a new field to the original structure of documents. This is done by the GENERATE action, which specifies the novel structure of the documents: notice the new rank field, whose value is the membership degree to the Wanted fuzzy set, obtained by means of the MEMBERSHIP_OF function. Finally, all membership degrees to fuzzy sets are discarded from documents by the DROPPING ALL FUZZY SETS option. An example of document in the output collection is depicted in Fig. 4.
- The SAVE AS instruction on line 7 saves the final temporary collection into the DetectedNUTS collection in the NUTS_Info database.

J-CO-QL provides many other statements, in particular in the rest of the paper we will make use of the EXPAND and GROUP statements (they will be described when they will be used). Nevertheless, the script presented in this section should have clarified how *J-CO-QL* supports fuzzy querying on *JSON* documents.

4   Introducing *GeoJSON* and the Running Example

This section briefly introduces the *GeoJSON* format; then, it presents the data set adopted as running example to show how the *GeoSoft* language works.

4.1   *GeoJSON*

GeoJSON is an interchange format for spatial data. It adopts open standards and it is used to represent geographic features and their non-spatial properties. *GeoJSON* is based on the JavaScript Object Notation (*JSON*) as host syntactic format, due to its simplicity and wide diffusion: this characteristic allows for processing *GeoJSON* documents as any other *JSON* document. Typically, it is used for encoding a variety of geographical information layers, i.e., aggregations of spatial features that provide a specific type of spatial information (e.g., roads, buildings, rivers, and so on). It is independent of any geographic coordinate reference system; however, most of *GeoJSON* documents implicitly adopt the World Geodesic System 1984 (WGS-84) and decimal degree units.

Currently, *GeoJSON* has become very popular in many GIS tools and services related to web mapping. It is actually used by Web applications as a standard format for exchanging geographical information layers in client-server communication; this is due to the fact that a *GeoJSON* document is a *JSON* document, so client-side libraries and platforms for web mapping written by means of the JavaScript programming language (such as *Leaflet*[6], *CARTO*[7], and *Turf.js*[8]) easily process it.

Another advantage of *GeoJSON* is that it is a human-readable format, since it is a plain-text format; however, this characteristic makes it verbose, because property names are repeated for each single feature, even though they all have the same properties. As an effect, *GeoJSON* documents can become much larger if compared to other formats for representing spatial data, such as *Shapefile*[9] and *GeoPackage*[10].

To illustrate the structure of a *GeoJSON* document, consider the document reported in Fig. 5a. Hereafter, a brief introduction to its structure is reported (more details can be found in [9]).

- A *GeoJSON* document is a unique, single and possibly-giant *JSON* document. At the root level, two mandatory fields are present: the `type` field has the `"FeatureCollection"` value, in order to denote that this is the root level (since am information layer is a collection of spatial features); the `features` field is an array of documents, each one describing a spatial feature.
- A document describing a single feature has three mandatory fields: the `type` field has the `"Feature"` value, in order to denote that the document actually describes a spatial feature; the `properties` field is a nested *JSON* document that reports non-spatial properties of the feature; the `geometry` field actually denotes the spatial property (also named "geometry") of the spatial feature.
- The `properties` field has not a specific structure; it is a list of possibly-complex properties, based on the *JSON* format.
- The `geometry` field describes the geometry of the spatial feature. The format encompasses points, line-strings, polygons and mixed geometries.

4.2 Running Example

In order to illustrate the goal of the *GeoSoft* language, and to let the reader understand it, a running example is adopted. The example originates from the *Eurostat* (the European Institute for Statistics) portal[11], which publishes many interesting data sets concerning the European Union. Among them, *GeoJSON* documents, describing European countries, are available. Specifically, we downloaded the *GeoJSON* layer[12] that describes the

---

[6] https://leafletjs.com/examples/geojson/, accessed on 30/10/2021.
[7] https://carto.com/developers/carto-vl/guides/add-data-sources/, accessed on 30/10/2021.
[8] https://turfjs.org/, accessed on 30/10/2021.
[9] https://www.statsilk.com/maps/convert-esri-shapefile-map-geojson-format, accessed on 30/10/2021.
[10] https://www.geopackage.org/guidance/modeling.html, accessed on 30/10/2021.
[11] https://ec.europa.eu/eurostat, accessed on 30/10/2021.
[12] https://ec.europa.eu/eurostat/web/gisco/geodata/reference-data/administrative-units-statistical-units/nuts, accessed on 30/10/2021. We opted for the 1:3Million scale since the *GeoJSON* layer at 1:1Million scale was too big to be stored into a *MongoDB* database.

```
{                                                    {
    "type" : "FeatureCollection",                        "type" : "FeatureCollection",
    "features" : [                                       "features" : [
        { "type" : "Feature"                                 { "type" : "Feature"
          "properties" : {                                     "properties" : {
            "CountryCode" : "BG",                                "CountryCode" : "BG",
            "GDP2017"     : 1011.36,                             "NUTSCode"    : "BG313",
            "GDP2018"     : 1260.6,                              "NUTSLevel"   : 3,
            "NUTSCode"    : "BG313",                             "NUTSName"    : "Vratsa",
            "NUTSLevel"   : 3,                                   "rank"        :  0.954458997 },
            "NUTSName"    : "Vratsa",                          "geometry" : {
            "Pop2017"     : 167.19,                              "type"        : "Polygon",
            "Pop2018"     : 164.1         },                     "coordinates" : [ [
          "geometry" : {                                            [ 24.323523,  43.697686],
            "type"        : "Polygon",                              [ 24.30067,   43.647582],
            "coordinates" : [ [                                     … ] ]                        }
                [ 24.323523,   43.697686],                       }
                [ 24.30067,    43.647582],                       { … }, …, { … }
                … ] ]                    }                 ]
        }                                              }
        { … }, …, { … }
    ]
}
```

(a) Excerpt of the reference   (b) Excerpt of the output
GeoJSON document.   GeoJSON document.

Fig. 5. *GeoJSON* documents for the running example, which describe (a) all level-3 NUTS in Europe and (b) those selected by the sample *GeoSoft* query.

geometries of the level-3 NUTS; they are depicted on the left side of Fig. 6. For each NUTS, the downloaded *GeoJSON* layer reports only registry properties (such as code, name, level and country code), while data such as population[13] and GDP[14] were provided in different pages as CSV (Comma-Separated Values) files, that were converted into *JSON* documents[15]. By means of a *J-CO-QL* script, which we do not report here since it is out of the scope of this paper, we were able to integrate the basic *GeoJSON* layer with the additional sources, to obtain a new *GeoJSON* layer that reports registry properties, population and GDP in 2017 and 2018 of level-3 NUTS. An excerpt of the reference *GeoJSON* document is reported in Fig. 5a.

5 *GeoSoft*: An SQL-like Language

Consider the *GeoJSON* document reported in Fig. 5a. A *GeoJSON* document can be viewed as a container of features. So, it is straightforward to guess that these features could be queried, so as to obtain a novel *GeoJSON* document (i.e., a novel container of features). The availability of a query language to perform such a query without the need to deal with technicalities concerned with processing of *GeoJSON* documents would significantly help analysts. However, we make a step forward: we consider not only querying but *soft querying a GeoJSON document*; we mean searching for features that meet a qualitative condition, in order to get a new *GeoJSON* document, in which

---

[13] https://ec.europa.eu/eurostat/databrowser/view/nama_10r_3popgdp/default/table, accessed on 30/10/2021.

[14] https://ec.europa.eu/eurostat/databrowser/view/NAMA_10_GDP$DEFAULTVIEW/default/table, accessed on 30/10/2021.

[15] for this purpose we used: https://www.convertcsv.com/csv-to-json.htm, accessed on 30/10/2021.

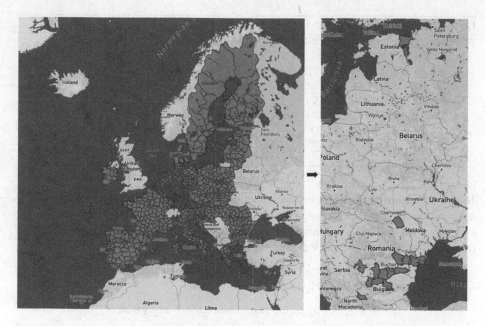

Fig. 6. On the left, the map depicting all EU Level-3 NUTS; On the right, the map depicting only the selected Level-3 NUTS.

features might be sorted in reverse order of importance (as far as the qualitative selection condition is concerned).

5.1 Semantic Model

The language we propose is named *GeoSoft*. It is strongly inspired by the well known syntax of the SQL SELECT statement, because it is quite familiar to analysts. However, we are introducing soft concepts to work on a crisp context. For this reason, we have to clearly distinguish the *external* and the *internal* semantic models.

External Semantic Model. *GeoSoft* is designed to work on *GeoJSON* documents, so as to generate new *GeoJSON* documents. Thus, the external semantic model (i.e., independent of what happens inside the query) is the following one.

- A *GeoSoft* query *gsq* can be seen as a function

$$gsq : GJ \to GJ$$

   where GJ is the domain of (crisp) *GeoJSON* documents.
- A (crisp) *GeoJSON* document can be seen as a "set of features" (if we ignore syntactic aspects), where a feature can be denoted as a tuple
   $f = \langle \text{properties}, \text{geometry} \rangle$ where properties and geometry are defined as in the *GeoJSON* standard (see Sect. 4.1).

Listing 3. Simple soft query in *GeoSoft*.

```
SELECT .CountryCode, .NUTSCOde, .NUTSLevel, .NUTSName
    FROM NUTSCOllection_GeoJSON@NUTS_Info
    WHERE Decreasing_Population AND Increasing_GDP
        FOR FUZZY SET Wanted
    ALPHA-CUT Wanted: 0.8
    ADD MEMBERSHIP_OF Wanted AS .rank
    ORDER BY .rank DESC
    SAVE AS DetectedNUTS_Geojson@NUTS_Info;
```

Internal Semantic Model. In order to meet the external semantic model, soft concepts must be confined within the *gsq GeoSoft* query. Thus, it is necessary to introduce the concept of *internal query*, denoted as iq, which works on a different domain than GJ (the domain of crisp *GeoJSON* documents).

- A *soft feature* $\overline{f}$ is a feature for which its membership degrees to some fuzzy sets are known. A soft feature is defined as a tuple

$$\overline{f} = \langle \texttt{properties}, \texttt{geometry}, \texttt{fuzzysets} \rangle$$

where `properties` and `geometry` are defined as in the *GeoJSON* standard. Each feature can belong to several fuzzy sets with a specific membership degree (the membership degree to each fuzzy set denotes the degree with which the feature belongs to the fuzzy set). In the $\overline{f}$ tuple, the `fuzzysets` field is a key/value map, that associates a fuzzy set name *fsn* to the membership degree of the $\overline{f}$ feature to the fuzzy set *fsn*.
- A *Soft GeoJSON* document $\overline{d}$ is a "set of soft features". The domain of *Soft GeoJSON* documents is denoted as SGJ.
- An *Internal GeoSoft* query iq can be seen as a function

$$iq : SGJ \rightarrow SGJ$$

but SGJ exists only within a *GeoSoft* query *gsq*. Consequently, by introducing two functions named *get* and *set*, it is possible to join the two semantic models. It is:

$$gsq = set(iq(get(d)))$$

where $get : GJ \rightarrow SGJ$ translates a *GeoJSON* document $d \in GJ$ into a *Soft GeoJSON* document $\overline{d} \in SGJ$ (*fuzzification*), while $set : SGJ \rightarrow GJ$ translates a *soft GeoJSON* document $\overline{d} \in SGJ$ into a (crisp) *GeoJSON* document $d \in GJ$ (*de-fuzzification*).

5.2 Queries

Based on the running example (Sect. 4.2), a sample qualitative query may be: *extract those NUTS (features) that, between 2017 and 2018, registered a significant reduction of population and a significant increment of GDP*.

Listing 3 shows the query as it would be if two linguistic predicates named `Decreasing_Population` and `Increased_GDP` were available.

The idea is the following: if we are able to evaluate the two linguistic predicates on each feature, we can evaluate a compound `Wanted` linguistic predicate; the membership value associated to this linguistic predicate denotes the degree with which the single feature matches the compound linguistic condition. Let us describe our idea in details.

- The `FROM` clause specifies the collection in the *JSON* document database containing the source *GeoJSON* document.
- The `WHERE` clause specifies the compound linguistic condition, by evaluating the membership degree for each single feature.
  The last part of the clause, i.e., `FOR FUZZY SET Wanted`, gives a name to the fuzzy set to which the membership degree is evaluated by means of the compound linguistic condition.
  Thus, the `WHERE` clause is now a "soft condition": it computes the membership degree of each $\overline{f}$ feature to a given fuzzy set. A single term t that appears without dot notation is assumed to be a fuzzy set name and its membership degree is retrieved from the $\overline{f}$.`fuzzysets` map (if it is not in the map, the 0 value is assumed as its membership degree).
- The `SELECT` clause specifies the properties of the feature to project on. Notice that property names are denoted by means of the dot notation, which refers to the $\overline{f}$.`properties` field as the root.
- The `ALPHA-CUT` clause selects only those features that belong to the `Wanted` fuzzy set with membership degree no less than 0.8.
- `ADD MEMBERSHIP OF Wanted AS` .`rank` specifies that the membership value of the `Wanted` fuzzy set becomes a new property in features, whose name is `rank`.
- The optional `ORDER BY` clause sorts the selected features by the novel .`rank` property, in descending order. This way, the output *GeoJSON* document will show in the first positions of the `features` array those features that are most relevant w.r.t. the query.
- Finally, the `SAVE AS` clause specifies that the resulting *GeoJSON* document must be saved into the `DetectedNUTS_Geojson` collection into the *JSON* document database.

Referring to the semantic model introduced in Sect. 5.1, the *internal query iq* is composed by the `SELECT`, `FROM`, `WHERE`, `ALPHA-CUT` and `ADD MEMBERSHIP` clauses; the `ORDER BY` and `SAVE AS` clauses falls into the *set* function, that *defuzzifies* the output document.

Linguistic Predicates and Fuzzy Sets. Linguistic predicates can be interpreted in terms of fuzzy sets, i.e., the satisfaction degree of a linguistic predicate corresponds to the membership degree to a fuzzy set. So, the previous soft query is correct only if features in the source *GeoJSON* document are provided with such membership degrees. However, features in *GeoJSON* documents are not provided with membership degree to any fuzzy set (i.e., $\overline{f}$.`fuzzysets`$= \emptyset$). So, apart from assuming that the membership degree for any fuzzy-set name not appearing in $\overline{f}$.`fuzzysets` is 0, it is necessary

Listing 4 Complete *GeoSoft* query.

```
                                                                          iq₃
SELECT .CountryCode, .NUTSCode, .NUTSLevel, .NUTSName
FROM
                                                                     iq₂
    (SELECT *
     FROM
                                                              iq₁
         (SELECT *
          FROM NUTSCollection_Geojson@NUTS_Info
          WHERE Has_Decreasing_Population(.Pop2017, .Pop2018)
                FOR FUZZY SET Decreasing_Population
         )

     WHERE Has_Increasing_GDP(.GDP2017, .GDP2018)
           FOR FUZZY SET Increasing_GDP
    )

WHERE Decreasing_Population AND Increasing_GDP
      FOR FUZZY SET Wanted
   ALPHA-CUT Wanted : 0.8
ADD MEMBERSHIP OF Wanted AS .rank

ORDER BY .rank DESC
SAVE AS DetectedNUTS_Geojson@NUTS_Info;
```

to understand how to provide features with membership degrees to fuzzy sets corresponding to linguistic predicates. The solution is to compute them by means of "nested *GeoSoft* queries", allowed in the FROM clause.

Based on the above-mentioned considerations, and supposing that fuzzy operators named Has_Decreasing_Population and Has_Increasing_GDP are defined, the soft query can be written as reported in Listing 4. Hereafter, we describe it.

- The innermost internal query (that we denote as iq_1) retrieves the source *GeoJSON* document from the collection named NUTSCollection_Geojson. This collection is stored within the database named NUTS_Info.
  The WHERE clause uses the Has_Decreasing_Population fuzzy operator to evaluate the membership degree of each single feature in the document to the Decreasing_Population fuzzy set.
  All features $\overline{f}$ are kept, but their $\overline{f}$.fuzzysets map now is no longer empty, since it contains the Decreasing_Population entry.
  As specified by the * character in the SELECT clause, all properties in the features are kept.
- The intermediate *GeoSoft* internal query (that we denote as iq_2) in Listing 4, receives the set of features generated by the innermost query iq_1 (as specified in the FROM clause).
  The WHERE clause evaluates the membership degree of a feature $\overline{f}$ to the Increasing_GDP fuzzy set, by means of the Has_Increasing_GDP fuzzy operator.

Again, the properties of the features are not changed and all features appear in the result set: simply, a new entry with key Increasing_GDP is now present in the $\overline{f}$.fuzzysets map of each feature.

– The outermost *GeoSoft* internal query (that we denote as iq_3) in Listing 4 is the same as the simple internal query reported in Listing 3, apart from the fact that the FROM clause contains the nested query discussed above.

Linguistic predicates in Listing 3 now have become fuzzy-set names, in that they have been evaluated by the two nested queries.

Clearly, after the evaluation of the WHERE clause, the $\overline{f}$.fuzzysets map of each $\overline{f}$ feature actually contains three entries; they correspond to three fuzzy-set names, which are Decreasing_Population, Increasing_GDP and Wanted. The last one is used by the ALPHA-CUT clause to select those features whose membership degree to the Wanted fuzzy set is no less than 0.8. Furthermore, the ADD MEMBERSHIP OF clause adds a new property to the ones specified in the outermost SELECT clause (in iq_3), by using the membership degree to the Wanted fuzzy set. Since this is the outermost internal query, its output must fall again into the domain of *GeoJSON* documents: as a consequence, the $\overline{f}$.fuzzysets map disappears in the f features of the output crisp *GeoJSON* document.

The reader can notice that internal queries can be compound too. In particular, Listing 4 is based on three internal queries iq_1 (the innermost), iq_2 (the intermediate) and iq_3 (the outermost), so it is $iq(\overline{d}) = iq_3(iq_2(iq_1(\overline{d})))$.

Currently, *GeoSoft* does not provide instructions to define fuzzy operators, since we assume they are already available in the execution environment. We will address this aspect too in our future work.

The above-described *GeoSoft* query works on the input *GeoJSON* document we built for the running example, an excerpt of which is reported in Fig. 5a. It contains 1169 features describing the level-3 NUTS depicted on the left side of Fig. 6; the *GeoSoft* query generates the output *GeoJSON* document (an excerpt of which is reported in Fig. 5b) that contains 14 features, each one describing a NUTS of interest, depicted on the right side of Fig. 6. These are the provinces in which a significant reduction of population from 2017 to 2018 corresponded to a significant increment of GDP, which is an interesting phenomenon to investigate.

6   Translating *GeoSoft* into *J-CO-QL*

In this section, we show how *J-CO-QL* can be used as the execution engine for *GeoSoft* queries; we will show how a *GeoSoft* query can be translated into a *J-CO-QL* script. As an example, we still refer to the running example and to the *GeoSoft* query presented in Listing 4. We divided the *J-CO-QL* script into 3 parts. Part 1 is named *preamble*: it is reported in Listing 5 and discussed in Sect. 6.1. Part 2 is named *core*: it is reported in Listing 6 and discussed in Sect. 6.2. Part 3 is named *tail*: it is reported in Listing 7 and discussed in Sect. 6.3.

Listing 5. Translation of the *GeoSoft* query: preamble.

```
1. GET COLLECTION NUTSCollection_Geojson@NUTS_Info;

2. EXPAND
     UNPACK WITH ARRAY .features
     ARRAY .features TO .feature
     DROP OTHERS;

3. FILTER
     CASE WHERE WITH .feature.item
        GENERATE {
          .type        : .feature.item.type,
          .properties : .feature.item.properties,
          .geometry   : .feature.item.geometry    }
     DROP OTHERS;
```

6.1 Preamble of the *J-CO-QL* Script

The *preamble* of the *J-CO-QL* script substantially corresponds to the *get* function intro-duced in Sect. 5.1 to define the semantic model of *GeoSoft*. The goal of the *preamble* is to get the input *GeoJSON* document, split each feature inside the *GeoJSON* document into a single *JSON* document, and transform each single feature document in a conve-nient way to be easily handled. The rationale of this sub-script is that a *GeoJSON* layer, which might include several features, is a single document, while *J-CO-QL* works on collections of documents.

Hereafter, we illustrate each single instruction in Listing 5. We refer to the *GeoSoft* query reported in Listing 4.

- The GET COLLECTION instruction on line 1 retrieves the content of the collection named NUTSCollection_Geojson, which is stored within the database named NUTS_Info. The collection name is specified in the FROM clause of the innermost internal query iq_1 presented in Listing 4. Notice that the collection contains only one document, that is a *GeoJSON* document, as the *temporary collection* generated by the instruction (in the future, we will address the situation in which several *GeoJSON* documents are stored in the same database collection).
- The EXPAND instruction on Line 2 unnests features from within the *GeoJSON* doc-ument in the temporary collection. Specifically, the UNPACK condition selects doc-uments containing an array field named features. The ARRAY clause specifies that items in the array field named features must be unnested: a new document for each item is generated; the TO keyword specifies that the unnested item must be included inside a structured field named feature. In each new generated docu-ment, the feature field contains two sub-fields: position denotes the position of the unnested item in the source array; item actually reports the content of the unnested item. The final DROP OTHERS clause, which in this case is ineffective, discards all documents in the input temporary collection that do not match the selec-tion condition.
- The FILTER instruction on line 3 transforms the documents in the temporary col-lection generated by the EXPAND instruction on line 2, in order to give them a sim-plified structure, suitable for the next part of the script.

Listing 6. Translation of the *GeoSoft* query: core.

```
4. FILTER                                                                    iq₁
      CASE WHERE WITH .properties.Pop2017, .properties.Pop2018
         CHECK FOR FUZZY SET Decreasing_Population
            USING Has_Decreasing_Population(.properties.Pop2017, .properties.Pop2018)
      DROP OTHERS;

5. FILTER                                                                    iq₂
      CASE WHERE WITH .properties.GDP2017, .properties.GDP2018
         CHECK FOR FUZZY SET Increasing_GDP
            USING Has_Increasing_GDP(.properties.GDP2017, .properties.GDP2018)
      DROP OTHERS;

6. FILTER                                                                    iq₃
      CASE WHERE KNOWN FUZZY SETS Decreasing_Population, Increasing_GDP
         CHECK FOR FUZZY SET Wanted
            USING Decreasing_Population AND Increasing_GDP
         ALPHA-CUT 0.8 ON Wanted
      DROP OTHERS;

7. FILTER
      CASE WHERE  WITH .properties.CountryCode,   .properties.NUTSCode,
                       .properties.NUTSLevel,      .properties.NUTSName
            AND KNOWN FUZZY SETS Wanted
         GENERATE {
            .type                     : .type,
            .geometry                 : .geometry,
            .properties.CountryCode   : .properties.CountryCode,
            .properties.NUTSCode      : .properties.NUTSCode,
            .properties.NUTSLevel     : .properties.NUTSLevel,
            .properties.NUTSName      : .properties.NUTSName,
            .properties.rank          : MEMBERSHIP_OF (Wanted)         }
      DROP OTHERS;
```

Specifically, the CASE WHERE condition, which is always true by construction, selects documents having the .feature.item field; the selected documents (i.e., all the documents in the collection, by construction) are restructured by the GENERATE action, in order to simplify them: all fields inside the .feature.item field are moved to the root level, so as the output documents have the fields named type, property and geometry.

The final DROP OTHERS clause is ineffective.

Apart from the name of the input collection (on line 1), the preamble is fixed and independent of internal queries within the *GeoSoft* query. We can say that it corresponds to the *get* function of Sect. 5.1, although to comply with the execution model of *J-CO-QL* it generates a collection of *JSON* documents.

Furthermore, notice that the ˜fuzzysets field (which is the counterpart of the $\bar{f}$.fuzzysets map), has not been considered yet. In fact, it is automatically added and removed by the *J-CO-QL Engine*.

6.2   Core of the *J-CO-QL* Script

The *core* of the *J-CO-QL* script actually corresponds to the n internal queries $iq_1, \ldots, iq_n$ of the *gsq GeoSoft* query. *J-CO-QL* instructions corresponding to each internal query are generated from the innermost iq_1 internal query to the outermost iq_n internal query. Listing 7 reports the core *J-CO-QL* script for the *GeoSoft* query presented in Listing 4.

– The FILTER instruction on line 4 corresponds to the innermost iq_1 internal query in Listing 4. For each document in the temporary collection (which corresponds to a feature in the input *GeoJSON* document), the instruction evaluates the membership degree to the `Decreasing_Population` fuzzy set. The soft condition expressed in the `WHERE` condition of q_1 is reported in the `USING` clause of the `FILTER` instruction. It exploits the fuzzy operator named `Has_Decreasing_Population` applied to the properties named, respectively, `.Pop2017` and `.Pop2018`. All property names are translated into the actual names of the corresponding fields, i.e., `.properties.Pop2017` and `.properties.Pop2018`, because feature properties are actually in the root-level `.properties` field.

The `CASE WHERE` condition selects documents in the input temporary collection having the fields named `.property.Pop2017` and `.property.Pop2018` (by means of the `WITH` predicate). The following `CHECK FOR FUZZY SET` clause *fuzzifies* the document, according to the *J-CO-QL* model presented in Sect. 3, generating the special `~fuzzysets` field that contains the field named `Decreasing_Population` whose value is the membership degree computed by the fuzzy operator `Has_Decreasing_Population`,

The final `DROP OTHERS` option is ineffective, since all documents in the input temporary collection are selected.

- The `FILTER` instruction on line 5 corresponds to the intermediate iq_2 internal query in Listing 4. Similarly to the `FILTER` instruction on line 4, it evaluates the membership degree of each document in the input temporary collection (the one generated by line 4) to the `Increasing_GDP` fuzzy set, by exploiting the `Has_Increasing_GDO` fuzzy operator. Notice again how the soft condition in the `WHERE` clause of iq_2 becomes the condition reported in the `USING` clause of the `FILTER` instruction.

We can observe that when a *GeoSoft* internal query keeps all properties (denoted as `SELECT *`), one single `FILTER` instruction suffices in the *J-CO-QL* script.

- The outermost iq_3 internal query in Listing 4 projects features on a subset of properties. In this case, two `FILTER` instructions are necessary.

The first `FILTER` instruction is on line 6. Its goal is to evaluate the membership degree of each document in the input temporary collection (the one generated by line 5) to the `Wanted` fuzzy set. Again, the soft condition reported in the `WHERE` clause iq_3 is reported in the `USING` clause: notice that linguistic predicates are not translated, since they correspond to fuzzy-set names previously evaluated.

The `ALPHA-CUT` clauses in the outermost internal *GeoSoft* query has a direct counterpart in the `FILTER` instruction: only documents having a membership degree to the `Wanted` fuzzy set no less than 0.8 are selected.

The final `DROP OTHERS` option is ineffective, since all documents that are present in the input temporary collection are selected by the `CASE WHERE` clause.

- The `FILTER` instruction on line 7 is necessary to end processing iq_3, because its `SELECT` clause projects features on a subset of properties and because the `ADD MEMBERSHIP OF` clause adds a new property to features.

Consequently, the `CASE WHERE` clause in the `FILTER` instruction selects those documents having the desired properties (translated into the actual structure of documents in the input temporary collection) and adds the `.rank` properties, by getting the membership degree to the `Wanted` fuzzy set through the `MEMBERSHIP_OF` function. In the `CASE WHERE` clause, notice the `KNOWN FUZZY SET` predicate:

it is a crisp predicate (in *J-CO-QL* the WHERE condition is a traditional Boolean condition, while the USING clause expresses soft conditions) that is true if the specified fuzzy sets have been already evaluated for the document (i.e., the fuzzy-set names appear as fields in the special ~fuzzysets field).

The final DROP OTHERS option discards all documents (if any) that are not selected by the CASE WHERE clause.

Consequently, the patterns we applied to translate a *GeoSoft* internal query iq into a fragment of *J-CO-QL* script are the following ones:

- A FILTER instruction corresponds to the soft condition in the WHERE clause of iq and/or to the ALPHA-CUT clause.
  The CASE WHERE clause selects documents having the properties that are referred to in iq;
  the CHECK FOR FUZZY SET and USING clauses correspond to the WHERE clause in iq;
  if present in iq, the ALPHA-CUT clause is present in the FILTER instruction.
- If the internal query iq projects features on a subset of properties and/or adds properties by means of the ADD MEMBERSHIP OF clause, a second FILTER instruction is present in the fragment of *J-CO-QL* script.
  The CASE WHERE clause selects documents having properties specified in iq;
  if the ADD MEMBERSHIP OF clause is in iq, the CASE WHERE clause is extended with the KNOW FUZZY SETS predicate;
  the GENERATE action projects the .properties field of selected documents, with those listed in the SELECT clause in iq and the ones added by the ADD MEMBERSHIP OF clauses in iq.

6.3   Tail of the *J-CO-QL* Script

The *tail* of the *J-CO-QL* script implements the *set* function introduced to explain the semantic model of *GeoSoft* in Sect. 5.1. Its main goal is to aggregate documents so far selected (and currently in the temporary collection generated by the last instruction in the core of the script) into one single *GeoJSON* document. It also *de-fuzzifies* documents, sorts them if the ORDER BY clause is specified in the *GeoSoft* query and saves the output *GeoJSON* document into the database.

The tail of the *J-CO-QL* script is reported in Listing 7.

- The FILTER instruction on line 8 prepares documents to be grouped into the output *GeoJSON* document. By construction, the CASE WHERE condition is true for each document in the temporary collection, because all documents have the three specified fields. The GENERATE action inserts a fictitious key field, with a constant value into each document; this field will play the role of grouping key in the next GROUP instruction. The other fields are those required by the *GeoJSON* standard for features and are left untouched. The DROPPING ALL FUZZY SETS option *de-fuzzifies* the documents, i.e., removes the ~fuzzysets field. The DROP OTHERS option is ineffective by construction. Remember that each single document in the output temporary collection is a feature to aggregate within the .features array field of the output *GeoJSON* document.

Listing 7. Translation of the *GeoSoft* query: tail.

```
8.   FILTER
        CASE WHERE  WITH .type, .geometry, .properties
          GENERATE {
            .key        : 1,
            .type       : .type,
            .geometry   : .geometry,
            .properties : .properties            }
          DROPPING ALL FUZZY SETS
        DROP OTHERS;

9.   GROUP
        PARTITION WITH .key
          BY .key INTO .features
            DROP GROUPING FIELDS
          ORDER BY .properties.rank DESC
          GENERATE {
            .type       : "FeatureCollection",
            .features   : .features             }
        DROP OTHERS;

10.  SAVE AS DetectedNUTS_Geojson@NUTS_Info;
```

- The GROUP instruction on line 9, rebuilds a unique *GeoJSON* document. First of all, it creates a partition of documents in the input temporary collection, in such a way that all documents are in one single partition; in fact, by means of the WITH predicate, all documents that hold a key field are selected. By means of the BY clause, documents in the partition are grouped based on the value of the key field: since we have only one constant value (generated by the FILTER instruction on line 8), all documents in the partition are grouped into one single document.
  The INTO clause specifies the name of the new array field that has to contain grouped documents: in this case, the name is .features (to comply with the *GeoJSON* standard). The DROP GROUPING FIELDS option discards the key field. The ORDER BY clause sorts documents that have been grouped into the new .features array in descending order (DESC option) of values of the .properties.rank field, as specified in the ORDER BY clause in the *GeoSoft* query in Listing 4. The GENERATE action maintains the features field unchanged and adds a new type field with "FeatureCollection" as value, as required by the *GeoJSON* standard.
  Notice that the new temporary collection now contains one lonely document that satisfies the *GeoJSON* standard.
- Finally, the SAVE AS instruction on line 10, saves the temporary collection holding the single *GeoJSON* document into the DetectedNUTS_Geojson collection, which is created into the NUTS_Info database as declared in the final SAVE AS clause of the *GeoSoft* query in Listing 4.
  Figure 5b reports the output document obtained by the script, which derives from the input *GeoJSON* document reported in Fig. 5a that we built for the running example.

As a result, we can state that the *GeoSoft* query can be actually automatically translated into a *J-CO-QL* script. This also proves that the *J-CO* Framework can be actually exploited as execution engine of domain-specific query languages designed to work on specific *JSON* formats, such as *GeoJSON*.

7   Conclusions

In this paper, we introduced *GeoSoft*, a domain-specific language for querying features described in a *GeoJSON* document. The paper introduced the language and the *J-CO* Framework, which we used as the execution environment for *GeoSoft* queries. The *J-CO* Framework is under development at University of Bergamo to be an advanced tool to integrate, manipulate and query possibly-heterogeneous collections of *JSON* documents, by means of its query language named *J-CO-QL*. In this paper, we demonstrate the feasibility of the *GeoSoft* language, by showing how it is possible to automatically translate *GeoSoft* queries into *J-CO-QL* scripts; indeed, scripts reported in Listings 5, 6 and 7 were generated by the prototype *GeoSoft* interpreter we recently built.

As a future work, we will continue developing the *GeoSoft* language, in order to provide users with sophisticated functionalities able to deal with geometries and to integrate features coming from several *GeoJSON* documents.

Acknowledgment. We warmly thank Luca Assolari, student of the Master Degree in Computer Science at University of Bergamo (Italy), who implemented the prototype *GeoSoft* interpreter.

```
geoSoft         : ( selectClause  ( orderBy )?  saveAs ';' )* ;
selectClause    : 'SELECT' properties
                      from
                      ( where )?
                      ( alphaCut )*
                      ( addMembership )* ;
properties      : '*' | property ( ',' property )* ;
property        : DOT_ID ( 'AS' DOT_ID )? | expression 'AS' DOT_ID ;
from            : 'FROM' source ( ',' source )* ;
source          : ID  ( '@' ID )? | '(' select ')' ;
where           : 'WHERE' condition ( 'FOR' 'FUZZY' 'SET' ID )? ;
alphaCut        : 'ALPHA-CUT' ID ':' number ;
addMembership   : 'ADD' 'MEMBERSHIP' 'OF' ID 'AS' DOT_ID ;
orderBy         : 'ORDER' 'BY' DOT_ID ( 'ASC' | 'DESC' )?
                      ( ',' DOT_ID ( 'ASC' | 'DESC' )? )* ;
saveAs          : 'SAVE' 'AS' ID  ( '@' ID )? ;
```

Fig. 7. *GeoSoft* grammar.

A   Syntax of *GeoSoft*

In Fig. 7, we present the syntax (grammar) of the *GeoSoft* language introduced in Sect. 5. The grammar is formulated in EBNF[16] notation according to the convention applied by ANTLR (*ANother Tool for Language Recognition*)[17]. ANTLR is a widely-known parser generator that denotes non-terminal elements (rules) in lower case, while

---

[16] https://en.wikipedia.org/wiki/Extended_Backus%E2%80%93Naur_form, accessed on 30/10/2021.

[17] https://www.antlr.org/, accessed on 30/10/2021.

terminal elements (tokens) are in upper case or directly declared between quotes. The *geoSoft* rule is the starting rule of the grammar.

For the sake of simplicity, we do not include the definitions of the `condition`, `expression` and `number` rules, but their meaning is denoted by their names. The `ID` and `DOT_ID` tokens denote the classic `identifiers`, respectively, not having (`ID`) or having (`DOT_ID`) a dot character as starting character.

References

1. Aufaure, M.A., Trépied, C.: A survey of query languages for geographic information systems, p. 3 (1996)
2. Bieber, M., Kacmar, C.: Designing hypertext support for computational applications. Commun. ACM **38**(8), 99–107 (1995)
3. Bordogna, G., Capelli, S., Ciriello, D.E., Psaila, G.: A cross-analysis framework for multi-source volunteered, crowdsourced, and authoritative geographic information: the case study of volunteered personal traces analysis against transport network data. Geo-Spat. Inf. Sci. **21**(3), 257–271 (2018)
4. Bordogna, G., Capelli, S., Psaila, G.: A big geo data query framework to correlate open data with social network geotagged posts. In: Bregt, A., Sarjakoski, T., van Lammeren, R., Rip, F. (eds.) GIScience 2017. LNGC, pp. 185–203. Springer, Cham (2017). https://doi.org/10. 1007/978-3-319-56759-4_11
5. Bordogna, G., Psaila, G.: Soft aggregation in flexible databases querying based on the vector p-norm. Int. J. Uncertain. Fuzziness Knowl.-Based Syst. **17**(supp01), 25–40 (2009)
6. Bordogna, G., Psaila, G.: Customizable flexible querying in classical relational databases. In: Handbook of Research on Fuzzy Information Processing in Databases, pp. 191–217. IGI Global (2008)
7. Bosc, P., Pivert, O.: SQLf: a relational database language for fuzzy querying. IEEE Trans. Fuzzy Syst. **3**(1), 1–17 (1995)
8. Garcia Bringas, P., Pastor, I., Psaila, G.: Can blockchain technology provide information systems with trusted database? The case of hyperledger fabric. In: Cuzzocrea, A., Greco, S., Larsen, H.L., Saccà, D., Andreasen, T., Christiansen, H. (eds.) FQAS 2019. LNCS (LNAI), vol. 11529, pp. 265–277. Springer, Cham (2019). https://doi.org/10.1007/978-3-030-27629-4_25
9. Butler, H., et al.: The GeoJSON format. Internet Engineering Task Force (IETF) (2016)
10. Cai, G.: GeoVSM: an integrated retrieval model for geographic information. In: Egenhofer, M.J., Mark, D.M. (eds.) GIScience 2002. LNCS, vol. 2478, pp. 65–79. Springer, Heidelberg (2002). https://doi.org/10.1007/3-540-45799-2_5
11. Cattell, R.: Scalable SQL and NoSQL data stores. ACM SIGMOD Rec. **39**(4), 12–27 (2011)
12. Costagliola, G., Tortora, G., Tucci, M., Busillo, M.: GISQL—a query language intepreter for geographical information systems. In: Spaccapietra, S., Jain, R. (eds.) Visual Database Systems 3. ITIFIP, pp. 275–286. Springer, Boston, MA (1995). https://doi.org/10.1007/978-0-387-34905-3_17
13. Egenhofer, M.J.: Spatial SQL: a query and presentation language. IEEE Trans. Knowl. Data Eng. **6**(1), 86–95 (1994)
14. Florescu, D., Fourny, G.: JSONiq: the history of a query language. IEEE Internet Comput. **17**(5), 86–90 (2013)
15. Formica, A., Mazzei, M., Pourabbas, E., Rafanelli, M.: Querying distributed GIS with GeoPQLJ based on GeoJSON, pp. 175–182 (2019)

16. Fosci, P., Marrara, S., Psaila, G.: Soft querying GeoJSON documents within the J-CO framework. In: 16th International Conference on Web Information Systems and Technologies (WEBIST 2020), pp. 253–265. SCITEPRESS-Science and Technology Publications, Lda. (2020)

17. Fosci, P., Psaila, G.: *J-CO*, a framework for fuzzy querying collections of *JSON* documents (demo). In: Andreasen, T., De Tré, G., Kacprzyk, J., Legind Larsen, H., Bordogna, G., Zadrożny, S. (eds.) FQAS 2021. LNCS (LNAI), vol. 12871, pp. 142–153. Springer, Cham (2021). https://doi.org/10.1007/978-3-030-86967-0_11

18. Fosci, P., Psaila, G.: Powering soft querying in J-CO-QL with JavaScript functions. In: Sanjurjo González, H., Pastor López, I., García Bringas, P., Quintián, H., Corchado, E. (eds.) SOCO 2021. AISC, vol. 1401, pp. 207–221. Springer, Cham (2022). https://doi.org/10.1007/978-3-030-87869-6_20

19. Fosci, P., Psaila, G.: Towards flexible retrieval, integration and analysis of JSON data sets through fuzzy sets: a case study. Information **12**(7), 258 (2021)

20. Galindo, J., Urrutia, A., Piattini, M.: Fuzzy Databases: Modeling, Design, and Implementation. IGI Global (2006)

21. Anderson, J.C., Lehnardt, J., Slater, N.: CouchDB: The Definitive Guide. O'Reilly Media, Inc. (2010)

22. Jacobs, B.E., Walczak, C.A.: A generalized query-by-example data manipulation language based on database logic. IEEE Trans. Softw. Eng. **1**, 40–57 (1983)

23. Kim, H.J., Korth, H.F., Silberschatz, A.: Picasso: a graphical query language. Softw. Pract. Exp. **18**(3), 169–203 (1988)

24. Mayer, B.: Beyond icons: towards new metaphors for visual query languages for spatial information systems. In: Cooper, R. (ed.) IDS 1992. Workshops in Computing, pp. 113–135. Springer, Glasgow (1992). https://doi.org/10.1007/978-1-4471-3423-7_8

25. Nayak, A., Poriya, A., Poojary, D.: Type of NoSQL databases and its comparison with relational databases. Int. J. Appl. Inf. Syst. **5**(4), 16–19 (2013)

26. Ong, K.W., Papakonstantinou, Y., Vernoux, R.: The SQL++ unifying semi-structured query language, and an expressiveness benchmark of SQL-on-Hadoop, NoSQL and NewSQL databases. CoRR, abs/1405.3631 (2014)

27. Psaila, G., Fosci, P.: Toward an anayist-oriented polystore framework for processing json geo-data. In: International Conferences on Applied Computing 2018, Budapest, Hungary, 21–23 October 2018, pp. 213–222. IADIS (2018)

28. Psaila, G., Fosci, P.: J-CO: a platform-independent framework for managing geo-referenced JSON data sets. Electronics **10**(5), 621 (2021)

29. Psaila, G., Marrara, S.: A first step towards a fuzzy framework for analyzing collections of JSON documents. In: IADIS AC 2019, pp. 19–28 (2019)

30. Staes, F., Tarantino, L., Tiems, A.: A graphical query language for object oriented databases. In: Proceedings 1991 IEEE Workshop on Visual Languages, pp. 205–210 (1991)

31. Zadeh, L.A.: The concept of a linguistic variable and its application to approximate reasoning—I. Inf. Sci. **8**(3), 199–249 (1975)

Author Index